Man [illegible]

SIR TERRY LEAHY [illegible] ge, Liverpool, and then we[illegible] Manchester Institute of Science and [illegible]ology, where he gained his BSc (Hons) in management sciences. He joined Tesco when he was 23, became the company's first marketing director and was responsible for the introduction of the highly successful Tesco Clubcard. As CEO he oversaw Tesco's expansion into everything from electrical goods to insurance, built a £1 billion clothing business and was one of the first to see the potential of the internet for selling groceries. He was knighted in 2002 for his services to food retailing and has received many industry honours and awards, including *Sunday Times* Business Person of the Year in 2010 and a Lifetime Achievement award from *Retail Week* in 2011.

Since Sir Terry stepped down as CEO of Tesco in February 2011 he has been in constant demand as a public speaker. He is also a senior advisor to Clayton, Dublier & Rice, the US private equity firm. In addition, he invests in entrepreneurial businesses and is involved with various charities.

Praise for *Management in 10 Words*

'a surprising and incisive management page-turner that has interesting things to say about everything from the evolution of British society to the art of transforming huge organisations.' – *The Economist* Books of the Year 2012

'Should be required reading for anyone running a business, or indeed any organisation' – Chris Blackhurst, *Evening Standard*

'An insight into Sir Terry's influences, his management style, the techniques he used to deliver results and his recollections on the genesis of some of his numerous achievements – *Management in 10 Words* is a revelation' – *The Grocer*

'Enlightening' – *Independent*

'This is the authentic voice of the man . . . the nearest any outsider is likely to get to understanding what motivated one of Britain's most successful businesspeople' – *Financial Times*

'in a complex world having some simplicity to build a management framework around is exactly what is needed . . . It is hard to argue with Sir Terry's choice of watchwords.' – *Developing Leaders Magazine*

'This book is proof that anything is possible if you put your mind to it . . . Leahy should be an inspiration that starting on the shop floor is as good a way as any to achieve one's hopes.' – *Management Today*

'political leaders could profit greatly from this book.' – Charles Moore, *Daily Telegraph*

Terry Leahy

Management in 10 Words

Published by Random House Business Books 2013

2 4 6 8 10 9 7 5 3 1

First published in Great Britain in 2012 by
Random House Business Books
Random House, 20 Vauxhall Bridge Road,
London SW1V 2SA

www.randomhouse.co.uk

Addresses for companies within The Random House Group Limited can be found at:
www.randomhouse.co.uk/offices.htm

The Random House Group Limited Reg. No. 954009

A CIP catalogue record for this book
is available from the British Library

ISBN 9781847940919

The Random House Group Limited supports The Forest Stewardship Council (FSC®), the leading international forest-certification organisation. Our books carrying the FSC label are printed on FSC®-certified paper. FSC is the only forest-certification scheme supported by the leading environmental organisations, including Greenpeace. Our paper procurement policy can be found at
www.randomhouse.co.uk/environment

Text designed by Christopher Wakeling
Typeset by Palimpsest Book Production Limited, Falkirk, Stirlingshire
Printed and bound in the UK by CPI Books Ltd

To Alison

Contents

PREFACE

When I joined Tesco as a raw but eager marketing man back in the 1970s, the supermarket chain was very much the poor relative in British retailing. Struggling to shake off its reputation as a discount store, it sold only food and it had no presence beyond the shores of the UK. Although it grew rapidly during the 1980s, in the mid-1990s it was still lagging behind the giants of Britain's high street: Sainsbury and Marks and Spencer. When I left Tesco in 2011, after 14 years as Chief Executive, the company had grown to be around six times larger than both companies. Now the third largest retailer in the world, with over 6,000 stores and operations in 14 countries in Europe, the United States and Asia, Tesco has access to more than half of the world's population, selling everything from cereal to insurance, mobile phones to bananas, clothes to iPads, in store and online, to millions of customers every week.

Tesco's turnaround, one of the most remarkable stories in British business, was thanks to a combination of factors: a relentless focus on delivering value to customers so as to earn their loyalty; constant innovation – loyalty cards, retail services, new formats; and, above all, a will on the part of its staff to succeed.

I had no intention of writing a book. I have to thank Danny Stern for encouraging me to develop ideas I had used for a series of talks into a book on management. My editor Nigel Wilcockson was a delight to work with. He was always encouraging, and I marvelled at his ability to shape my efforts into a coherent structure and style. I can't thank George Bridges enough: he was a constant support, providing invaluable help, advice and suggestions.

I have been very lucky to have worked at Tesco, and could not have chosen better people to work with. To name them all would require a book in itself. To name but a few would cause needless offence to those whom I omit. I cannot begin to number the many – certainly, hundreds of people – who helped me at Tesco over 30 years. Most offered small acts of kindness; many gave significant help; some friends and colleagues offered years of patient support and guidance.

Most of all I have to thank my wife Alison and our children Tom, Katie and David, from whom I have only known love, support and laughter.

INTRODUCTION

The room was full of the men and women who run the British government. The question these senior officials asked me was the same one that I have faced time and again. 'So how did you do it?' What was it that turned Tesco from being a struggling supermarket, number three retail chain in the United Kingdom, into the third largest retailer in the world?

'It's quite simple,' I said. 'We focused relentlessly on delivering for customers. We set ourselves some simple aims, and some basic values to live by. And we then created a process to achieve them, making sure that everyone knew what they were responsible for.'

Silence.

Polite coughing.

Someone poured out some water.

More silence.

This was the Civil Service at its most civil. 'Was that it?' an official finally asked. And the answer to that is 'yes'.

This book is about the lessons I learnt as Tesco grew. Some of what follows may strike you as simple and obvious. Yet as I have met and worked with people from different cultures worldwide, I have been struck by how basic, simple truths about life – not just business – have been forgotten or are dismissed as 'too obvious to matter' by clever people who mistake 'simple' for 'simplistic'. We have allowed ourselves to think that, because the world in which we live is complicated, the solutions to problems must be complicated as well.

This leads many people to think that as they are powerless to overcome the problems they face, solving them is someone else's problem – your boss, their boss, the country's leader, the United Nations: anyone but them. Meekly agreeing that the world is a difficult place and challenges are too difficult to overcome, they think that ambitions are too far-fetched to achieve. Whether it is in business or politics, the private sector or the public sector, too many people accept their lot. It is time to think again.

Yes, the world is complicated. Some of the global challenges we face – population growth, climate change, how to regulate a global economic system – are, of course, complex problems. In business, the impact of the digital revolution, the labyrinth of regulations and laws, the intricacies of the financial markets – all these things and more make life a tangled web. Yet whether it is tackling a global challenge or a company's management problems, good, durable solutions are simple solutions. They are ones that we can all understand and, more often than not, they are based on clear values and principles that everyone can grasp.

I learnt those basic lessons as we turned Tesco into the company it is today, overcoming some of the complex challenges we faced. This book is an attempt to share these lessons with you. I have grouped my thoughts around ten words, which together form the barest essence of what my experience has taught me. I suspect this wish to distil ideas to their simplest form does reflect something about me: I am described as being blunt and to the point. That's true: when something matters I say things as I see them, which at times may cause offence, but avoids misunderstanding.

And that brings me to what this book is not.

It is not a history of my career at Tesco, although obviously what follows is rooted in my experience working there for more than 30 years. The Tesco story continues, and my part in it was just that: a part. Tesco's success – as I hope you will see from what follows – is not thanks to one person, but hundreds of thousands of people, working hard together towards a common goal.

Any book about my career might risk giving the impression that Tesco's success is solely thanks to me. Indeed, reading and re-reading this book, I am concerned that at times I might give that impression still. So let me apologise, before you even get to Chapter 1, if that is the case. Hubris is a common fault, and one I hope to avoid.

You cannot run a business without making mistakes – and I certainly made my fair share: my first advertising campaign as Marketing Director; our failed attempt to create restaurants in our stores; our unsuccessful launch in Taiwan. The list is long. It also reflects the fact that business is all about taking risks. Decisions that involve no risk are not decisions that will enable your business to grow. The trick is to learn from mistakes so that they don't prove fatal.

If I were put on trial for the errors I made at Tesco, I'm sure my lawyer would be able to mount a defence for some and have to enter a guilty plea for others. My purpose in this book, however, is not to promote or defend decisions I made, but to impart the lessons I learnt over the course of my career. I'll leave it to others to be the judge and jury.

Nor is this book just about retailing – although many of the lessons are rooted in retailing. I hope the lessons are applicable whatever you do, wherever you work. Do not read the words 'the customer' and think 'I don't have customers, so this is irrelevant to me'. Almost every organisation has a customer. In the private sector, some companies may talk about their clients or 'buyers': they are customers. In the public sector, although often no money passes hands, citizens are usually customers of the services they use, having paid for them through their taxes. I write 'usually' as sometimes there is no choice of service: citizens have to accept what the state's organisation gives them. If they are to succeed, even these organisations must have clear aims, processes and some of the other characteristics I will address later.

Nor is this book solely for those perched precariously on the top rung of management, in some vast organisation nervously looking down and wondering 'Where next?' Many of the observations are directly relevant to managing any endeavour, large or small.

I hope – I stress, hope – that even if you do not think of yourself as a manager, you might find what follows just a little bit useful in your day-to-day life. If you work in a tiny firm, or are part of a small team, the chances are that you have to handle relationships with people at work, face difficult decisions and need to create and implement plans. This book might help you. It is not some magical elixir, the snake oil salesman's 'secret to success and happiness'. If it was, you would soon be asking for your money back (and as retailer I see refunds as a sign of failure). Let me disappoint you now: there is no silver bullet that will hit the bull's-eye of a successful life or business. Anyone who tells you otherwise is lying. But there are some simple truths which, combined with hard work, increase the chance of success. That is all.

I should add to my list of 'nots' that this is not a book about Terry Leahy. I am a private person – much to the irritation of the many journalists whose kind offers of a 'personal interview' with them to talk about 'my life' I have declined. I feel uncomfortable telling people about my life partly because I don't see it as any of their business, and partly because I cannot believe anyone is that interested.

All that said . . . I fear that you need to know a little about me to understand why I have written what follows, as all of it is tinged with my beliefs and values. So, with my teeth slightly gritted, here is a potted history of Terry Patrick Leahy.

My father was born in County Sligo, Ireland, one of ten

children. Those who could migrated to America. My father was planning to go there too but his love of gambling on greyhounds diverted him: having won some money on a dog race, he left Ireland for Liverpool instead. Had that dog lost, I would probably have been an American.

A carpenter, he joined the merchant navy when the Second World War broke out, and sailed on the Atlantic convoys. His ship was torpedoed, he was hit by shrapnel but survived. He then contracted tuberculosis, and his injury meant he could not work as a carpenter again. Instead, he became a greyhound trainer. Dogs and gambling, washed down with quite a bit of drink, became his way of life. He was a kind and intelligent man. I would sometimes go with him to the tracks, some of which were unlicensed, rough-and-tumble places – I remember one man turning up with a grievance and a gun.

My mother is also Irish. Born in County Armagh to a farming family, she was used to prodigious hard work from an early age. She became a nurse, and went to England where she worked in Exeter during the Blitz. Moving then to Liverpool, she met my father in Toxteth and that, as they say, was that. I was the third of their four sons, born in 1956 in Belle Vale, Liverpool.

We lived on a council estate in a prefab house. Made in parts and then assembled on site, these homes were built in their thousands after the Second World War for people left homeless thanks to wartime bombing. Cheap but cheerful, painted chipboard on the aluminium walls, freezing cold in winter, ours had the luxury of a fridge and an indoor toilet.

Working class – although 'sometimes working' is probably a better description of my father – we never had much money. We bought a TV in 1962, but we didn't have a car for years, we never went on holiday and I don't remember having many clothes: I think I wore my school uniform most of the time until I was about

16. That said, we never went hungry. Bacon, egg and chips almost every night, fish on Friday, our diet was by today's standards simple and basic. I don't remember eating rice, but I do remember eating my first bowl of pasta (aged 18) and my first yoghurt.

Food played a big part in my childhood. I would often go shopping with my mother, perhaps because I have a gene that draws me to shops, or maybe my mother saw me as the daughter she never had. The nearest shops were in a row of prefabs, each smaller than our house. Dark and small, crammed with stock, each was known by the shopkeeper's name: Ronnie the butcher, Harry the sweet shop, George the grocer.

My first school was a local Catholic primary school. I didn't much like it at first, and regularly ran away. I was a slow reader: we had no books at home and I found school work unfamiliar. Fortunately, even though there were 50 in a class, the school was blessed by having inspirational teachers who discovered I was bright and managed to help me win a scholarship to the best school in Liverpool, St Edward's. It was a fee-paying school; the council funded my place.

St Edward's was my lifeline. My family, like almost all the others on our estate, had no contact with the professions, managers, businessmen. It was a 'them and us' culture. We would always be us, and they would always be them. That was life, and there was no point fighting against it. Leave school at 16, get a job – any job – and that was it. Looking back, it is ironic that we all hero-worshipped the socialist, Labour MP for the neighbouring constituency, Harold Wilson, who was then Prime Minister. Wilson had broken free of our world, gone to Oxford University and then up and up. He was the one who got away – one of the few, a rare exception. Or so we believed.

My teachers – many of whom were Christian Brothers – taught me otherwise. Day after day, explicitly or implicitly, I learnt that if you worked hard, you could do as well as anyone else in life. I resisted their efforts to begin with, and as a result I felt their leather strap more than once. Rebellious, I bumped along at the bottom of the class for a few years, being a bit of the class clown. When I came to do my A-levels, I discovered I had things to say on important subjects, but the people at the bottom of the class weren't taken seriously by their peers. So I applied myself to my work, and lapped up my geography, history, economics and general studies textbooks. I even won prizes, something which still probably perplexes my teachers.

At that time Liverpool's industry was imploding while its culture was exploding. My early school years were spent listening to local pop groups – Gerry and the Pacemakers, Freddie and the Dreamers and, of course, The Beatles – while Liverpool's docks, the source of so much of its wealth, began to fall silent. Opportunity was draining away. One summer, on holiday from school, I wanted a job but there was none to be had. So I took the bus a couple of hundred miles to Wandsworth in South London. Knocking on doors of businesses in the area, I found a job at Tesco in a large local shopping centre. My job was to stack the shelves of tea and coffee. I quite liked the job except for the store's background 'muzak', which played the same songs time after time. When I left I did not think I would be heading back.

My original plan when I left school was to become an architect as I liked the creativity the profession involves, but I failed to get the O-level grade I needed in art so that was ditched. My next plan was to become a lawyer, but I was told that my O-level results were probably not good enough for me to consider going to law school. My mind turned to management – quite why I am unsure, as I had absolutely no idea what management was other than that it sounded interesting, demanding and challenging. So I applied for and won a place to study management sciences at the University of Manchester Institute of Science and Technology. Although homesick and quite daunted by the institution itself, I was by now confident academically. The inspirational teaching I had there, especially from Roland Smith and Cary Cooper, taught me the importance of simplicity and focus – especially focus on the customer.

Armed with my degree, I applied for a number of jobs at glamorous consumer goods companies. And I was rejected. So I joined the Co-op instead, and spent my time travelling around the country selling delicatessen goods – cold meats, cheese and so on – to their trading societies. Trying to tell the hard-nosed mining communities of Yorkshire that they should try crottin cheese, dry-cured meat and olives was challenging, but fun. That said, I felt the company was going nowhere because of its fragmented structure and complicated ownership. I applied for a marketing job at Tesco in 1979, while applying at the same time to join Alcan Foil – a brand that I thought was on the up. Tesco rejected me. Fortunately, they then thought the person who actually got the job was so good that they immediately gave him something else to do. Thanks to his brilliance, I found myself being offered the job I'd previously failed to get. I joined Tesco, and stayed for the next 33 years.

To complete the picture, you should know that I am married to Alison, a doctor, and we have three children.

Trying to analyse the impact your background has had on your own beliefs and view of life is bound to be flawed. You cannot be both judge and jury. But if I lie on the psychiatrist's couch while playing Sigmund Freud at the same time, I suppose my upbringing taught me a few things.

First, the importance of good manners, education, hard work, common sense and respect for others. These are the bedrock of any family, community, company or society.

Then there is a yearning desire to succeed come what may. From an early age, I learnt that if I wanted to achieve something, I had to look to myself. Self-help, not 'please help', was the mantra. Failure meant insecurity, a life stuck in a rut and no money. I soon realised that success demanded giving one's all and taking risks. Our school motto was 'Courage through faith'. Faith in one's God, faith in oneself: I suppose I have both.

After that, a deep wish to help give everyone, no matter their background, a better life. I never saw much attraction in politics. I was too shy to stand on the politician's soapbox. In politics there also seemed to be too much talk and not enough action: too many promises, too few results. I wanted to do something lasting, something that I could point to.

And finally, my Liverpudlian roots gave me a lifelong devotion to its best football club, Everton.

While reading this book, you will see that I have drawn on the experiences and writings of a number of people. Forgive me if you therefore find some of the things I have to say 'unoriginal'. My excuse is that in our search to be 'original', to be 'new' all the time, we risk overlooking the experience and wisdom of the generations that have gone before us.

Some of the sources I have drawn on are those written by the diamonds in the rough of the enormous industry of 'management consultancy'. Others are military leaders, foremost among whom is Field Marshal Viscount Slim, whose memoirs of his time commanding the British Fourteenth Army in Burma in the Second World War have had a big impact on me. He transformed a demoralised, defeated army into a formidable fighting – and ultimately victorious – force. Obviously the parallels can only be pushed so far – apart from anything else, Tesco was never beaten or demoralised – but many of Slim's experiences have struck a chord with me and influenced the way I think.

This may sound all rather clichéd, but the similarities are there: generals command many thousands of men in fast-moving situations, in which clarity of purpose and process is critical; running big businesses is not that different. What is more, the military (usually) have no time for management niceties: in battle, you need to be short, sharp and to the point. Imprecision kills. That simplicity and focus is something I like and respect. Finally, I should confess my interest in military history: maybe beneath every shopkeeper's counter lies a field marshal's baton.

Before you read on, you need to know one other thing about me. I am an optimist. I believe our best days lie ahead, largely because humans the world over are driven by a simple hope day after day: a better life for themselves and their families. Motivated by that universal wish, I've never lost my belief that if people are free and have both confidence and opportunity, they are capable of incredible things. Idealistic that may be: but better to be that than pessimistic.

So to those who think 'I can't achieve my ambitions', I say think again. A good education, a stable family: yes, of course these help to provide the bedrock of a successful life. But if you are not blessed with these things, never become the prisoner of your background. The past is just that – the past. Don't let it limit your future. As I will spell out in the pages that follow, there are plenty of ways in which each one of us can improve our chances of success. Success depends on what lies deep within us. If you spend your life never daring to go where your hopes and dreams might take you, you will end your days deep in a dark valley of frustrated hopes, looking up at what might have been. You are ultimately responsible for your own actions. Only you can decide the path you take. Misfortune and mistakes will knock you back, but keep on moving, look up, and turn the page.

1 Truth

Organisations are terrible at confronting the truth. It is so much easier to define your version of reality, and judge success and failure according to that. But my experience is that truth is crucial both to create and to sustain success.

Confronting the truth is painful. To confess even to yourself, let alone others, that your job is not as great as it might be, that an investment is not paying off, that your company is slipping or that you could do better at work – any admission of imperfection or inadequacy is hard. And once the words have passed your lips, all sorts of questions raise their ugly little heads. Why has this happened? What did you do wrong to make this happen? And what are you going to do about it? Change jobs, sack people, restructure the company? All that spells change for you and, most likely, for someone else. Change is difficult. Change thanks to a mistake you made is doubly hard.

So the easy option is not to confront the truth, but to let things potter along as they are. Of course, if it is a car or house you are unhappy with, well, that's something that you can take in your stride. But if it is a job that is going nowhere, or a company or team at work that is steadily slipping, that's something that can erode your confidence and gnaw away at your soul. The sense of purposelessness, knowing you could do better, leaving work each day not sure of what you have achieved – all this is demoralising, depressing, crushing even.

Almost worse is when you sense that everyone in the organisation is thinking the same thing: that the latest strategy is not going to work, the so-called 'performance indicators' are meaningless, and that the organisation has lost its way. But, inevitably, no one is saying so. The longer the silence lasts, the harder it becomes to confront the truth and face the consequences. As a result, the more likely it is that nothing is done – until it is all too late.

The world over, organisations of all kinds are terrible at confronting the truth. It is so much easier to define your version of reality, and judge success and failure according to that. Management screens and filters out what it doesn't want to hear.

To acknowledge a problem would mean having to take an awkward decision or face an unpleasant meeting that would make you unloved and unpopular, and who wants to be that? Worse, truth can expose failure – the f-word, feared by everyone. Slowly and imperceptibly, the 'bunker mentality' descends, blinding management to reality. Those on the board convince themselves that there isn't really a problem, or that the problem everyone is talking about has been concocted by those who are analysing, commenting and often criticising the organisation: journalists, pressure groups, politicians, customers. Whatever is happening, the board persuades itself, it certainly isn't the fault of management. Then, inexorably, the world closes in and the problems grow. By now management knows it has to be seen to be doing something and to be in charge of 'events', so it indulges in frenetic (and often pointless) activity and initiatives.

Paradoxically, the more successful a business becomes, the easier it is to justify not seeking out the truth and taking difficult decisions. If all the indicators are pointing to success – your share price, sales, membership, and so on – why fill the world with gloom and doom? Why bother changing things when you are doing so well? Success breeds complacency, a sense that the world in which you became successful will not change, so neither should you.

The truth is not something you usually associate with retailing. It's a word you normally connect with the law or religion – perhaps too big and worthy to grace the shopping aisles. But my experience is that truth is crucial both to create and to sustain success. And certainly, when I consider how Tesco was in the early 1990s, finding the truth was absolutely essential: it was the only way we would get out of the rut of being a middle-ranking UK supermarket.

A brief bit of history. Tesco began life when Jack Cohen used his gratuity from Army service in the First World War to set up a market stall in the melee of the East End of London. Cohen bought tea (at 9d – old pence – per pound, selling at 6d a half pound)[1] from T E Stockwell. TES plus the CO of Cohen produced Tesco – although Cohen was the driving force. On one day alone, Cohen sold 450 pounds of tea from his barrow. Cohen had a natural flair for retail, an eye for a bargain and a strong belief that low price, and nothing else, was the secret of good business. Once he bought a consignment of Danish cream from a half-sunk ship and sent it to his shops with an order 'Take off the labels, get a tin of Duraglit from the shelves to clean off the rust and sell these for 2d a tin'.[2] Another time he bought a consignment of Polish cigarettes allegedly made of lettuce leaves which, according to one Tesco employee, 'reminded me of nothing more than the old herbal cigarettes which we smoked behind the lavatory at school'.[3] To 'Slasher Jack' (as he became known), quality played second fiddle to price: 'Pile it high, sell it cheap' was his motto, with 'Always keep your hand over the money and be ready to run' a favourite maxim.[4]

With Cohen's forceful character, flair for business and sheer energy, Tesco grew. By the mid-1950s it had 150 stores. Its first supermarket opened in 1956, and in 1961 Cohen asked the comedian Sid James, star of the Carry-On films, to open the UK's then largest supermarket, a Tesco in Leicester.[5] By the time Cohen – then Sir Jack – retired in 1970 and handed over the reins to his sons-in-law, Tesco had over 800 stores.

But a bigger Tesco was not a better Tesco. Cohen had been Tesco – and therein lay the problem. His forceful, somewhat cowboy personality gave the chain its identity, complete with a reputation for flouting planning regulations and for board meetings that descended into verbal fisticuffs, or worse. But basing a company's culture on the founder's personality is not always a recipe for continued success. As Britain started to become richer and an ever-expanding middle class more affluent, Sir Jack's Tesco began to look rather jaded. Soon, the competition was running rings round Tesco. Sainsbury was building new supermarkets in the south of England, while Asda was building big new stores and selling food at low prices in the north.

The fact that Tesco survived at all is thanks to Ian MacLaurin and his senior team, David Malpas (his Managing Director) and John Gildersleeve (a rising star). In the years immediately after Jack Cohen's departure, the focus on price had dimmed, and too much faith had been placed in the Green Shield stamps marketing scheme. (Customers would be given stamps to reflect the value of their purchases, which they could then trade for more goods.) Rumours swirled around that a tobacco company had thought about buying Tesco, but had then decided that it might be bad for its brand! Ian took the bold step of abandoning Green Shield stamps, and returned to aggressive price cutting. At the same time, his team took the edge off the 'pile it high and sell it cheap' image by creating better own-label brands and a healthy-eating programme, and a focus on fresh foods. On top of that, they focused on building out-of-town superstores, to meet the demands of the growing number of car-owning shoppers. In the three years to 1990, turnover went up by more than 50 per cent, profits more than doubled and operating margins passed six per cent. Tesco's space – the total size of all its stores – was growing by almost ten per cent per year.[6] Reporting on Tesco's results in 1990, one national newspaper said:

> A decade ago Tesco was the modern equivalent of a music hall joke. But now it is Tesco which is laughing – all the way to the bank . . . the transformation of Tesco is a remarkable success story.[7]

Just when things were going so well, however, Britain fell into recession. After years of shoppers 'trading up', now they were looking for bargains, which created opportunities for Aldi and Lidl, limited-range discounters newly arrived from Germany. Tesco tried to protect its margins by cutting costs – for example, by reducing the number of tills open at any one time. The problem with this approach was that it chipped away at the quality of customer service and so dented customers' loyalty. Things were made worse by escalating interest rates. Tesco customers were badly hit. Sainsbury's customers, by contrast, suffered rather less: they were older and better off than Tesco customers, fewer had mortgages to pay and more enjoyed income from savings. Suddenly, the Sainsbury juggernaut seemed invincible and unstoppable. Confidence in Tesco's strategy gave way to doubt. Phrases like 'on the up' were replaced by 'losing its way'. Tesco tried various new initiatives but they proved as effective as shooting peas at tanks. It seemed the company had, in the words of seasoned observers, 'reached something of a dead end'.[8]

And so, by 1992, morale was flagging and a sense of crisis was beginning to set in. Sitting at my desk at Cheshunt one October day, I was suddenly summoned upstairs for a meeting with Ian MacLaurin. I walked in to find David Malpas there too. I immediately thought I was going to be fired. We were losing customers and I shared more than just some of the responsibility – at the time I was Commercial Director of Fresh Foods, buying and selling a large part of what Tesco sold. Instead, they asked me if I wanted to be Marketing Director and on the board. A promotion.

The colour drained from my face. The only thing I felt missing from the room was a poisoned chalice. But I accepted. I had just been made an offer I could not refuse. There was no choice.

Although it sounded powerful, the role of Marketing Director had been created for me and so was untried and untested. On my first day I had no team, no meetings scheduled, just an empty office. For someone who is not innately confident, and who likes the structure that action points, agendas and plans bring, I found it all deeply unsettling. But the lack of paraphernalia that usually goes with a new job gave me something I now realise is the most precious thing of all – time to think.

My task was quite simple: to find out why Tesco was struggling, and fix it. For months if not years my gut had been telling me that there was something wrong with our approach to our business. Although Tesco was a retailer, we hardly ever took any account of what our customers thought. Yes, we did customer research, we talked about what focus groups told us, we discussed how sales had risen or fallen, but the truth was that the customer was not driving the business, day in, day out.

'Customer satisfaction' was seen in a silo, the responsibility of a department to address, not something that the whole company should focus on – no more important than, say, process and logistics. Tesco's approach was not unique. The retail industry had become fixated with its own operations: a customer was sometimes reduced to an anonymous unit who bought our goods.

This grated with the most basic lesson of all that I learnt studying marketing at university: successful companies do not just focus on what their customers want, but put the customer at the centre of all they do. The customer should drive the entire business. We – the management of not just Tesco, but other retailers – were not thinking as consumers, and were not asking basic questions about what our business was all about.

Worse still, we at Tesco were fighting our competitors on their terms, judging ourselves against their performance, playing catch-up with their initiatives. We religiously followed what was called a 'benchmarking strategy', looking at what other retailers were doing well and (to quote Ian MacLaurin, who is honest to a fault) 'we just copied what they did unashamedly'.[9] We were playing 'Follow My Leader' – which is not the way to get ahead.

So I began with nothing more than a hunch: that if we listened to our customers, they would give us the route map to success. But to prove this theory correct meant getting to the truth, the very essence of what those customers thought about not just Tesco, but what role a company like Tesco could play in their lives. Routine customer research would not do this. To get under the skin of our customers I needed to turbocharge our research, and needed time to do that.

Up against me were calls for 'something to be done now – this instant'. It's a familiar occurrence. Failure provokes panic, initiatives get launched, 'strategy groups' are formed as people mistake action for progress. People think that they have no time to stop and think through the basic questions that they must address – such as 'What is the purpose of the organisation?' – when there is nothing more important than getting to the truth behind the failure.

I lost count of the number of times people popped into my office to ask me 'What are you going to do, Terry – the board are keen to know?' In those first few months I had not the faintest idea, but I nevertheless played my part by launching several initiatives. The problem, of course, was that they were all tactical rather than strategic and, as a result, they failed to make any impact at all. More peas shot at tanks. Meanwhile, in the City, while the stock market rose by 20 per cent in 1993, shares in food and drug retailers fell by 20 per cent, with Tesco among the hardest hit.

With our share price in the doldrums, I criss-crossed the country, sitting in countless focus groups of shoppers, hearing what they had to say about Tesco. I was frightened that I was going to find that the Tesco business model was a busted flush. Logic said that if people wanted quality they would surely go to Sainsbury, and if they wanted cheap products they would shop at a discounter: why would they come to Tesco? Worse still, the German discounters were prowling the UK market – and we could become their lunch.

So I decided that we needed to commission the biggest piece of consumer research in the history of Tesco. It was an unnerving strategy, since I knew it would involve turning over a stone that was almost certainly hiding some nasty surprises. I doubt that I would have had the courage – or authority – to do that if Tesco had been pottering along gently. The fact that I could is testament to Ian MacLaurin's leadership. He was not merely prepared to face harsh truths: he actually wanted to do so. Failure, or a threat to one's very existence, is a terrific spur to radical action, so long as you have the authority and credibility to do what is required.

It transpired that underneath the stone did indeed lurk some horrible things. The unvarnished, unedited truth about what customers thought of Tesco was painful to hear. In short, they thought we had deserted them. We had stopped concentrating on their needs, and had become obsessed with being like Sainsbury and Marks and Spencer. Tesco just wasn't Tesco anymore. We had lost something of our soul, our values and with that our customers' loyalty. At a time of recession we should have been there for these customers, offering them good value products at prices they could afford. But we weren't. If they could afford it, they would go to Sainsbury or Marks and Spencer; if not, they went to the discounter. Tesco's prices weren't low enough, and we had concentrated too much on better productivity at the expense of customer service. The logic was irrefutable. A customer in our Trowbridge store in Wiltshire summed it up for me: 'I like Tesco, but I just can't afford to shop here anymore.'

But were we doomed? No. Customers wanted to come back to us. For them, we were their local store – but they needed a reason to return. We needed to earn their custom, and prove that we were on their side.

The reactions of these customers tapped into something deep within me. Their hopes and dreams were not far-fetched: all they wanted was help in making their pay packets go further, so that they could buy their kids new shoes, save up for a holiday, treat themselves to a night out at the cinema. As someone who had been brought up modestly but well by parents on tight incomes in Liverpool, I felt a natural affinity with what these customers were telling us.

More than that, the fact that the customer was not at the centre of our business was, to me, a hangover from the years when people were expected to take it or leave it, when 'luxuries' (things that today we take for granted) were the preserve of the rich, and everyone else would be left to press their noses against shop windows, looking in awe at what they could not afford. I was convinced that our customers' simple wish for a better life gave Tesco an opportunity – and a mission: to give everyone quality and choice, irrespective of their income. All they wanted was the ability to look forward to a treat, to have that little bit extra. Tesco could make a real difference by making products both more affordable and more interesting. Yes, we would want to provide for those on middle or upper incomes – but we also needed to be there, through thick and thin, for those on small incomes, those who had to watch the pennies at the end of the month. Tesco needed to be genuinely classless.

Eventually I was ready to present my findings. Walking into the boardroom on a spring day in 1993 I could sense the atmosphere was tense: the directors clearly feared that I might tell them that there was an insurmountable problem, or I might have simply failed to find an answer as to why Tesco was struggling. I then gave my presentation, painstakingly taking them through the research and my recommendations. The point I tried to hammer home was that we must be prepared to do whatever was necessary to make Tesco the natural choice for ordinary people. We did not face an intractable problem, but there was no silver bullet either. Instead, there were lots of little things that we must do for the customer. I referred to them as 'bricks in the wall'. They would involve lots of innovation, I said, and would bring forward in the near future big changes – including a better price list and much improved service.

When I had finished, there was a palpable sense of relief. David Malpas reflected the views of many, saying 'It's a really bad problem, but it's much better once you know the cause and feel you can do something about it.'

That meeting showed the power of the truth – and the natural authority of the customer. Anyone who argued with the findings was arguing with thousands of customers. There could be no second-guessing about what customers might think about our business, or why our business might be slipping. It was all there, in horrible, grisly detail: you could see exactly what we were doing wrong. And yes, it was 'we'. There was no point trying to pass the buck, to claim that if only logistics improved availability, all would be fine. The truth was that customers had lost trust in us, and no amount of new products on our shelves, or clever one-off marketing tricks, or better logistics would save us. We had to go back to square one.

Acting on the truth

Square one meant recognising that customers are the most reliable guide that any business has. They would lead us out of the quagmire we were in. Once we had accepted that they were the voice of truth, however, we had to stick with them. We had to lock their views, demands and wishes into every aspect of how we did business, and how we thought about our business. There was no going back to the old habit of ignoring them.

Putting the customer at the core of everything we did may sound exceptionally obvious – yet how many organisations truly listen to what their customers, clients or users think of the service or products they provide, and then act on what they hear? Schools, manufacturers, charities, professional services, suppliers of all kinds: every organisation has its customers, most will claim to 'know them', few actually do, and even fewer respond to what customers tell them. With a wave of the hand, managers will say 'Of course we do research', but when you press them you often find that the research they commissioned is either being used to support a belief that has already been formed, or is sitting in some drawer, once read and now gathering dust. As a result, these organisations inhabit a twilight world in which the truth is a feeble light. In every area – from retail to town planning – progress is too often impeded by research that does not really drill into what people think.

By 'knowing your customer', I mean that you have to get behind their views on everything about a product or service, discover any frustrations they might have about what is on offer, and understand what really makes them tick – their emotions, hopes and fears. Our research at Tesco taught us about a whole range of issues – whether customers were scared about losing their jobs, what small luxury they yearned for but was just beyond their weekly budget, whether their family ate as one or individually, even the level of irritation they felt at using a trolley that didn't steer properly. Those who embark on this sort of quest for knowledge soon realise that it is endless: 'the customer' – the parent or patient, the businessman who buys a service, the single woman in search of the latest fashion – these people's wishes, tastes and emotions never stop changing and are often utterly unpredictable. If you take your finger off the customer's pulse, you quickly lose all sense of what makes their hearts beat that bit quicker.

Managers may see the importance of objective enquiry, but simply be unwilling to commission – or ignorant of the need for – research that drills down deep enough to find the truth, and gives sufficient insight to provide a reliable basis for making decisions. This is not merely bad management, but unjustifiable in today's world where there are countless means of researching what is going on in people's minds and hearts, enabling one to understand what thought or emotion is driving a particular action. There is quantitative or qualitative research (jargon for opinion polls and gathering a representative sample of people together to discuss issues in a structured way). On top of that is image, attitudinal, behavioural research. You can do research on the phone, in person and, of course, online. The internet means research takes far less time – you no longer feel that by the time it is done you are reading last month's newspapers. You can recruit a representative sample of customers quickly, and their feedback is instant.

I don't want to give the impression that Tesco had never undertaken any market research until I became Marketing Director. In fact, we had been honing our skills since the early 1980s. The problem was that the research we did in the early days wasn't exhaustive enough and, more crucially, it wasn't sufficiently central to the decision-making process. It often gave us much needed insight, but, as Tesco's fall from grace in the early 1990s shows, not enough and not quickly enough. Crucially, it wasn't embedded in the company's DNA, so the customer's view was not the starting point for everything we did.

That said, we did make some advances in the early days. During the 1980s, for example, I brought in at Tesco the 'trade-off research model' which had originally been created by Ford Motors. It may sound a rather jargon-ridden research tool, but it was actually a very clever approach to creating and sustaining competitive advantage. Ford wanted to make sure the new Fiesta they were developing would compete strongly against the market-leading VW Golf. This posed a challenge. When you buy a car, you look at all manner of attributes: the power of the engine, how safe it is, how soft the seats are, the size of the boot, will it fit your child's pushchair and the weekly shop, how many miles does it do to the gallon . . . the list is endless. Ford needed a reliable way to rank the relative importance of each attribute so they could ensure the Fiesta was market-leading.

They created a research process which forced customers to choose between pairs of attributes in multiple combinations until a clear ranking emerged. Which is more important: the size of the engine and fuel consumption, or safety and space? The outcome gave Ford the insight they needed to focus their efforts so the car fulfilled most consumers' greatest needs.

I found that the same approach could be applied to how a customer chooses between stores. Think about how you decide which supermarket to visit. You will weigh up and compare all manner of different characteristics. Choice of goods versus price of goods. Convenience versus quality. Quality versus price. We came up with our own system, which allowed us to rank those factors that influenced customers to choose one particular store in preference to another. As with a car, the list was long – especially when you started to get into 'fresh fruit and veg versus a good range of beer and wine', or 'fresh bread versus all I need for my baby'. Our findings enabled us to understand why some shoppers preferred Sainsbury to Tesco. It emerged, for example, that they wanted better quality and fresh food. This gave us the insight we needed in the 1980s to develop the type of superstore that would enable us to tackle Sainsbury's dominance. Sainsbury were so far in front of Tesco at the start of the process that, although we closed the gap during the 1980s, we never did quite remove their lead. But by the end of the decade, we were seen as a coming force, even if we did then lose our way for a while in the recession that followed.

There's no doubt that this robust research technique helped us improve our decision-making. Yet even the best research (which this was for the time) has its limits. What you see and learn is framed by the method you use and the questions you ask. You may have perfectly accurate research as far as it goes, but it may still not necessarily give you a true picture of your situation. Like shining a narrow torch beam in a dark room, you only see what the beam illuminates. You do not see all that is there.

Aware of this potential shortcoming, I realised that we needed something else to help us get into the minds and hearts of our customers, and understand the deeper emotional and rational forces that guided their behaviour. Instead of listening to customers through the rigid framework of prepared questions and pollsters' analysis, I wondered why we did not just gather customers together and let them talk – talk about anything, and see what emerged. I had the chance to put this thought into action when I became Marketing Director in 1992, by creating what became called Customer Panels. Every store in the country was asked to run a session of panels: one panel for daytime shoppers, one for evening shoppers (each group comprising 30 or so people) with a panel of store staff in between. The sessions were run by the store manager but moderated by a specialist team from head office. We invited other head office departments to attend and contribute.

In many respects, these panels would not pass the strict definition of research. I doubt that all the groups were a truly representative sample of our customers. Yet they gave us an invaluable, subjective insight into how our customers *felt.* Customers would just talk and talk, about their lives, their work, their home, their family, their money problems. They would talk about what they had seen on TV, where they had been on holiday, the latest gossip in the papers and, of course, shopping. They would talk about Tesco, the company, as well as their own local Tesco. They told us what they liked, what they didn't like, what they needed and how we could help. They said how we compared to other stores, what we were good at and where we needed to improve.

The personal testimonials provided much more colour about how ordinary people get by, and so were more compelling than dry research. The young man in Hemel Hempstead (just outside London) who seized on a single price, out of 40,000 products, which formed his entire view of our prices – and it was no use anyone explaining averages to him. The pensioner who hated paying for carrier bags, even though they cost us tens of millions of pounds to provide. The mum who was really upset by sweets at the checkout, as they provoked her children to pester her to distraction as she tried to pack and pay for their shopping. Often there were one or two strident voices – usually men – who began to dominate the panel. Others would listen quietly, and then gradually start to counter the more extreme views. The really powerful points were seldom from the strident but from the accumulation of stories, where the same point was made in different panels and in different ways all over the country.

This was the 'wisdom of crowds' in action. Those who are sceptical about following the customer (or patient, or voter) argue that people have such contradictory requirements that no organisation can take account of all their needs and demands. To that extent, the sceptics argue, those who know – the experts – should be left to decide. Beneath the sceptics' view of customer research often lies a fundamental lack of trust in people, and a misplaced belief that central planning – not the market – can deliver what people want. I believe in trusting people. Talk and listen to a sufficient number of people, and you find that patterns emerge, extremes are filtered out and you get simple, powerful insights that management sometimes misses.

We held our panels across the country and, later, we would introduce them across the world. In the 1990s I went to dozens of them, sitting anonymously at the back. Leaders are expected to be at the centre of the action, usually talking. The best leadership I ever gave was to be in the background, listening, and allowing the customer to be the leader instead.

In the early days I certainly found it difficult listening to the painful truth about Tesco's shortcomings. I found it even more difficult that criticisms were coming from our customers, who we thought we had done so much to please. But soon after I had been told the worst, relief took over as I realised that what they were criticising could be fixed. Indeed, the very fact that they were telling me suggested they hoped – and thought – that things could be fixed. Relief gave way to excitement as we started to work on the things that needed to be done.

Based on what consumers told us, we embarked on a wholesale period of change to turn the business around in the 1990s. Out of all the things we did, the most important change was in how we thought. In simple terms, we reversed the flow of the company: instead of our work ending with the customer, it started with the customer. That basic principle embodied our desire to avoid letting them down again. We would do everything and anything to ensure that we knew what customers needed, and that we gave it to them before any of our competitors did.

When the customer spoke, we listened. When the customer asked for something, we did it. When they said something was wrong, we fixed it. No questioning whether they were right, no second-guessing. We believed our customers knew best what they needed in their lives. Our job was to give them what they wanted.

Customers were always demanding of the business but they were not unreasonable. They felt a sense of ownership and had a strong sense of what was fair. They knew that businesses did not have a bottomless pit of cash to spend on stores or to cut prices. (Whenever I hear campaigners and politicians insist that more money be spent on everything, I think it would be good to have ordinary customers there to temper their demands.) They had a remarkable understanding of the problems that management faced in solving problems.

By listening to them so closely, we came to understand what changes we needed to make to the business. In just three years those changes not only fixed the problem but catapulted us past our competitors to become market leader – a position which we have kept to this day.

The introduction of the Value product range in 1993, with its distinctive simple, no-frills packaging, is a prime example of a clear strategy that emerged from listening to our customers. By creating a new economy range for the company, we were sending a clear signal to hard pressed consumers: 'We are on your side in tough times – you do not have to shop at the discounters.' A year later we introduced the 'one in front' checkout service which removed queuing from British supermarkets for the first time.

The principle was simple. A customer approaching the checkout should only see one person in front of them. If there was more than one, the checkout manager should open another checkout. And then, in 1995, we launched the Clubcard loyalty scheme which had the most far-reaching effect of all (and which I will cover in more detail later).

All these initiatives involved major investment and risk. Value lines threatened to bring about a spiral into a destructive price war with competitors. Removing queuing required thousands of new staff and cost ten per cent of our profits. There was no absolute guarantee that we would recoup all our expenditure through greater footfall in our stores, even though the programme was thoroughly trialled under the watchful eye of Philip Clarke (who succeeded me as Chief Executive). Clubcard was the riskiest of all. We stood to lose 25 per cent of our profits. What's more, if competitors followed suit, we might simply end up in a zero-sum game: no increase in industry sales and a quarter of the profits given to the consumer.

It's not surprising, then, that each of these major steps, critical to our success, had detractors within Tesco – and among our shareholders. Yet their arguments were usually based on a hunch, a resistance to change, an aversion to the truth. We had the truth on our side: the incontrovertible evidence, as a lawyer would say, that this was what customers wanted. We were not arguing that we should – or could afford to – write a blank cheque to meet every customer demand, there and then. (Customers are sensible: they know that companies cannot do that, and have to make a profit.) Rather, we had to listen, respectfully, to what customers wanted and resist the temptation to dismiss out of hand their demands as impossible to meet. We then had to ask ourselves whether we could deliver some or all of what they wanted and make money at the same time.

The research showed clearly that the status quo was not an option. 'No change' would have meant, in time, 'no Tesco'. When it came to introducing the changes, we were also helped by being the first to move. Without any doubt, our customers knew that we had done this for them. After all, we were not compelled by law, regulation or the competition to do these things. None of our competitors was changing in the way we were. So customers gave us credit for that, and we began, bit by bit, to regain their loyalty.

Better still, when our competitors did decide to follow in our footsteps, customers realised it was not because these companies cared, but because they had been forced to play catch-up with Tesco – so they did not gain loyalty. 'Me too' responses to the competition are rarely well executed, perhaps because the company's heart is not really in the move. Their employees know that the only reason they are changing is that a competitor has wrong-footed them and they feel they must follow suit. Customers then pick up on this lack of enthusiasm.

One of the first things we changed in response to what customers told us was the design and layout of our stores. At the time I became Marketing Director, our stores were the most expensive in the industry. We had lavished money on them to create the latest, sleekest design – a design that was much admired and copied around the world. The only problem was that we had built the stores without asking customers the basic question 'Would you like to shop in this kind of store?' Yes, a pretty basic point, but somehow one we had forgotten.

When we actually did ask customers about the stores, the answers that came back were a shock. Far from trotting out the architectural world's plaudits, people told us they didn't like the stores one bit. They thought them to be slightly cold, unwelcoming and a bit industrial, more like warehouses than nice retail stores. We had opted for low ambient lighting and spotlights to pick out colourful displays: all very chic, thought the designers – but customers told us it was too dark. We had sleek stainless-steel refrigeration without doors, even for frozen food – cutting-edge stuff – but unsurprisingly customers complained that it made the stores cold. We had added twists and turns in the floor layout to give each department a special identity: customers thought it was confusing.

Our architects and designers were certainly talented but – and a very big 'but' – they were designing in a vacuum. Maybe they thought 'We know enough about customers to design a store without talking to them.' Arguably our management had allowed them to design stores for us, the managers – whereas we should have been crystal clear from the start that they were building for the customer.

We had to turn that way of thinking on its head. Initially, the architects and designers resisted this incursion into their creative independence. Yet once they were given a different brief, based around the customer, these same designers produced outstandingly successful stores.

Before we could design new stores, however, we had to fix the ones already open and causing the problems. We started by talking to customers, via Customer Panels, and to our staff to get their thoughts and ideas about what could be done to improve things without involving massive outlays of cash. None of the changes that we then put into effect in response to their feedback was revolutionary. We brightened up the stores with better ambient lighting and some warmer paint colours on the walls. We lowered the grocery shelving so people no longer had to struggle to reach the top shelf – this also helped to make the aisles seem wider and brighter. We simplified the layout by straightening up displays. We improved signage and opened up the entrance, taking away clutter so that it seemed more spacious and welcoming. We added wipes for trolleys, extra bags for packing produce and baby-changing facilities in the toilets. We modified car parks, with better signs and a different layout to improve circulation.

Change, change and more change. Yet none of it cost very much: we had a limited budget per store and it never came under pressure. The programme needed someone who had lots of common sense and was a good manager – one of our retailers, Gordon Fryett, was a perfect choice. And the customers liked it. By implementing their ideas, we had given them a tangible sign that Tesco was trusting and focusing on them once again after years spent trying to copy Sainsbury and Marks and Spencer. They could see that we had spent some money to make shopping easier for them – and it was not obvious how we would make money out of it. This impressed them. By proving that we were motivated by their needs more than simply to make money, customers started to think about their relationship with Tesco differently. We communicated this change through the very successful 'Dotty' advertising campaign, featuring Prunella Scales (who starred in the TV sitcom *Fawlty Towers*). 'Dotty' was a hard-to-please customer, and each advertisement introduced a new innovation from Tesco to address one of her many quibbles and which, together, made shopping better for customers.

Today, New Look (as the initiative was called) seems a tiny step, barely worth a footnote in the history of Tesco. Yet changing the layout of stores to reflect customers' wishes had a profound effect on the future of the company. Without really knowing it, we had been transformed by this one, seemingly small innovation, from a good retail business to a potentially great marketing company – a company built around customers, completely different from the Tesco of the 1980s.

That was step one. From then on, customers were the starting point for all the major decisions we took – and the source of wisdom and advice as to how to solve seemingly intractable problems.

By the 'noughties', for example, we were finding that some of our stores no longer reflected the demography of the communities they served. This matters hugely to any retailer. If your shop stops being a mirror image of the community, it no longer connects with local people, nor does it penetrate into the life of that community in the way a successful store always should. An alien implant, without any relevance to customers' way of life, their culture or their budget, the store begins to lose its appeal.

We had always relied on the UK's National Census to help us decide where a store should be located, how it should be designed and what ranges it should stock. The problem was that the Census is only conducted once every ten years – and is not always that precise to begin with. Moreover, the cultural makeup of the UK has been changing fast in recent years, with people coming into the country from many parts of the world. Our data was simply not reflecting this.

This problem was thrown into sharp relief when we decided to rebuild our store in Slough, just west of London, in 2005. Just walking round the neighbourhood at the time revealed how much the community had clearly changed since the time of the 2001 Census. (Between 2003 and 2006, the percentage of children in Slough's schools who did not speak English as their first language rose by almost seven per cent – one of the highest rises in England.[10] One primary school took in 50 Polish children during a single term.)[11] Yet it was equally clear that our store did not reflect these changes in the community. Nor, it was apparent, would one of our typical brand-new, shining hypermarkets connect with Slough's multicultural markets and streets with their ethnic communities, consisting of over 30 nationalities,[12] that made up about 40 per cent of the borough's population.[13] Our existing store wasn't serving our customers; our plans for a new store wouldn't work either.

So the entire company put in a massive effort to understand the community, holding numerous Customer Panels and talking to local community leaders of the immigrant population to find the truth about what customers in Slough wanted. Customers told us they would like much more of the cuisine they were familiar with (in bulk so that it was at much lower prices), clothing that reflected their traditional fashions, and their holidays and festivals celebrated in store. Not only did all our marketing have to change to reflect this, but we had to build a whole new supply chain to source different food products, consisting of more than 1,000 new items, from India, Pakistan, Bangladesh and Poland. The store had to be significantly redesigned and we brought local traders to operate parts of it – for example, the meat counter and also a new shop selling traditional Indian desserts. This was something we had never done before.

When the new store opened, it was a huge success. Its atmosphere and pace, the mix of customers and staff really reflected the local community and, as a result, its sales were more than double that of its predecessor. None of the changes we made would have occurred to us had we relied on the Census. What drove them was a direct engagement with people and a willingness to look and listen. We learnt a valuable lesson, too: the success of the Slough venture completely changed how we did business, not just there but across the UK. We knew that if Tesco was to remain the first choice of ordinary families, we had to change to meet the needs of a new and vibrant, diverse society.

As time passed, we realised not just that customers were our route to solving problems, but that they could give Tesco a cutting edge, too. A few years after we launched New Look, we asked customers to help us plan the refurbishment of existing stores as well as the design of new ones. Any store is a very busy place – trucks delivering goods, spillages and breakages, mums with pushchairs – so they take a lot of wear and tear, and demand more than just a lick of paint every so often. At Tesco, every five years we spruce up a store and give it the most up-to-date marketing look, and every ten years we have to replace most of the internal equipment such as lighting, air conditioning, refrigeration and so on. With a lot of stores, that means we are running a big programme of refits all the time, investing over £200 million a year in the UK alone on major refits to over 100 stores, and much more abroad.

However, the sheer quantity of refits meant that the team at the centre gradually slipped into a one-size-fits-all mentality, rather than applying the general design principles of New Look and then demanding in addition that each refit should be appropriate for the individual store. In so doing we managed both to disrupt the business through constant repairs and adjustments and to displease our customers: they made it clear to us that they did not always like the refurbished stores at the end of it all. In other words, the investment sometimes destroyed value.

We could have simply ignored what we were being told and ploughed on regardless. After all, refurbishment programmes are essential: stores age so quickly that if you do not remodel and refresh them, they quickly lose custom, undermine customer loyalty and become a drain on the company. Delay costs money. But I felt we had to involve our customers more directly. Before a store was due for a refurbishment, I suggested, could we not convene a Customer Panel, explain to the customers what we were trying to do, tell them how much money we had and how much various things cost to change, and then ask them to pick the most important changes that they would like to see in the store?

You might think this was a very bad idea. Customers are not store planners and they don't know the first thing about format – so why hand them the cheque book? What do they know about marketing? How can they possibly spot the latest trends? And anyway, when has free advice ever been worth listening to?

Our people, understandably, thought the same thing. They were slightly concerned and nervous – and, I suspect, wondered 'What's Terry up to now?' But it says a lot for the trust that the marketing team and planners put in customers that they nevertheless ran the panels I proposed and, with only the lightest of guidance, gave the customers the chance to speak their mind openly. And the result was better than I could possibly have hoped. Customers loved the chance to influence the remodelling of their stores: for many, it was like being able to refurbish their home, with the added advantage of not having to pay for it. Moreover, most had a strong, personal incentive to get involved for the simple reason that most consumers tend to do their shopping at one store (though they may use others) and so have a vested interest in how it is set up. The result of all this consultation: a big improvement in sales performance and a rise in customer satisfaction.

There was also another outcome – one that I hadn't expected. To get the new store they wanted, customers proposed spending on average only half of what we typically spent on store refurbishment. Although they were spending our money, they showed the wisdom of people who have to manage a household budget in which every penny counts. They didn't want to spend money on frills if that money could be spent on price cuts. Fancy wine racks, shiny new lights, designer counters – people told us that they did not want the things that a designer might understandably have assumed they would. And that truth saved us more than £1 million a store.

Another insight, a moment of truth gleaned from a Customer Panel, gave birth to a whole new range of food. During the mid-1990s, when I was attending numerous Customer Panels, discussion quite often turned to special dietary needs. If truth be told, until then the concerns of people who had allergies had been a very small blip on our radar screen. Our market data hardly recorded the products they bought – it was a minuscule market. However, from the customer's standpoint it was clear that things looked very different. If one family member had a special dietary need (a gluten allergy, say), that would determine where the whole family shopping trip was done.

It's blindingly obvious when you think about it: no parent wants to shop in one place for some of the family and then have to go to a different outlet to find things for a child with an allergy. What they'll tend to do instead is to take all their shopping to a retailer who stocks the special product or products they require and who can also supply the needs of the rest of the family. In other words, the search for special products comes first and the rest of the family shop follows that. The practical result is that the store that can supply a few pounds worth of special dietary products is also likely to gain the £100 or so that a family will spend on their weekly shop.

Obvious that may be, but at head office no one had really thought much about these families, nor about the special dietary needs market itself. They saw the small size of, say, the gluten-free market, and didn't appreciate the larger scale expenditure that went with it. Nevertheless, although the logic of what we were discovering was strong, I struggled to get a good response to this insight. We were not organised – or perhaps not willing

– to handle the consequences. To create entire ranges for people with allergies would cut right across our market structure: all our ranges, our brands, the lot. And yet, at the same time, the quantities of product we would want to stock would be too small for the individual buying managers to focus on.

Then I got help from one very special customer. Patricia Wheway shopped in our stores and her child, George, had a gluten intolerance. She is a very determined woman. Unable to buy what she wanted, she got herself an appointment in my office. She explained the problem, said we should deal with it by hiring her and promised she would then create a range for people like her son. If I truly believed in trusting the customer, what could I say but 'yes'? So we took Patricia on, gave her some support and she set about developing the first comprehensive, mass-market range for people with dietary needs. The range was called Free From and, although not in itself enormous, was very substantial by the standards of the time. Contemporary in feel and well marketed, it was sold in one place in each store so that it was clearly visible. It was a life-saver for all those families like Patricia's who wanted these foods at affordable prices in their local Tesco. What's more, sales were terrific.

We set a trend. Evidence of the enterprise's success was that our competitors came into the market with their own ranges, prompting a big growth in investment in the sector, transforming the level of choice and availability. I am eternally grateful to Patricia, who went on to have a successful career with Tesco, for what she taught us.

The whole experience served to confirm my conviction that if you listen to customers, and act on the truth they tell you, you will be amazed at what can happen. By the same token, if your business or organisation has lost its way, and you fail to ask the customer – or client or citizen – why they have lost trust in you,

you will never get to the truth as to why you are failing. You may convince yourself that you have come up with a 'strategy', but the chances are that it will be the wrong one, based on cosy assumptions, not hard fact. Without realising it, you will take the wrong action, and go in the wrong direction for want of a true compass bearing. Once you get that true bearing, however, you have taken the first step towards recovery.

A willingness to confront the truth, no matter how painful the immediate consequences might be, became an integral part of the culture at Tesco. Things inevitably went wrong from time to time, as things inevitably do. My view was that to ignore events, or to duck or fudge decisions, was a sure way to store up problems for the future. Acknowledging setbacks and meeting them head on was – and remains – key. Being honest is the only way to retain people's trust, one of the most valuable commodities any manager or leader has. It is always far better to suffer the short-term pain of admitting to a mistake than enduring the long-term agony that comes from trust leaching away as your staff, or your customers, no longer believe you are willing to face up to and tell them the truth.

The bigger truth

By the time I became Chief Executive in 1997 Tesco had more than turned the corner: we had overtaken Sainsbury, our arch-rival. However, I was determined to underpin the business with a renewed sense of purpose and mission to prevent the problems of the early 1990s from happening again. We needed to move forward as one cohesive body, in which everyone knew the answer to the big question 'What is Tesco for?'

The larger the organisation, the greater the challenge it is to find that fundamental truth, the answer to the question 'What are we all doing here, day in day out?' The chances are that no one dares even ask it. The result is that organisations, and especially businesses, can become lifeless, soulless places, in which people undertake processes without the faintest idea what the overriding purpose is. People come in to work each day simply to do something – sometimes quite boring tasks – to support themselves and their families. I am not belittling their commitment for a moment. Everyone needs to make a living and every parent wants to be able to support their family. But every person I have come across wants to have a sense that their job, however superficially mundane they might think it is, is helping to achieve a wider purpose than simply bringing in the weekly pay packet.

Field Marshal Viscount Slim's book *Defeat into Victory* contains the best description I know of why it is so critical to clarify the purpose of any organisation, and to give those who work within it a truthful, simple answer to the question 'Why are we here?'

Slim's argument is simple. Armies (like businesses or any organisation) are only as strong as the morale of those who work within in them. 'Morale is a state of mind,' he wrote.

> It is that intangible force which will move a whole group of men to give their last ounce to achieve something, without counting the cost to themselves; that makes them feel they are part of something greater than themselves. If they are to feel that, their morale must, if it is to endure – and the essence of morale is that it should endure – have certain foundations.

Slim then lists the foundations of morale as 'spiritual, intellectual, material'.

> Spiritual first, because only spiritual foundations can stand real strain. Next intellectual, because men are swayed by reason as well as feeling. Material last – important, but last – because the

> very highest kinds of morale are often met when material conditions are lowest.[14]

Top of Slim's list of foundations for morale is that 'there must be a great and noble objective' – the answer to the question 'Why are we here?' The answer to this is not anything easily quantifiable. It needs to appeal to the heart, not just the head. And it must endure beyond the next battle – or the next set of financial results.

So far as my own company was concerned, no one had asked the question 'What is Tesco for?' It was a struggle to come up with a satisfactory answer. Nevertheless, I knew that for any company or organisation, while the great and noble objective need not be novel, it must have two essential qualities.

First, it must be lasting. The objective must endure, and have within it the capacity for renewal. If it is only attached to a product – a new computer, a new car – it will last for as long as the product is new, and then shrivel away, leaving the husk of a purposeless organisation. Second, this noble objective must be just that: noble. It needs to deliver an emotional benefit, not a purely rational one, to those on whom the organisation most relies. For companies, these people are its customers, its staff and its shareholders. They all must feel drawn to the company or organisation.

Note the absence of the word 'profit' here. Companies that focus solely on the bottom line rarely endure. The bottom line is a short-term measure, and such companies will sell the long term to buy short-term success. However, if you focus instead on delivering benefit for customers, you are more likely to deliver long-term satisfaction, which is the durable way of building lasting profits.

Jim Collins has written extensively and eloquently on this

subject. He cites George Merck II, of the pharmaceutical giant Merck and Co. 'We try to remember that medicine is for the patient . . . It is not for the profits. The profits follow, and if we have remembered that, they have never failed to appear. The better we have remembered it, the larger they have been.'[15]

'Medicine is for the patient'. Like so many truths, it sounds so obvious that it is hardly worth stating. Yet as the sale of goods and services has become ever more sophisticated, the processes by which they have been manufactured or marketed have overshadowed these simple truths. Leaders of companies – and other organisations, come to that – have focused on what they are selling, not whom they are selling to.

So as we grappled with the question 'What is Tesco for?', I gradually realised that the answers were scattered around us. We were there to serve people – not to sell products. We wanted to create value, not simply to deliver profit. And we wanted to create an emotional bond between ourselves and our customers, so that they would return to us, time and again. This long-term custom would provide the basis of lasting success.

Putting those pieces together, I concluded that our core purpose was 'to create value for customers to earn their lifetime loyalty'. Nothing about what we sell. No mention of profit. No sense that we deserve anyone's custom. Instead, a total focus on customers, and our wish to earn their loyalty to Tesco. Better still, by embodying what I and my colleagues believed in, the days when we set our objectives in response to our competitors' actions were well and truly over.

For something that had such profound consequences for Tesco, agreeing on this core purpose was a surprisingly straightforward exercise. I drafted it, my team discussed it, and that was it. No long-drawn-out strategy days, no endless meetings with flip charts. The impact of the research we had done in the mid-1990s meant we all saw it as obvious that the company was there for customers, and that our ambition should not be to win their custom today or tomorrow, but to win it for a lifetime.

This core purpose is, to me, a great and noble objective. Positive, ambitious, it reflects a simple aim I have always had: to help make ordinary people's lives that bit better. Above all, it was drawn from the simple truth that loyalty underpins every successful organisation.

2 Loyalty

Winning and retaining loyalty is the best objective any business – indeed, any organisation – can have. The search for loyalty has, at its heart, an age-old idea: you reward the behaviour you seek from others.

Sales, market share, profits, satisfied staff, good returns for investors, an excellent reputation: businesses face a number of competing aims. They all matter, but which matters most? This not a hypothetical question. While it's possible to pursue multiple desirable objectives, all managers are forced, time and again, to favour one objective over another. Often they will not make a decision explicitly, in a meeting, but will be rushed into making a choice in the pell-mell of everyday business. Given these various pressures, it is vital to have a single objective that overarches all others, giving everyone a compass to guide them.

Without question, winning and retaining loyalty is the best objective any business – indeed, any organisation – can have. It can be captured in a simple question every time anyone has a decision to make, whatever business or activity they are in: 'Will it make people more loyal to us or not?' Much has been written about the importance of people's loyalty to a business or organisation, especially by Frederick Reichheld. He understood that loyalty is about people – all the people involved with a business – and is a reciprocal bond. To build customers' (and employees') loyalty to a company, you have to be loyal to them, come hell or high water.

The search for loyalty has, at its heart, an age-old idea: you reward the behaviour you seek from others. If a business rewards the behaviour it needs to prosper and grow, it will produce a positive response which over time is loyalty. That behaviour may be employees' hard work, commitment and innovation; long-term investment in a business, even during tough times; or a willingness to return again and again to buy your goods or use your services. Schools have loyal parents; companies have loyal shareholders; charities have loyal donors; retailers have loyal customers. The one common characteristic of each group is that they are willing to support that organisation, and their loyalty is being rewarded by that organisation – be it through its performance, its dividends or its quality of service. That might mean the company has to cut prices when times are tough, or incur new costs to improve the quality of service. To create a loyal workforce, the management has to realise that while money and benefits are obviously critical, so too are the values by which the companies operate. And to create loyal investors, management has to deliver a long-term plan for sustainable growth.

Yet, despite the importance of loyalty, analysts usually look at other factors – immediate profit, return on capital, earnings per share – when trying to work out if a business has a future. Think about this for a moment, and you will realise how strange it is to ignore loyalty. In the last half of the 20th century, the West saw the market for goods and services become more crowded, with customers increasingly able and prepared to move from one provider or brand to another.

In the closing years of the last millennium and the start of the new one, the rapid spread of free markets, spurred on by the digital revolution, has led to still more choice and information. In 1980, there were about six major blue-jean brands: by 2010 there were estimated to be more than 800. Between 1999 and 2002, the amount of information communicated by print, film, magnetic and optical storage was the equivalent of 37,000 times the total amount of information in the US Library of Congress (which contains 17 million books). Between 2002 and 2010, this amount of information is estimated to have grown tenfold.[1] All this choice, all this information, increases the temptation for customers to shop elsewhere, testing their loyalty.

Think about the impact this has had on your own life. Whether you are buying a car or choosing where to shop for a meal; deciding what cereal to buy or where to go on holiday – the choice is endless and, thanks to the internet, is now literally at your fingertips. So for a company or organisation to flourish and grow in this world, it has to form an attachment with you and earn your loyalty, so you instinctively return to shop at its store, invest in its stock, donate to its campaign, use its services.

This attachment is partly rational. You buy a product because you know it works. You invest in a company because you have looked at its accounts and know it is well run. You send your child to a school because you know it has a great ethos and gets good results. But emotion is at work too. The product, company, organisation has values that you share or with which you can identify.

These two attachments – one rational, one emotional – breed loyalty. And they are seen in organisations that create real benefit for their customers or users. The value that is created may be quantifiable (in terms of price, return on investments and so on) and functional (in terms of reliability or convenience, for example). At the same time it will have an intangible, emotional element to it. These factors fuse together, building loyalty which in turn generates more custom, more profit and investment, a better service and a deeper sense of loyalty.

Profit follows from this; it does not lead it. And there is no doubt in my mind that the economic benefits of focusing on loyalty are very compelling for any business. The difference between loyal and disloyal customer behaviour is not marginal in terms of profit: loyalty is the biggest driver of profitability. If you keep customers for longer, you do not have to spend money trying to replace them so often. Most businesses – even the best ones – lose a lot of customers over time. When it comes to competitive markets like retail the turnover in customers is much higher than most people assume: the rate at which a business loses customers can be several per cent per month. Some businesses, such as mobile phone companies or car insurers, may turn over their entire customer base in two or three years. So even a small improvement in loyalty can have a big impact on the number of customers you have to replace each month.

Acquiring new customers is not cheap – it is probably the biggest expense a business has. Some financial service businesses routinely spend half their gross margin on customer acquisition. Reaping the rewards of that investment, and seeing those newly won customers contribute a profit, can take years – and, frustratingly, just as you think you have won their loyalty and are making a profit, you find some of them taking their business elsewhere. If a company can retain those customers even for just a fraction longer when their custom has become profitable, it can make a dramatic difference to the bottom line.

Achieving this goal is becoming harder by the day. The digital revolution, of course, is one reason: as I have already said, people now have more choice – and with it more power – than ever before. The death of deference is another factor. People no longer feel that you should 'know your place in society' and 'take it or leave it'. They have a sense that they are entitled to choice, and also a quality of service and care (be it from a company or a public organisation). The knowledge that they can easily take their custom elsewhere, and that rival companies are fighting for their attention, has taught people that their loyalty has a price – and they try to ratchet that price up.

Some businesses react to this challenge in entirely the wrong way: they think it's enough to create a tempting deal to lure new customers. In fact, this deal will probably be the best one that those customers will ever receive from the company and so, perversely, the businesses that adopt such a strategy actually find themselves rewarding customers for being promiscuous and switching their custom from one business to another. Customers' behaviour changes accordingly: it begins to make perfect sense to become 'first-time customers' permanently, constantly switching to get the very best deals. The car insurance industry is prone to this type of behaviour. Many insurers offer their best prices to new customers whom they do not know, rather than to the customer they already have and whom they do know. By rewarding disloyalty, and switching rewards from old customers to new ones, such companies descend into a dangerous spiral, losing loyal customers and chasing disloyal ones. The right approach to take is almost the opposite: of course, you need to reward every customer – but you should especially reward those who have proved their loyalty to you by returning time and again to buy your products and services. The more you know your customers and how they behave, the more you can afford to invest in the most loyal.

By rewarding loyalty, companies grow faster. If company 'A' is losing ten per cent of customers and gaining twelve per cent of new customers, it has a two per cent growth rate. If company 'B' gains twelve per cent of new customers but only loses five per cent, it is growing at seven per cent. Translated into a stock price, those different growth rates could easily see company 'B' valued at two or three times company 'A'. You might say company 'A' should just recruit more replacement customers, but the more of these customers a company needs the more expensive they become, to the point where they actually become unprofitable to recruit and the company cannot make up the growth shortfall.

Loyalty spurs growth in another way, too: loyal customers spend more. Tesco measured functional loyalty (how much of a customer's expenditure we captured) and emotional loyalty (how committed they felt toward us). There was a strong correlation between the two. We found that the more customers shopped with us (or bought a service from us), the more they trusted us. Because they trusted us, they were also more inclined to try other or new products we had to offer. It was a virtuous circle that benefited us as we expanded. At one point, we were concerned that as Tesco broadened what it had to offer – into insurance and mobile phones, for example – our customers might find aspects of the service unsatisfactory, weakening their loyalty to the entire Tesco brand and their willingness to shop with us for food. The reverse turned out to be the case. The customers who bought a wide range of products and services from us also gave us the biggest share of what they spent on food.

Those loyal customers cost less to maintain. They knew the business and liked it. They even knew the staff and liked them. They complained less, returned fewer products and needed less assistance. They often brought out the best in staff. They gave more positive recognition and feedback, making the team feel valued, raising their self-esteem and their sense of pride in their employer.

Loyal customers do a company's marketing themselves. After all, nothing beats a third-party endorsement from a customer: each syllable of praise is worth far more than any marketing, advertising or offer. These people become more than a business's ambassadors: they become its family. They will even stick up for the company when it is criticised, pointing out all the useful things a company does for customers and communities when others might not notice. All successful businesses face detractors who dislike the business for a whole host of reasons, and are committed and vocal in expressing their grievances. The uncommitted customer is not going to moderate those arguments – but the loyal customer will.

A business that values loyalty above all else does not focus on trying to win some customers simply because they have deeper pockets or are less sensitive to price than others. Our thinking was that although everyone has different needs and budgets, we had to find a way of creating some value for all of them, and ensuring that each time they shopped at Tesco they felt some benefit, however small. That way, they would reward us by becoming that bit more loyal. The reward for us might not be large – many people are on tight budgets – but for Tesco just as much as the customer, every little helped. So we always tried to use techniques and create offers that built loyalty among as many of our customers as possible, whatever their budget. We tried not to discriminate against any customer. Almost any business, large or small, a global chain or a high street boutique, should try to tap that sense of aspiration everyone has. Even if someone does not have the money to buy a product at the moment, the successful retailer should not spurn a customer. 'Everyone is welcome at Tesco' was our powerful message – we were inclusive, not exclusive.

That applied to our employees as much as our customers. Loyal employees benefit a company – or any organisation – in many ways. The more experience someone has at handling customers – be they shoppers or citizens – the greater their skill at retaining their custom (or fulfilling their needs) and building loyalty. As a business attracts and keeps new customers, so it can afford to attract and retain the best employees – and build their loyalty. The longer someone stays with a company, the quicker they can fulfil tasks without impairing quality. Better productivity and efficiency generates sustainable profits which makes it easier for the company to attract (and I use the word carefully) investors who share the management's core purpose. And by retaining good employees, you ensure that their experience and insight is passed down to new recruits – the best kind of training you can give them.

How do you build a loyal team? Part of the answer is to create the right culture: by having a core purpose that motivates people – something more than simply 'the better you do, the more you will be paid'; by setting clear values that show that everyone is treated fairly and with respect; and by trusting people to do their jobs – and allowing them to make mistakes. A loyal team is one that is not riddled with cliques, nor a sense that one group is benefiting from success more than others. Everyone needs to be given the chance to progress and helped to do so. Everyone needs the chance to own a share in the long-term financial success of the business, with profit sharing, share options or pensions. By the time I left Tesco, five of the eight executive directors had worked their way right up the company, and Tesco had more employee shareholders than any other company in the country.

Creating loyal investors is more difficult. Obviously every investor wants to see a return on their money. Yet, once again, those who simply want profit in the short term and try to force a company's management to deliver that return will land up creating an unsustainable business. Loyal investors are there for the long term. That means management needs to seek its investors with care, and then treat them as partners in the business, sharing problems and challenges with them just as one would with senior management. The best investors are those who understand and accept that it takes time for a business to create loyalty among its customers, but that in the end loyal customers provide the highest return on investment.

Building loyalty among employees and shareholders is critical, but creating customer loyalty is the key to success. That simple observation is the basis for Tesco's core purpose: 'to create value for customers to earn their lifetime loyalty'. To achieve that, however, you have to know your customers inside out.

Following the customer

Businesses that are loyal to their customers let them drive the business. There are no other hands on the steering wheel, no back-seat drivers shouting out conflicting directions. To achieve this relationship, a business must understand its customers – who they are, how they live, what they need. The richer your data, the more you can respond with innovations to appeal to them. That way, you can create an attachment which, if sustained, turns into loyalty.

Traditional customer research – for example, focus groups and opinion polls – can help but its power is limited. Such research can never tell you precisely which customers are your loyal customers, what their habits and tastes are, and how best to reward their loyalty. You have to rely on people's stated opinions about their needs and behaviour, and there is no way of checking to see if they acted as they said they would. Did they actually shop with you – and, if so, did they buy what they said they would?

Someone might spend a considerable part of their disposable income with a company each year, and yet that company might have absolutely no idea who that person is. A young mum, a student, a pensioner? Always loyal, or tempted to buy elsewhere? If they jump ship, will the company notice, let alone know why? If they stay loyal, will the company know how to thank and reward them? To achieve the level of insight to answer such searching questions, you require an entire system dedicated to identifying and rewarding loyalty. Tesco's success is largely built on such a system: Clubcard.

Clubcard's mother was failure. In 1993 Marks and Spencer was Britain's most profitable retailer – and it had only recently been overtaken by Walmart as the world's most profitable.

J Sainsbury was the most profitable grocery retailer not just in the UK but in the world. Britain was proud of both Marks and Spencer and Sainsbury, icons of British business and beloved of the middle classes.

Meanwhile Tesco, as I wrote earlier, was struggling in a period of recession. Unpopular with middle-class customers, it was also coming under pressure from discount retailers newly arrived from Germany. *The Times* delivered a particularly harsh, damning verdict: 'if you want quality shop at Sainsbury, if you want price shop at the discounters. Tesco is stuck in the middle. Who needs to shop there?' In 1993, Sainsbury had a market value of £8.5 billion, while Marks and Spencer's value rose to over £12.5 billion at the end of the year. Tesco seemed stuck in the doldrums, with a market value of about £4.5 billion. To us, Marks and Spencer and Sainsbury appeared unassailable.

Fast forward to the end of 1995, when Tesco overtook Sainsbury both in market share and stock market value to become Britain's number one grocery retailer. Two years later, Tesco surpassed Marks and Spencer to become the UK's number one retailer. From that day to this, Marks and Spencer and Sainsbury have never been able to challenge Tesco for market leadership. By 2011, Tesco had grown to be around six times larger than both companies. This turnaround, described by some as the most remarkable in British business history, was thanks to a number of changes we made. But the launch of the Clubcard in February 1995 was, in my view, undoubtedly the most significant.

Clubcard was one of the world's first shopper loyalty cards. At its heart lies a very simple idea: people join and receive a one per cent discount off their shopping as a reward. In return, we gather vital data generated by our checkouts about the products the customer buys. So simple – so why hadn't it been done before, and why was Tesco the first?

Technology has a lot to do with it. Viewed from today's vantage point, life without the internet, email, Facebook and online shopping seems almost unthinkable – let alone life without computers. And yet, until the 1990s, the biggest obstacle that prevented a company from collecting and analysing data about its customers was the high cost of computing for an organisation. When I joined Tesco in 1979 there was just one computer for the whole company. Occupying a whole floor of the building, The Computer, with its air conditioning and special security, was more pampered than the staff. A young, eager marketing executive, I was desperate to analyse who bought what products, where and when – but that was almost impossible. I had to ask The Computer department (note, not the marketing department) for very limited, specific pieces of data on the shipment of a product (not its sales) and wait in a queue for the request to be processed – as The Computer had to do all manner of other things too. By the time I finally received any information it was as up to date as last month's newspapers – in other words, pretty useless.

The bar code – which beeped into life when a packet of Wrigley's chewing gum was purchased in 1974 – began to create new possibilities. For customers, those little black lines meant shorter queues and quicker transactions, as most prices no longer had to be rung up on a till. For the retailer, the bar code created data, and lots of it. Retailers could at last capture product sales in detail. Yet problems remained. The cost of storing data was so high we could only keep limited amounts of analysis, and the rest was lost. Worse, the data told us nothing about the actual customer buying the product. We could learn about sales of shampoo but nothing about the people using the shampoo (other than that they probably had hair). Was it a man or woman, old or young, married or single, buying lots of it for a family, or just for themselves?

This lack of knowledge did not just frustrate me, but grated with all I learnt at university. The central principle of marketing is simple: find out what customers want and give it to them. But how could I, or Tesco, do that if none of us knew who the customers were, and what they were buying? Research existed – and we did plenty of it – but, as I have already said, the sort of research that is limited to opinion polls of a few thousand customers which is then interpreted by pollsters is of questionable value. It tells you what people say they've done or will do, not necessarily what actually happens. Moreover, it doesn't enable you to reward loyalty.

My frustration with this inability to thank loyal customers was also provoked by my experience of working for the Co-operative Movement in Manchester, where I had begun my career in 1977. Owned by its customers, the Co-op spread through Scotland and northern England in the first half of the 19th century as the Industrial Revolution gathered pace. Mill workers wanted an alternative to the mill owners' shop in which to spend their hard-earned wages, and so they set up their own store, the Co-op. The profits of the Co-op stores were distributed to their owners, the workers, by way of a dividend roughly in proportion to the amount they spent in the store. This early form of a loyalty scheme suffered from the same problem I encountered years later at Tesco: the Co-op never analysed any data, so it never knew who its most loyal customers were, what they bought, when they shopped and so on.

By the early 1990s, thanks to the exponential increase in computing power predicted so presciently by Gordon E Moore, new possibilities emerged. Computers could now handle the mountains of data about an item's movement produced by the bar code. There was even the possibility of linking an item's movement to individual customers as long as we had a way of identifying them.

Turning this problem over in my mind, I wondered whether Tesco could not reinvent the Co-op membership scheme based around modern computing power. By linking the identity of customers to their purchases, we would not merely understand their behaviour but be able to respond by improving what Tesco offered – be it beer, cereal, fish fingers, nappies or anything else. I cannot claim I was the only person thinking this. I read in 1990 that Bury Co-operative, an organisation of just a few stores, was trying to create an electronic membership scheme. Nothing came of that plan, but it showed me that I had to act before others did.

At this time I was head of buying Tesco's fresh food, a role that included product marketing. There was no marketing director as such. The job of marketing the company was being carried out by someone else who also had other responsibilities. While we were travelling together one day by train, I took the opportunity to suggest my idea to him. He turned it down flat, for perfectly understandable reasons. He remembered that Tesco had jettisoned a huge stamp-collecting loyalty scheme (Green Shield stamps) in 1977. Moreover, he recalled that the scheme had had a down-market image and defined what was not a successful period for Tesco, to put it mildly. Our CEO, Ian MacLaurin, had bravely staked his career on getting rid of it. This executive was not going to commit professional suicide by announcing to the CEO that loyalty schemes were now a good idea.

I was frustrated, but not for long. The company's growing financial woes in the 1990s gave it the spur to look for new answers. My promotion to Marketing Director gave me the opportunity to suggest what they might be. When I presented my idea the board of Tesco was cautious, if not sceptical. There were several objections. If the entire retail industry issued a loyalty card it would be hard to see what advantage Tesco would be left with. The one per cent discount was a problem: it might not seem a lot, but at the time most retailers were making pre-tax margins of around four per cent, so – on paper, at least – 25 per cent of profits were at stake. Next, it was far from clear at the outset what level of discount would be enough to attract customers to become members. Most executives actually felt that one per cent was far too little and the likely discount would need to be at least double that – between two and five per cent. If they were right, that would be the end of Tesco's profits.

Nevertheless, I ploughed on, buoyed up by what customers were telling us, and got approval to trial the scheme quietly in just a few stores – three at first, to get something organised, then around ten more in order to get meaningful results. Sales rose. Better still we discovered that, when we introduced discounts of one and two per cent, the lower discount was just as effective as the higher discount at recruiting customers. Hours of forensic analysis, trying to calculate what level of sales and what type of discounts would have the greatest impact on customers, paid off.

And then there was the data. Although collecting it proved quite costly, at least there was plenty to analyse. If we mined it properly and systemically, I was convinced that the insights we would gain would cover the investment many times over. What clinched the scheme for me, though, was the customers' reaction: they loved it. It might have been a simple 'thank you', and might not have been an enormous one, but they had never been thanked personally before – certainly not with the old loyalty stamps – and that mattered. Our thanking them for their loyalty strengthened their loyalty towards us.

The decision whether or not to launch Clubcard nationally was to be taken at our annual strategy conference in November 1994. This involved the whole board of Tesco, outside directors included. Although I had presented to this group many times over the years, and had attended the last two conferences as a director, I still found it an unnerving experience to come into a room full of my bosses. I knew they should be judging my proposal purely on its merits, but I felt – probably correctly – that they were judging me as well. (When I became CEO, I always tried to reassure people that we were discussing the issue at hand and making no judgement on them. I was only partially successful. When you are in the middle of a fierce debate, it's hard to remember that the criticisms are aimed at the argument you are advancing, and not at you.)

Given what was at stake – we were all conscious we were discussing a major strategic move – it was a surprisingly calm meeting. And even though I was a young marketing director who was suggesting that we should reinvent a failed initiative and take the business in an entirely new direction, I was amazed at the support I received. The decision to go ahead was unanimous. For Ian MacLaurin it was a brave move. Having scrapped the last loyalty scheme, he was now authorising a new one. Other grocery companies might have been beginning to think about a loyalty card – some were even trialling it – but we were the first to risk taking the plunge.

Now it was a race against time. Once it became clear we were going ahead, it seemed quite likely that our competitors would try to beat us to it. The board showed great faith in its young marketing team, the average age of which was only 30, led by me, a 38-year-old. We were left to our own devices, the only order being to move quickly to a national launch. This meant developing the concept, the systems, the advertising at breakneck speed. All this, plus a multitude of details, had to be nailed down without anyone having had any experience of this type of venture, nor any scheme with which to compare it.

We launched in February 1995 with a big campaign and a lot of national publicity. The UK consumer has a special relationship with its supermarkets, which play a much larger role in the national consciousness than in other countries. Sometimes this can be a problem but, for the launch of Clubcard, it meant a huge publicity boost. From first thing in the morning, the launch was all over the national TV news, as well as the next day's papers.

And on the day of launch we got what turned out to be a huge break. Sainsbury, still the industry brand leader, finding itself under pressure for an immediate public response, dismissed Clubcard as nothing more than 'electronic Green Shield stamps'. We couldn't believe our luck. This apparent knee-jerk response bore all the hallmarks of an organisation that, although currently reigning supreme, was fast becoming an *ancien régime*. Instead of stopping for a moment to ask whether customers might like this idea and wondering what they might learn from the opposition, Sainsbury had decided to dismiss our initiative out of hand. It reflected a lack of strategy on their part, and spoke volumes as to their attitude towards the competition. It also taught me an important lesson: it is always better to look for the strengths in a competitor's innovation than the weaknesses. You may feel better attacking a competitor, but in the long run it is wiser to learn from them.

Sainsbury's response also showed the risks inherent in modern communication. All too often in business and elsewhere, something unexpected happens and you are pressed for an immediate response. Your professional PR advisers say 'Just as nature abhors a vacuum, so does the media – if we don't fill it, our critics will.' Yet silence is sometimes the very best course of action: it keeps your options open. If you don't have anything to say, either say nothing or tell the simple truth: 'I will tell you what I think when I've had time to consider it.' (The truth has, for some reason, come to be regarded as problematic in modern communication.) 'Electronic Green Shield stamps' may have sounded like a good, well-crafted riposte, but it marked the start of Sainsbury's descent from the summit of British retailing.

We were in a London hotel, briefing the media, when I heard about Sainsbury's reaction. A naturally cautious person, I look behind every event to see where the bad news lies. But I knew that we had just had an amazing piece of good fortune. The press would pounce on the statement. The more Sainsbury had to defend it, the more it would have to become their strategy. It would be a brave Sainsbury executive who could then say 'I think that Clubcard move was a good idea by Tesco, we should do one.' Consequently, we were granted a vital period in which to establish a lead. As it transpired, Sainsbury did eventually launch a loyalty card but by the time it appeared, it seemed a rather belated attempt forced on it by Tesco rather than a bold initiative conceived for its customers.

The national launch of Clubcard was, if anything, even more successful than the trial. Sales surged ahead. Not long after its launch, I remember looking at the latest industry figures, crucial statistics which allow retailers to compare their weekly sales growth against the average of the industry. In a mature industry like retailing, one or two per cent either side of the industry average is what you would normally expect to see; anything more and something very unusual is happening. That morning, we were 11 per cent ahead. I knew at that moment something had changed in the industry for ever, and my life along with it. Gaining an unstoppable momentum, we overtook Sainsbury in that same year and became market leader – a position we still held when I left in 2011.

Our success was thanks to getting two fundamental things right. Customers received a loyalty discount irrespective of how much they spent: the scheme was not an incentive to spend more or drum up more business. It was a thank you, pure and simple. Second, the discount did not increase the more you spent. We did not reward big spenders over low spenders. There were strong arguments for a progressive scheme but we wanted to make it clear that every customer was valued. 'Everyone is welcome at Tesco' – a value which I will talk about later – became embodied in the scheme. We were inclusive and classless.

The benefit of Clubcard was increasingly felt over the following years. The scheme grew fairly quickly to ten million members (there are around 26 million households in the UK),[2] creating the mountain of data of which I had always dreamt. At first, this proved a real headache. We had never really appreciated what would actually be involved in handling so much data in order to unearth meaningful insights. So we hired a young entrepreneurial couple, Clive Humby and Edwina Dunn, who had just founded a data mining business. DunnHumby taught us how to analyse data and bring it to life. (They did it so successfully, we eventually bought DunnHumby and it is now one of the world's fastest growing data analysis businesses.) Their analysis meant we could see, as we had hoped, who our customers were; what they bought; how they shopped; when they shopped.

At first, this meant we could see what Mr, Mrs, Master or Miss Smith was buying, second by second. One of our team spotted that a celebrity, who was promoting a competing retailer, was shopping at Tesco – and suggested that we leaked this fact to the press. Although this might have given us a day's good headlines at the expense of that competitor, I was queasy about this. The short-term gain would, I feared, be overwhelmed by long-term pain of having to explain how we protected people's personal data.

Indeed, this episode flagged in my mind the need for us to give every customer peace of mind that their personal shopping habits would not be shared with anyone – including people within Tesco.

Within months of Clubcard's launch, we therefore made the data anonymous, stripping Mrs Smith's name from data that recorded her purchase of chicken, washing powder, coffee, mince and onions, so that no one could ever see what she bought. Instead, we grouped the data according to consumers with common characteristics, where and when they shopped and what they bought. (This was long before there was any legal protection of personal data, so there was no obligation for us to do this.) As a result, in 16 years of Clubcard, we have never had an issue with data privacy, and yet we still have the opportunity to tailor information and marketing from the knowledge of what small groups of people are interested in.

Originally, we grouped customers by life stage: students, young singles and so on or by relative affluence (using their post-code) in order to produce summary analyses of purchasing behaviour. Gradually, however, we came to realise this was a rather artificial way to handle the data, and in time we settled on a classification that was authentic and actually more useful. We defined people by what they bought: not so much 'you are what you eat', more 'you are what you buy'. Vegetarians, people on a budget, devotees of finer foods, munchers of quick snacks – these were just some of the classifications of types of customers we used, and they changed over time as we discerned there were more subsets of behaviour. The richness of the data stunned senior managers who had been in the business for a lifetime. At the end of one of DunnHumby's first presentations of Clubcard's insights, Ian MacLaurin exclaimed 'I've just learnt more about my customers in the last 30 minutes than I have done in the last 30 years.'

Of course, just gathering data and knowing more about

groups of customers does not in itself create loyalty. Loyalty is created by the way in which you respond to the things you learn about people: lots of little things which may not amount to much individually but added together create the feeling that Tesco understands customers' needs better than other retailers, and tries to help them. This tailoring of our 'offer' has multiplied the productivity of our marketing investments – new store launches, customer recruitment, individual product promotions and defending our stores and products from our competitors – by between three and ten times, depending on the particular type of investment.

For example, when used to defend a store against a new competitor opening a store down the road, Clubcard is three times more effective than conventional methods, such as paper vouchers. By knowing which customers had been attracted to the competition, and what factors might have influenced them, we could make sure we looked after them and encouraged them to come back once they had tried the new store.

Since we now knew what things people liked to buy, we could offer targeted promotions on those items. Seeing an offer on something you frequently buy as opposed to one on something you rarely or never purchase is inevitably far more attractive to you – and thanks to Clubcard this offer can therefore be ten times more effective than an indiscriminate one. Seeing an offer on a related product that you may not yet buy, but other people like you buy, builds loyalty. We could also make sure that we always stocked items – a particular type of jam, a certain make of razor – for which customers would never accept a substitute. They might not be good sellers, but they were nevertheless important to people – and their availability also built loyalty.

These insights enabled Tesco to build a direct relationship with an individual customer. The core communication has been Tesco's quarterly mail outs, when customers receive their

Clubcard rewards, targeted coupons and other information about things we think they will be interested in. Each mail out is unique to each customer and there are, consequently, tens of millions of versions, containing hundreds of millions of pounds of rewards and product offers. Unsurprisingly, they are eagerly awaited – it is one of the few times the mail brings money rather than a bill. The Clubcard mail out revolutionised the sales promotion industry. Traditionally, untargeted promotional offers had a response rate of barely one per cent: with targeted Clubcard product offers this response rate was transformed up to anywhere between 10 and 30 per cent – 10 to 30 times better.

Another scheme, Clubcard Rewards, was designed to build loyalty, but in a counter-intuitive way. Recognising that customers obviously buy goods and services outside Tesco, we decided to help them with their purchases there too. Clubcard Rewards allows customers to redeem their bonuses against, for example, a trip to the cinema or a driving lesson for a teenager, a holiday or a meal at their favourite restaurant. As Clubcard customers can make up around 30 per cent of the clientele at these leisure outlets, we found we could buy these services in bulk and pass the savings to our members.

The story of Clubcard obviously continues. It is now online and on mobile phones – particularly useful for self-scanning checkouts. Wherever Tesco operates, there is Clubcard, helping us understand the differences in shopping around the world, increasing the speed at which we learn and enabling us to deliver for customers. In China, 6.7 million customers have one. In Thailand, 5.2 million. All in, almost 43 million people around the world have a Tesco loyalty card.

There have been many loyalty cards that have sought to imitate Clubcard. Few have lasted as long, and even fewer have made a real difference to the fortunes of the company that has launched them. What has made Clubcard so successful for Tesco is that it transformed the way we worked. We made loyalty and data insight absolutely central to everything we did, reflecting our all-consuming obsession to understand the customer and make sure that insight shaped all the big decisions we took. Getting the data, interrogating it, gaining the insight is only half the task. Putting it at the heart of decision-making is the other – perhaps more important – half.

The Clubcard story may be about retailing, but the lessons it teaches can be applied in almost any organisation. It shows how fresh thinking can overturn the existing order and strip long-entrenched market leaders of their supremacy. Every organisation has customers – be they shoppers purchasing goods or parents using a school. Every organisation today has data. Clubcard showed how data can give any organisation new insights, and help any company to compete in new ways and overcome the disadvantages of a lack of scale, an unfashionable reputation and lower profitability than its competitors. Yet 15 years after the launch of Clubcard, only a fraction of the organisations I encounter have begun to tap the potential that data can offer. Consequently most organisations are, at best, not realising their full potential, while many continue to drift.

Above all, Clubcard taught me a simple truth: people like to be thanked, and if they are thanked, you begin to earn their loyalty. This may be a simple truth but its power, as our competitors found to their costs, can be profound.

Spotting trends, building loyalty

Clubcard became the bedrock of our success, and the data we reaped from it drove our business. Over the years, however, I became aware that mountains of data can blind managers to deep, long-term shifts in how people behave – often because these shifts don't superficially seem to have anything at all to do with your particular area of business. They're the sort of changes that happen almost imperceptibly, ultimately tricking people into thinking that life was always like that or – at the opposite extreme – making them wonder how things could have changed so radically without their really noticing. To spot these changes, you need to resist the pressure that exists in every organisation to look down and blinker yourself to life outside. Life around you – a news story about something on the other side of the world, or a chat with your friends at the pub – may seem irrelevant to your work and organisation, but it may well reflect a trend that will change your world entirely.

One example of this kind of profound, societal change has been the trend, repeated in every developing economy, of more women going out to work – and, in particular, working women with children. In the USA, the percentage of married women in the workforce rose by about 25 per cent between 1960 and 1990.[3] (Even more dramatic, the percentage of married women who were in work and had children under the age of six rose from 19 per cent in 1960 to 64 per cent in 1995).[4] The same happened in Britain. In the early 1950s, less than a quarter of married women were in the workforce: by 1991, half were.[5]

Businessmen and especially politicians were slow to recognise the impact this would have on all aspects of life. The debate about whether women should stay at home and look after their children distracted people from the effect this change was actually having on society and behaviour. Both parents going out to work, more single, working parents – for many consumers and families, this meant one thing: increasing wealth but decreasing time. Meanwhile there was more shift and flexible working, making it harder for many households to find time to go out to shop. Today, talk of the 'work–life balance' is commonplace. But it took years for this debate to begin – and years for retailers to respond. In particular, it was a long time before retailers considered keeping their shops open for longer.

For generations in England, shops had opened typically from 8am until 6pm, and were closed all day Sunday and for half a day during the week. (John Lewis was actually closed all day Monday even though they were the UK's largest department store chain.) Some larger stores might open until 8pm on Thursday or Friday. (In Germany, the restrictions were even more severe: stores were closed on Saturday afternoons as well.)

This practice had hardly changed in a century. It was based on the idea of a nuclear family, in which the father went out to work while the mother stayed at home, ready to rush out and do the shopping when the shops opened. Some of the restrictions were based on the long discredited economic idea that consumer demand is somehow fixed, and that if you increased supply (in this case the number of hours that shops are open) you would simply put up retailers' costs without any increase in sales. Tesco was one of first to respond to society's changing habits. We began in the 1980s by extending weekday opening hours until 10pm. Then we opened late on Saturday evenings. Both moves were popular with customers, especially the increased shopping time on Saturdays. Sales increased. We were creating a real benefit for them, which meant we earned their loyalty.

Local councils were not convinced. Many restricted our opening hours, so certain were they of the domestic needs of the homes and citizens they served. As a young researcher I was always keen to know how they gathered this 'knowledge'. I never found out. Their decisions seemed to be driven by the loud complaints of a few and the resigned indifference of the many consumers who were never consulted.

These authorities could be tackled on a case by case basis, but not when it came to Sunday trading. Opening on Sunday was forbidden by law under the 1950 Shops Act.[6] To retailers and consumers, who understood that longer opening hours were helpful to the modern busy household, it seemed completely logical that shops should also be allowed to open on a Sunday. Yet two arguments persisted. First, that Sunday was special as it was a day of religious observance. Second, that Sunday should be a family day – a day of rest – and that therefore people, especially women, should not be placed in a position where they were encouraged to shop or forced to work. These core beliefs, strongly held by many in Parliament and the British 'establishment', were not shared by wider society who did not regard shopping as a threat to these traditions.

We had evidence for this. Scotland, which has its own legal system, did not prohibit Sunday trading. So we could demonstrate that, north of the border, shopping was a modern pastime for most people. It was exactly the sort of thing they wanted to be able to do on their day of rest. And staff liked working on Sunday: we only used volunteers (of which there were plenty) and we paid them a higher rate, which was appreciated. As one woman pithily observed when asked if working on Sunday took her away from being with her husband, 'You mean me slaving over a stove while he's down the pub? I'd rather have the money.'

So we campaigned hard for Sunday opening, because we knew customers and staff wanted it – it was a way to build loyalty with them. Success, however, would not have been possible without the support of the shop workers' union USDAW. They had always been implacably opposed to Sunday opening and lobbied MPs to support their position. Their intentions were heartfelt and genuine: they believed they were working in the best interests of their members. Our experience of Sunday opening in Scotland, however, was sufficient to demonstrate to them that their misgivings were not going to materialise. Staff told them how useful it was and how they enjoyed the opportunity to work on Sunday.

To USDAW's eternal credit, in the middle of an intense national political battle on the issue, they changed their position to support Sunday opening. Saying 'I got it wrong' is always difficult; doing so on the national stage is doubly so, particularly in an era when those engaged in political debate see it as weakness ever to admit they have made a mistake. As a result, the legislation went through and shops opened. It was a huge success: Sunday became the busiest day of the week in terms of hourly sales – and, over time, many other countries around the world followed in our footsteps.

Tesco then went further. Thinking particularly of customers who had difficult shift patterns, we found a way of opening most of our stores 24 hours a day. In reality 24-hour operations had existed in our stores for years, as most cleaning and stocktaking was done through the night when stores were closed. So we did a lot of clever reorganisation to allow us to get the store ready for the next day while customers shopped. For example, before 24-hour shopping, we used to restock a whole store in one go. We changed this to target one section of the store at a time, to minimise disruption to customers. Always being open provided a tremendous service. Think about getting Calpol for your crying baby – or having somewhere simply to take your baby who is up all night; being able to get food after a night shift; stocking up on provisions on the way back from the airport or during Ramadan after sunset. Today, people take all this for granted, just as they take for granted being able to do online shopping or banking any time of the day or night. This experience paved the way for the world of e-commerce, in which the consumer never sleeps. I doubt it would have developed so well or so rapidly if the retail industry had not first learnt this lesson: you have to be ready for business when it suits the customer, not when it suits you.

The common thread running through the story of opening hours is not just 'change to reflect customers' wishes'. It goes deeper than that. Only by thinking like your customers, and understanding how they feel, can you begin to earn their loyalty. You are changing not simply for their custom, but to strengthen that critical emotional attachment to your business in a way that has lasting value. That means getting under their skin, seeing how they behave, how they act.

Most managers today will say that they listen to those who buy or use their services. They may well do so – but do they act on what they learn, or are they merely going through the motions? I cannot claim that Tesco was perfect: I had constantly to remind colleagues of the need to base decisions on customers' views and behaviour. I suspect most companies are the same, however 'customer focused' they claim to be. But at least most of them now try.

The same cannot be said for vast swathes of public sector, taxpayer-funded organisations. The public sector is, of course, unlike the private sector in many ways. Public organisations often lack the clear lines of accountability that exist in companies: public servants have to contend with the competing agendas of politicians, regulators, unions, civil servants, the media as well as – and usually at the bottom of the heap – citizens. The ability to plan for the long term is hampered by the electoral cycle: a strategy can be reversed overnight when a new government or council is elected. A private company can raise money on the stock market to pay for a new investment, or cut one area of activity to pay for another: for a public sector organisation, the quest for 'extra resources' takes time and political guile. If a company wins more customers, it is able to invest and grow; good schools and hospitals, by contrast, are not properly rewarded for attracting more pupils and patients (though, in fairness, this is changing). Linked to this is the belief that the pupil's parents and the patients don't know what's best for them and therefore should not be given real choice to drive the allocation of resources as a customer does in the private sector.

In the public sector, if no market exists, it is difficult for a manager to discover what citizens think of a service. Many public bodies may go through the motions of 'consultation' or 'polling' citizens, but they are really on 'transmit' – telling their staff what to do without much regard for what the user thinks or wants. Yes, there are exceptions to the rule: local government in Britain is increasingly aware of the views, needs and behaviour of the citizens it serves. Maybe this is because, compared with national government, it can focus on delivering a relatively small number of services to an electorate who live within a relatively small space. Yet how many public organisations try, day after day, to put the citizen first in every aspect of what they do?

A new local school or hospital? Ask the teachers and parents, or nurses and patients, how it should look and challenge them to suggest how to save money. A new strategy for a city's healthcare? Ask patients what is most important to them. New opening hours for a public service? Ask citizens what times are most convenient for them. This is the attitude and frame of mind that should permeate the public sector. By focusing people's minds on the fact that it is their money being spent, and involving them more in how it is spent, governments and taxpayers might get better value for money.

By putting the citizen first, both the culture and the structure of organisations needs to change, so that the citizen really is in the driving seat. I believe that if people are given the right information and a real ability to choose, they are able to decide on the right school for their child or which hospital to go to. Such an approach would undoubtedly ruffle the feathers of those with vested interests. It would unquestionably mean new processes would have to be created and fundamental structural changes would need to be made. For having been told that citizens want 'X', there can be no quibbling or inflexibility over delivering 'X'. You have to do it.

Some have accused me of being obsessive, fanatical even, about focusing on the customer. I plead guilty. Only then can you understand enough about them to earn their loyalty – by doing the small things that show you care. And putting your trust in the customer gives you the courage to strive for audacious goals.

3 Courage

Good strategies need to be bold and daring. People need to be stretched as they can do more than they think. Goals have to cause excitement, and perhaps just a little fear. Above all, they need to inspire, and present an organisation with a choice: have these great ambitions, or remain as you are.

Courage usually makes people think of war or disease – heroic feats under fire, or resolute defiance when suffering from a terminal illness. Death is normally not far away.

So courage is not a word one usually associates with business, or running any organisation. When you think of men and women sitting in meetings, selling goods and services or making things, you don't often think of them as courageous.

Yet although we might think of physical acts of valour as signs of courage, to me courage is really mental, spiritual and moral. In the face of the unknown, risks and opposition, courage means being certain that you are right – in terms of fact and values. You are sure, both in your head and heart, rationally and emotionally, that you are doing the right thing. If you have that certainty, the possibilities of what you can achieve are limitless. Conversely, without that kind of courage all your grand ambitions for your organisation, all the good intentions you might have to make a lasting difference to people's lives, crumble away.

Viscount Slim wrote elegantly of this 'moral courage'. Few people have it naturally, he believed, so it had to be taught. Most people learn it in their youth, from their parents, teachers or church. Failing that, in some cases Slim said it required an adult to undergo 'some striking emotional experience – something that suddenly bursts upon him'.

I would not describe myself as naturally brave. Far from it: I am both shy and cautious. I only embark on a course of action when I think I am sure of the consequences and have assessed the risks. But I would admit to being driven by a fear of failure, and a wish not merely to achieve one set of goals but to continue to succeed. Experiencing failure and still pursuing audacious goals is, arguably, a form of courage.

When I became Tesco's Chief Executive in February 1997

we lacked clear, overarching goals that would deliver our core purpose in the long term. All the data we had from Clubcard, and all our research, told us clearly what consumers wanted there and then. Convenience, shops that sold food and other products (books, electrical goods, clothes and so on – called 'non-food' by retailers). We needed to respond to customer demands, as well as bigger trends that were also emerging in the UK and globally.

Technologies were converging: although the mobile phone and internet were in their infancy, it was clear that they would transform how people lived (of which more later). In the UK retail sector, we knew that if we were to prosper in the long term we did not just have to beat the US giant Walmart on our home turf (they were eyeing up our market in 1996), but we also had to grow our business. That meant entering new areas – like financial services and telephones – which were traditionally seen as off-limits for 'supermarket chains' like Tesco. We realised that we had to succeed where others had failed overseas – establishing profitable, long-term businesses in Europe and, quite possibly, beyond.

These trends and challenges swirled around in my head for months before I became CEO. Waiting to catch a plane to Ireland, I had what I can only describe as a moment of clarity: I realised what our strategy must be, and wrote it down in the back of my diary. Calling the goals I set Tesco 'courageous' may well sound self-congratulatory. At the time, they were seen by many as naive. Yes, Clubcard had given me a feather in my cap, but now I wanted to push things further. When I unveiled our plans, there was a sense of stunned disbelief. For this is what I set out to achieve.

First, I wanted us to be the number one choice in the UK. At the time, we were still second to Marks and Spencer and had only recently overtaken Sainsbury. Most observers thought that our lead was temporary – particularly with the Walmart whale swimming our way.

Second, I wanted us to be as strong in non-food products as we were in food. Given that, at the time, our non-food sales were a tiny three per cent of our overall sales, this was ambitious.

Third, I wanted to develop a profitable retailing services business (such as finance or telecommunications). In 1996, Tesco offered no such services at all.

And finally, I said, I wanted us to be as strong internationally as we were domestically – and to have as much retail space overseas as we had in the UK. At that point, less than one per cent of our space was overseas (and we were planning to sell that the next year).

In the classic TV comedy *Yes Minister*, the senior civil servant Sir Humphrey says that the best way to convince a government minister that their proposed course of action is unwise is to describe their decision as 'courageous'. I suspect Sir Humphrey would have said the same about my goals.

Yet the reality is that good strategies need to be bold and daring. People need to be stretched as they can do more than they think. Goals have to cause excitement, and perhaps just a little fear. Above all, they need to inspire, and present an organisation with a choice: have these great ambitions, or remain as you are – fine, but small; treading water, not making progress; being part of history, not making it; in people's lives, not improving their lives.

Bold ambitions usually require great change. This creates resistance which tests a leader's energy and will. Lord 'Jacky' Fisher was one of the greatest reformers of the British Navy in its history, responsible for – among other things – building the *Dreadnought*, which transformed naval warfare before the First

World War. Fisher's audacious goals were matched by his impatience for action and indomitable energy. 'To get a fighting Navy we must be ruthless, relentless, remorseless in our Reforms,' he wrote. 'Stagnation is the curse of life.' 'Mad things come off.' 'Big risks bring big success.' Here was a man who would let no one stand in his way – it took the King to instruct him to stop working on Sundays. One of his favourite texts was from St Paul's Epistle to the Philippians: 'This one thing I do, forgetting those things which are behind, and reaching forth unto those things which are before, I press toward the mark.'[1]

This restlessness and energy, and a sense that 'more' is never quite enough, is not to be ungrateful or unappreciative of people's hard work. It simply recognises that, if you want to keep growing, you have to set people's sights higher and higher still. Having climbed one mountain, it's not enough to say 'That's it, let's stop here and admire the view'. You need to look to the next highest peak, and head for that. When Tesco became the most successful retailer in the UK, we could have said that was good enough and rested on our laurels like Marks and Spencer and Sainsbury. We didn't. Likewise, when the electrical manufacturing company Tokyo Tsushin Kogyo had become a successful company in Japan in the late 1950s, its co-founder Akio Morita upped the ante, signalling this by changing the corporation's name – to Sony. 'It became clear to me that if we did not set our sights on marketing abroad, we would not grow into the kind of company [Masaru] Ibuka and I had envisioned.'[2]

Pressing ahead was the only option open to Tesco when I became Chief Executive. I realised that if we stayed as we were, we would enter a grey twilight of competing solely in the UK. The alternative was to dare mighty things, expanding overseas or into new markets. Daring mighty things – be it in trade or any other area of human activity – will always cause anxiety and fear.

The temptation to opt for the quiet life has existed ever since trade began. In the 14th century, an Italian merchant in the Tuscan town of Prato, Francesco Datini, received the following letter from a fretful business partner:

> Francesco, I have heard that you wish to embark on a new enterprise. Before God, I beseech you, open your eyes wide and look well to what you do! You are rich and at ease, and not a boy any more, that you should need to undertake so much – and you know that we are all mortal, and the man who does many things will assuredly meet with disaster . . . Imagine how Donato Dini must feel, who is now over seventy, and because he has tried to do so much is bankrupt, and has only five soldi left for each of his lire![3]

This is all too familiar – translate it into today's jargon and you have a typical note put out by financial analysts. The company's senior team is too old to try to set out on this new venture; it is doing too much; it is doing fine as it is; and look at what happens to others who have done the same thing. Advice: sell the stock. (Just so you know, Datini ignored these words of caution: he set up new businesses in Pisa, then Florence, then Genoa, then Spain, and after that the Balearic Islands. And that's not to mention his business in Avignon, and his trade with Black Sea ports and in the Balkans. International businesses are hardly new.)

So I was determined to set an ambitious strategy. Having agreed it we did not change it. From that moment on we knew what we wanted to achieve. In fact, we were so convinced that we scaled down our strategy unit. Strategy should come from the very top of any organisation, and once set should not be tinkered with. Leaders who put their faith in strategy units are abdicating their responsibility. An organisation with lots of 'strategists' is sending a clear signal to the world: we don't know where we are going.

Our energy instead went on telling our teams what we were setting out to achieve, and the part that they would play on the journey. Our efforts to make sure everyone understood our strategy, and their own part in it, helped us grow fast. What followed were years of intense change, innovation – and mistakes. In setting such bold aims, we knew we had to take risks, and that we would fail in some of the things we set out to achieve.

Failure: a word that strikes terror into people's hearts. Failure is frightening, of course, but it has to be confronted. You cannot have success without the possibility of failure. Perhaps there are people who are not frightened by failure; those who know that fear and press ahead regardless are the courageous ones.

I was, like anyone, haunted at times by the spectre of failure – certainly in my early years at Tesco when I could not afford, quite literally, to lose my job. Yet this fear was always outweighed by other emotions: at first a driving passion to make things better; later, a wish to turn Tesco into a world-class business and a realisation that to achieve that, we had to take risks and suffer setbacks. And what's the worst that's going to happen? Effort and money may be wasted and some people will feel embarrassed, but that's about it. Now think of the consequences of not innovating, not taking a step into the unknown, not trying something new: nothing will change, you will not have tried to make a process more productive, you will not have attempted to do something new that could create more value for the business. I'm not suggesting wild ventures into the unknown. If you take any risk, you need to plan and take precautions. The greater the risk, the greater the precautions you must take. Yet doing nothing is often the greatest risk of all.

Many wise heads have seen the benefits that failure can bring so long as – and this is the crucial bit – lessons are learnt. The Italian economist and philosopher Vilfredo Pareto was one: 'Give me a fruitful error any time, full of seeds, bursting with its own corrections.' Warren Buffett, the renowned investor, is another: with less of a rhetorical flourish, he has said you should 'start out with failure, and then engineer its removal'.[4]

The Toyota car company (about which a lot more later) took this message to heart after the Second World War. Traditionally, car production lines could only be stopped by a floor manager to correct a heinous mistake (and with severe consequences for the worker concerned): the result was that many cars were produced with faults, which had to be corrected down the line. Taiichi Ohno (the Japanese businessman who is considered to be the father of the Toyota Production System) turned this on its head, giving every worker the power to stop the line if a mistake was made or a fault spotted. When that happened, the entire team would come over and work on the problem. No problem, error or mistake was treated as a one-off, random occurrence: each was seen as an event that had to be engineered out of the system. Ohno invented the 'five why's?' – interrogating the cause of every fault until its ultimate cause had been identified and fixed.[5] At first, this approach meant the line was stopped frequently – and production suffered. But in time, as the company learnt from failure, the stoppages became less frequent, and the quality of the cars improved.

This shows the power of learning from failure. It also demonstrates the importance of giving individuals responsibility and control over what they do. When you set tough, demanding goals for an organisation, it is imperative that everyone feels empowered to do whatever is required to meet the challenge expected of them – to take risks and so, inevitably, to get things wrong sometimes.

Having the courage to aim high, to learn from mistakes and take people with you is not – and should not be – the prerogative of large companies, nor is it or should it be confined to the private sector. It can be achieved anywhere, in companies and organisations of all sizes and aims. I myself have had direct experience of pursuing audacious goals in very different arenas. In the business arena there was Tesco's decision to create a new format of stores in the USA and to move into providing not just goods but services in the UK. In the public arena there has been my involvement in the regeneration of my home town, Liverpool. Vastly different goals, organisations and pressures, but all requiring a degree of courage.

Braving new frontiers

By definition courageous acts or audacious goals take you into uncharted territory, beyond the safe borders the organisation has set for itself. As a Chief Executive you are taking a gamble that the business is capable of doing more than it thinks possible, that you know where the limits of business lie, and how far you can push it before it snaps.

One such decision I took was to create a new chain of Tesco, called Fresh and Easy, in the USA. To this day, that decision is viewed as rash by some. The sceptics argue that Tesco's strategic expansion into non-food, financial services, Europe and Asia already represents a very ambitious programme; that the USA is a notoriously difficult market for British companies to enter; and the Fresh and Easy format is completely untried.

There are indeed many cautionary tales to deter Britons – especially retailers – from setting up shop in the USA. The lure is understandable. A common language, a culture that Britons feel they understand, exposure to numerous American brands and companies who have invested in the UK – Ford, McDonalds, Coke, Apple, Mars, Kellogg, Boeing, Gillette: Britons can easily delude themselves that life on the other side of 'the pond' is not really that different, and that competing there cannot be that hard. Therein lies the problem. These apparent similarities have blinded companies to the numerous differences. Midland Bank's acquisition of Crocker National Bank in California, Sainsbury's purchase of Shaw's Supermarkets: there is a long list of British companies which have bought US businesses, assuming these businesses would give them the springboard to replicate their British success in the USA – only to discover that the firm and the market are different.

This failure has not been for want of studying the USA. For generations, British retailers have beaten a path to the USA, the epicentre of consumer culture. The USA was home to the world's first self-service supermarket, which had the unlikely name of Piggly Wiggly.[6] Its development of self-service, getting the customers to push carts around and select their own products, is seen by some as the greatest breakthrough in service productivity since the Second World War. (Piggly Wiggly must have been a particularly creative place, because they actually had two concepts for a self-service supermarket. The other one involved the customers sitting at stations and the products moving past on conveyors.) British success, however, has been in taking lessons learnt in the USA and applying them to the UK – not vice versa. For example, in the 1940s Tesco's founder Jack Cohen visited those shiny new emporiums. Given that food rationing had just ended in grey, post-war Britain, for Cohen this clearly seemed like a visit to paradise.

> There were gleaming palaces, well lit, roomy and clean. One of the most impressive developments concerned the packaging of

> goods. New materials, radical new designs, bright labels, clear price markings, and the women not only carried baskets, they pushed trolleys. It was utopia for a retailer . . . The noise from the cash registers was music to any trader's ears.[7]

Unsurprisingly, he brought a form of the self-service supermarket back to Britain. 'This was to be the start of the consumer revolution' he later said. 'Our willingness to plunge into self-service when many others hesitated provided our credentials for championing the consumer cause after all those bleak years of control'.[8]

The extent to which UK retailers hold our US counterparts in awe is reflected in the fact that, just four years after joining Tesco as a lowly marketing trainee, even I was sent on a retail pilgrimage to the USA to examine the wonders and learn the lessons of American retailing. My one-week tour cost more than I earned in a year, so I felt a heavy responsibility to study hard, criss-crossing the continent and visiting all the foremost retailers of the time. I was bowled over: the USA of the early 1980s seemed the land of plenty compared with recession-torn Britain. (After an afternoon windsurfing in La Jolla, California I even contemplated emigrating.) Not long after this visit we formed a co-operative research group with a number of American supermarket chains, and for many years we held exchange visits. We learnt to look at the US market through American rather than British eyes, while the Americans gave us their critique of the UK market.

Like many British companies, Tesco's interest in the USA was based on our assumption that our first foreign investment would be made there. Over the years the visits became more about acquiring a company than study tours. We looked hard at many targets and, as Tesco became bigger and stronger, more targets looked to be within our grasp. And yet we never did buy a business. Instead, Tesco began its international expansion with forays into smaller emerging markets with less formidable local competition, like Korea, Malaysia and Turkey. Although these countries were unfamiliar to a British supermarket chain we felt our expertise could make a greater impact there than in the furnace of the US market. And we learnt important lessons: the need to look for the differences in culture rather than the similarities (which were few in any case) and the need to devise a retail strategy to cope with those differences. Our experiences in these countries changed the way we looked at the USA. Rather than taking false comfort from the apparent similarities, we instinctively knew that we should view America as foreign, and we therefore began to look for the differences.

At this point – the mid-1990s – the US supermarket industry was ageing. It was no longer the place where you instinctively looked for companies that were at the cutting edge of innovation in food retail. (Walmart was still predominantly a retailer that sold not food but general merchandise.) When I look at a company I always ask myself whether I would be happier owning it or competing against it. By the time I was CEO we had reached the point where we thought it might be better to compete directly with American supermarkets rather than buy one.

Far from rushing into a crowded, highly competitive marketplace, we looked long and hard at possible opportunities. Gradually some features of the market began to emerge which we thought we could exploit. First, the rise of Walmart had increased the emphasis on low prices – but with some trade-off on quality. Niche players like Whole Foods Market had developed to fill the quality gap but they were upmarket with prices to match. Second, the vast continent of America poses a real logistical challenge for fresh food distribution. The problem of moving goods over large distances and through so many retail outlets helps to explain why, over many years, food has tended to be quite highly processed and treated with preservatives. Third, the huge success of 'big box' retailing (supercentres and retail parks), based on the formula of cheap land, cheap petrol and low operating costs, meant that local neighbourhood retailing had not really attracted investment or innovation for many years. By contrast, in every other market where we operated, convenience was the fastest growing segment of the market.

We decided to focus, quite simply, on creating a new type of store. The USA certainly didn't need another supermarket chain; by some estimates they already had eight times more retail space per head of the population than the UK had. (Compared with the UK, land in the USA is plentiful and planning regulations are light so it is easy to open new retail space.) Nevertheless, crowded though the market might be, we felt there was room for a new format that offered something different. People will always shop with you if you can show how you are making their lives that bit better than the competition. Customers do switch, and if you get it right, you can quickly build on success. Mainstreet USA is full of examples that bear this out: Costco, Trader Joe's, Walmart and Whole Foods all grew rapidly to challenge traditional supermarkets.

The question, then, was could we develop a format that offered a different combination of price and quality – the high quality of Whole Foods at the low price of Walmart? Could we offer fresher, more natural food without artificial additives, flavourings and preservatives? Could we offer this in a store in the local neighbourhood which was convenient to reach and to use?

To achieve all this would be a tall order, but we were sure that it would be a real draw to customers – a genuine innovation in food retailing that would be seen as new and different, not just more of the same. It would have to be niche: the size of a convenience store means it obviously cannot stock everything and cater to every need. But if the combination of price and quality was right, if it could appeal across the entire market, across all income groups and all age groups and all ethnicities, this would not be a tiny sliver but a big niche in the market – and in a market as vast as the USA, a big niche allows you to build a very big business indeed.

Our courage was strengthened by Tesco's experience elsewhere. Although the format we had in mind would be unique to the USA, we were sure that it played to some of our strengths. Fresh, natural, additive-free food has to be shipped quickly, which means you need a dedicated supply base and just-in-time logistics: we had plenty of experience building such systems in the densely populated UK. We also had experience of commissioning own-brand freshly prepared foods. And we knew how to operate smaller stores – our Metro and particularly our Express stores were highly profitable and growing rapidly in every one of our markets around the world.

Of course, the model would need to be highly efficient from end to end, from the farm, via the factory and central depot to the store – all on a single, highly responsive, purpose-built system. Products would have to be produced and delivered just in time in trays, straight onto the shelves. There could be no frills – no coffee bars, service counters or an endless range of brands. Such a tightly run and streamlined venture required bespoke features: central distribution, a dedicated supply base, unique replenishment systems and our own kitchen, located next to our central distribution depot and producing 30 per cent of everything sold in a store – juice, salads, ready-made meals, meat and produce. Upfront investment would run to hundreds of millions of dollars.

The first phase alone would involve setting up a dense network of up to 400 stores, and we would need to roll them out swiftly to achieve break-even point as quickly as possible.

The stores themselves needed to be small (about 15,000 square feet including the warehouse) so that they could be located right in the neighbourhood. Their size meant the range of goods on offer would need to be slimmed down to just 4,000 products – some famous brands but mainly our own brand: enough for customers to do their weekly shop. The stores would have self-service checkouts, with staff assistance as required. This would, of course, save money. But we had also discovered that customers who used self-service checkouts greatly appreciated it when help was nevertheless on hand and spontaneously offered. They acknowledged that we were going the extra mile for them.

All this had to be designed from scratch. We researched everything with customers, step by step, and then built what we learnt into the design. We even got our staff to live with families for a spell to find out how they shopped and what they needed – it was incredibly kind of the families to put up with the intrusion, and the insights they provided us with were invaluable. We then built an entire prototype of a store and invited customers to walk around it, shop for things and then tell us what they liked or disliked. This all happened before we formally decided to launch in the USA, so it had to be done in secret: we built the store inside a warehouse in an industrial district of Los Angeles, shipping in a lot of equipment and product. This naturally aroused a lot of local interest. 'What are you guys doing there?' our team kept being asked. 'We're making a movie,' we said – which struck the residents of Los Angeles as a perfectly plausible reply.

Feedback from customers was really encouraging: they noticed and liked the low prices and the clean, simple layout. We did lots of desk research, modelling the format with as much objectivity as possible to test the idea to destruction.

Obviously the brand had to be more than a network of stores. A brand has to have a personality to which customers can relate. Tim Mason, my Marketing Director, moved to the USA to become the CEO of the Fresh and Easy project and was an ideal choice to create the Fresh and Easy brand. He built a strong set of internal values about the company and its customers. Fresh and Easy was to be about fresh, natural food at great prices; it would be part of your local neighbourhood and would boast good environmental credentials. The name 'Fresh and Easy' started out as a working title for the project but it was better received in research than any other option because it simply stated what the store was about – good food and easy shopping – so it stuck.

Having done all our preparation, we decided to go ahead. The risk was very real: this was an untried format in a very crowded and competitive market. However, it was a calculated risk: after the initial upfront cost, most of the investment would be in new stores and their launch could be calibrated according to performance. What's more, even if the entire investment ultimately had to be written off, it would not threaten Tesco's underlying viability; to that extent it was a much safer option than, say, spending $10 billion or so acquiring a major player in the market. The upside was very considerable: even a niche format in the USA could become a business of the size of Tesco in the UK. It was also an investment which balanced the fast growth but higher economic and political risk of our expansion into the developing markets of Asia. Pressing ahead, pressing towards the mark, demanded courage – but we had done our homework, we knew what we were up against, and we were not betting the farm.

So we went public, explained what we were about to do and began to build the systems, logistics and manufacturing facilities and acquire the store sites. We had chosen to start in the Western United States. We based the depot and central kitchen east of Los Angeles to supply the city, San Diego, the Central Valley, Las Vegas and Phoenix. These last three, in particular, were fast-growing areas of affordable houses and employment growth. Much of our network was planned for this expansion – new communities still being built.

The first stores opened in autumn 2007. The timing couldn't have been worse. The western world was entering its worst recession for 70 years. Much of our target market was descending into a full-blown depression. The western United States had been booming when we decided to launch, but boom was rapidly turning to bust thanks to its being at the epicentre of the sub-prime housing collapse – something no one had predicted in 2005, when we decided to invest. Instead of filling up, many of the new communities started emptying out as the value of homes sank below the value of their mortgages and unemployment rose. Yet by then we were committed: the factories and depot were built, we had constructed many of the stores and we had taken firm leases on many others.

In retail, newcomers really feel the full force of a downturn. People don't try new things in tough times. They hunker down, draw in their horns and concentrate on spending less, not seeking out new tempting experiences. All this added to our woes, and we would have faced a serious problem but for one thing – the most important thing. Those customers who tried the stores absolutely loved them. They got the idea, loved the low prices, the great food and the quick shopping. Most of all they loved the service and the staff – a direct outcome of all the work Tim Mason had put into branding and values.

In these difficult, early days our most loyal advocates were the customers (who became 'Friends of Fresh and Easy') and the staff. For the latter it was the best place they had ever worked in: they really believed in the store and its values and were determined to make it a success. The stores in the more established communities in LA and San Diego were hit but not decimated by the downturn. They performed well enough to suggest that, in better times, the enthusiasm of staff and customers would translate into a viable business.

So we pressed on. We slowed the expansion. We were learning a lot – not everything is successful when an idea meets reality. We fine-tuned the choice of products, and made the store decor warmer and livelier. The original break-even date had been set for 2010. Now it would be 2012.

Fresh and Easy's success at the end of 2011 was encouraging. Sales were growing rapidly and the brand was growing in confidence. As the economic headwind slowly became a tailwind, I thought Fresh and Easy was well placed to benefit – thanks largely to the courageous people who stepped forward to turn an ambition into a reality. Many observers remained sceptical. For them it was not an audacious goal but a major miscalculation of the US market and the capabilities of Tesco. At the end of 2012, my predecessor took the decision to pull the plug and 'review' the entire operation. Whatever the rights or wrongs of this decision, investing in the US was my responsibility as CEO and a clear example that goals are easy to set, incredibly difficult to achieve and must carry a clear accountability.

Defying convention

For any organisation, expanding overseas is a risky business. You have to contend with new cultures, tastes, laws and regulations as well as a completely different economic background. Another type of risk is to move into an entirely new domain of activity, which changes the very nature of the organisation itself. You are going from an area in which you have a lot of experience to one in which you have little or none. Such diversification puts you head to head with a new set of competitors who know the market and have established customers, and also know all about its regulation, technology and systems. If they win, your reputation, brand, and customers' trust can all take a knock.

In retail, this diversification began in the middle of the 1990s. Until then, conventional wisdom had it that retailers sell things, not services. Customers went into a store with their hard-earned cash, chose what they wanted from a display of products, handed over the money, and that was that. So far as Tesco was concerned, that meant food and beverages, and sometimes cosmetics and medicines. In other words, Tesco was where you went to feed yourself and the family: end of story.

That innate conservatism was the product of generations of people behaving and thinking in the same way. It blocked out the possibility that things could be done in a different way, and hid the potential for new business that was under our noses.

For a retailer like Tesco, that mentality posed a challenge. As a traditional retailer in an increasingly competitive market, how were we to grow in the UK? The opportunities for traditional supermarkets that mainly sold food were diminishing thanks to regulation and growing competition. Like all CEOs, I suspect, I carried that nagging concern around with me all my waking hours. Even the good days were tempered by the thought 'Yes, this week's sales may have been good, but where is future growth going to come from?' I had always worked on the belief that if I simply followed the customer, watched how their lives were changing and what new needs they had, then that would give me the ingredients for growth. That meant we had to be ready and willing to change our business enough to be the one who could satisfy those needs for the customer.

By the time I became CEO, the UK economy – like many others – was changing fast. The service sector was becoming increasingly important. In the early 1960s consumers spent over 40 per cent of their income on food alone. By the 1990s that had declined to ten per cent. Even if you added clothing and all general merchandise, retailers of products were confined to a declining minority share of consumer expenditure. In developed economies, consumers were actually spending more on services than they were on products. And propelling those cold statistics were people's hopes, dreams and desires. This was brought home to me graphically when the mobile phone revolution began. Suddenly we were witnessing a society where some consumers were able and prepared to pay more for a single mobile phone call than they spent on food for the whole week.

Retailers were obviously aware of the service sector – banks, insurers and, as they emerged, mobile phone companies – but we placed them in another mental silo marked 'not us'. They were seen as irrelevant to the industry, just another part of the economy. This increasingly struck me not only as absurdly out of date, but also as a flawed business strategy. Retailers who sold products had no choice but to think of a way to retail services as well. Otherwise, growth would be much harder – if not impossible – to achieve. Retailers like Tesco would be left scrabbling over the scraps of the high street, food and drink, while the service providers would be feasting on their new-found markets.

Some argued that developing economies provided us with a respite. That had an element of truth in it. Most household expenditure in these countries still went on food and everyday essentials – a factor that strengthened our decision to expand into the developing markets of eastern Europe and Asia. But this state of affairs would not last forever; as these economies became more prosperous, consumers there would also spend more on services. So no change was, as usual, not an option.

One other feature of services struck me as interesting. Over the years, product marketing had become fragmented and broken up into specialist areas. There were very few manufacturers who still sold the products they made, and there were very few retailers who did anything other than distribute products. Some luxury goods brands did both, but they were a minority. In contrast, services were still largely integrated. Bankers and insurers, for example, still had large networks of banks and offices to market and distribute the products they developed (such as loans, mortgages and insurance), to acquire new customers and serve existing ones. In many cases half of their margin was taken up in distribution and customer acquisition. I wondered whether a separation between the origination and development of products (the manufacturing) and distribution and customer acquisition might lead to a better, more efficient business model as it had with the marketing of almost every other product, from tomato ketchup to toothpaste to Toyotas. If so, that could spawn the emergence of large discount retailers of services along similar lines to product retailing.

On my mental radar screen were the biggest industries: banking, insurance, telecommunications, and also entertainment and leisure. I did, in addition, consider education and health but came to the conclusion that these vast enterprises were complicated by uncertain regulation and, obviously, politics. Our own experience of developing a pharmacy service that could dispense prescription drugs had given us more than an inkling of the problems that might arise. Our customers wanted pharmacies in our stores, not least because our stores stayed open for longer than traditional chemists. The regulatory authorities, however, distorted the market by not granting licences to supermarkets for reasons that seemed at best arbitrary: they forbade any competition (which kept the price of medicine unnecessarily high) and, perversely, penalised success by charging a higher price for medicines for higher volumes purchased. This turned the economy of scale on its head, as the more you bought, the more you paid. So I soon ditched the idea of any involvement there. As far as other areas of the service economy were concerned, I knew we had to find something in each one that would give us an advantage over the incumbents, and some chance of success against them.

We found it thanks to Clubcard, Tesco's loyalty scheme. It allowed us to form an affinity group, a club of people who became our most loyal customers. These customers gave us our special advantage. Instead of going into service markets we didn't understand, looking for customers we didn't know, we could just concentrate on our own customers, the ones we knew very well, and provide services for them which they would help us design.

From the moment we launched Clubcard in 1995 and saw its power, we began to ponder how it might help us to offer services. And, as usual, the answer came not from a consultant, but from the customer. Within a few months of Clubcard's launch, our research revealed a startling question customers were asking: 'Can we not use Clubcard to pay for things at the checkout?' The proverbial light bulb was lit.

That shows the great thing about customers. They were untroubled by, and probably unaware of, the enormous consequences and vast logistical difficulties entailed in that simple statement, which effectively meant they wanted Tesco to be a bank. Yet what they were saying was both simple and honest. It was then up to us to decide whether their view should be ignored or acted on, whether it was a bounty or a burden.

Tesco, a bank? In the 1990s most people would have said 'You're mad.' And that is what many people did say when we first considered it. Shopping with us for food obviously meant customers needed to trust us. But asking them to trust us with their money? This was trust on a different order of magnitude. The slightest slip could jeopardise our entire relationship with them, and damage our brand overnight. A 'leap of faith' does not do justice to size of the risk we felt we were taking. We all had to draw deep on our courage, and our belief that we were doing the right thing.

Quite apart from the strategic risks we faced, there were numerous logistical and regulatory issues that we had to overcome. If customers were to use Clubcard to pay for goods, we would need a banking licence. We would have to learn how to be regulated as a bank. We would also have to change all our checkouts to be able to transact with the Clubcard, as we had only intended it to collect data. The obstacles looked immense, but the power of the idea made overcoming them that much more important. So we decided to give it a go. Sufficient customers wanted it, and the potential long-term opportunities it might provide were vast.

After a rapid period of development we launched Clubcard Plus in 1996. Like Clubcard, it enabled the customer to earn points and Tesco to gather information, but this card had the added feature that it could also be used to pay for goods. The customer arranged a monthly transfer from their current account based on their estimated spend on groceries. They were rewarded with extra points and we paid interest on any balance. It was a much better deal than they received from any bank account.

Even though the product could only be used at Tesco, it proved popular. We therefore decided to push on and launch a wider range of products and services. We created a partnership with the Royal Bank of Scotland (which was, at that time, a venerable Scottish institution with little presence in the rest of the UK). They were able to provide a good deal of the expertise we lacked, and could reassure the banking regulator when our new joint venture applied for a banking licence. We quickly broadened our offering, adding a credit card, a savings product, a lending product, car insurance and home insurance.

No one had ever done anything on quite this scale before. Banks had opened branches in supermarkets around the world but no supermarket had actually gone into banking and insurance so directly. Unsurprisingly, some media commentators gorged on speculation about whether the very idea of trusting a mere supermarket with your money was too much for people. This reflected the same ingrained thinking that many business analysts had about what was 'normal'. What they didn't know, of course, was that this idea had not been dreamt up by us, but by our customers themselves. So long as they trusted us to do a good job in terms of service, simplicity and value, that was enough.

And we did a good job. We set new attractive rates and a new standard of service. The products were simple to understand, with no hidden charges or conditions buried in the small print, for which the financial services had a bit of a reputation. Thanks to a series of successful product launches, within a few years we had begun to win up to ten per cent of the entire market share for some financial products. This was some feat for a new entrant into a sector as huge as financial services – especially as we were only targeting our own customers, for whom we became the brand leader in financial services.

Our success was largely because our approach was in tune with old-fashioned banking: know your customers, encourage them to save with you and insure with you and support them when they need to borrow. Because we were able to use Clubcard to get to know our customers better, this gave us an advantage in terms of the risk we were taking. We didn't need to build a massive bank overnight, with all the risks that would entail. Instead we could build steadily and take a patient, long-term view. The bank has grown consistently since it was created, even through the terrible financial crisis of 2008. In 2009 Tesco bought out RBS and began to expand the bank with products and services designed specifically for the Tesco customer base. With more than five and a half million customer accounts, one of the most encouraging features of the Tesco bank is how it has increased customers' loyalty to the whole Tesco business. What once seemed courageous and, to some, foolhardy, now seems common sense.

'Make no little plans'

'Make no little plans. They have no magic to stir men's blood and probably will not themselves be realized' was a sentiment expressed by Daniel Burnham, the American architect and town planner whose grand schemes reshaped Chicago and Washington – to name just two of his many achievements.[9] This sentiment should run through any plan. Every initiative comes up against snags, problems and people's innate fear of change. Small plans end up being salami-sliced into tiny ones. Only if you think big, and plan bigger still, do you stand a chance of seeing real change.

The history of my home town, Liverpool, reflects this scale of courage and ambition. While I love the north-west of England, it has never been blessed by geography or climate. For centuries the town – as it once was – struggled to make any impression on the nation, much less the world. Even though King John granted the town a royal charter for trade with Ireland in 1207,[10] nothing much happened for a very long time. In 1700 Liverpool was still a sleepy backwater of just 5,000 souls.[11]

And then, in the late 18th and early 19th centuries, in the region around Liverpool, a remarkable series of inventions and innovations in power generation and manufacturing began the first industrial age, the effect of which was truly global. For hundreds of years, two-thirds of global wealth and output had been in the east, centred on China and India. That was reversed by the Industrial Revolution in this tiny corner of a small island off the corner of Europe. Liverpool became the seaport for the Industrial Revolution – at one point in the 19th century it handled 40 per cent of the world's shipping.[12]

The city began to experience the sort of explosive growth one associates with China today. By 1800 the population had increased to about 80,000, and by 1900 it had increased almost nine times to just over 700,000, staking its claim to be the second city of the British Empire after London.[13] The merchants of the city grew rich and endowed it with magnificent Victorian buildings, galleries and museums.

Its decline was as rapid as its ascent. During the 19th century, the great families of Liverpool began to see London as the place they must be. In the 20th century shipping relocated to countries with lower costs and less onerous regulations, and when the UK joined the European Union the focus for British trade shifted to the east of England. Meanwhile, the impact of the Industrial Revolution had long since spread around the world, ending Liverpool's dominance. By the last decades of the 20th century the city had reached a low point. By 2001, its population was roughly half of what it was in 1931.[14] Between 1961 and 1985, the number of jobs in the city fell by 43 per cent, and the unemployment rate increased from 6 to 26 per cent.[15] It was one of the poorest places in Europe.

As the millennium approached, Liverpool's problems grew. To the litany of unemployment, family breakdown and crime were added riots and a far-left, socialist council who bankrupted the city and almost split the UK Labour Party. Liverpool, once the face of Britain's commercial might, became synonymous with inner-city decline.

Liverpool's problems appeared so intractable that they started to be accepted. Anyone who suggested that things could be turned around seemed, at best, naive. What was needed to counter this attitude was real courage: courage to overcome not just the politics of the place, but the sense that Liverpool's decline was inevitable and the best that could be done was to 'manage' it. And amazingly a group of people did exist who had this courage. They set up an organisation called Liverpool Vision, a joint venture between the public and private sectors that was designed to stimulate economic growth through physical regeneration of the city centre. In 2001 I was invited to be a director.

I felt a bit of an outsider as I had left the city almost 25 years before, but in fact that actually helped me – and I hope them – as I was able to reflect how the rest of the world saw Liverpool. Working for a city is like working for a firm or an institution: if you are caught up on the inside it is difficult to face the truth and see yourself as others see you. You can always find a reason as to why a specific criticism is inaccurate, or how it is already being addressed.

Thanks to all the bad publicity it was getting, the city had lost sight of its strengths. After a century of decline, people had only ever known things getting worse and could never think of things getting better, let alone plan on that basis. Government thinking and policy did not help. Ministers – of all political persuasions – provided a lot of much-needed, well-meaning support, but all of it was built on the assumption of managed decline. This fostered a dependency on government handouts and sapped morale, confidence and energy. I was much more optimistic. My business had taken me around the world, and I knew Liverpool punched above its weight in terms of its culture and historical legacy.

Two men in particular were responsible for turning Liverpool Vision's courageous goals into reality. Our company was ably led by a quiet Liverpudlian, Joe Dwyer, who had spent his life in the building industry. Meanwhile, the city had just hired a dynamic Chief Executive, David Henshaw. Liverpool Vision lived up to its name: to undertake no less than a complete replanning, regeneration and rebuilding of the entire city centre. More than that, the vision included a determination to attract the funds that would actually turn the plan into a reality.

The city's economic problems helped us in one way. Liverpool had been depressed for so long that many of its finest, grand buildings remained – there had never been the demand to demolish the old in a rush for the new and the modern that had occurred in other cities. There were even bomb sites left over from the Second World War, still largely untouched after 60 years. These included a unique, 40-acre plot right in the heart of the city.

This site became the linchpin of the master plan. The city council had previously asked for an expert's advice on the maximum potential demand for new shopping space in the centre of Liverpool. Taking into account the city's economic decline and relatively impoverished status, the answer came back that 250,000 square feet was the maximum area required – and a development of about that size had in fact opened up. We didn't agree with this. Our view was that if we got the scheme right, it would create new demand and begin the process of moving Liverpool back up the retail hierarchy. Luckily, one of the wealthiest men in Britain shared our view. The Duke of Westminster agreed that Liverpool needed to think big, and his company put forward a scheme for the rebuilding of the entire 40 acres, using 20 different architects to recreate the old street layout. The scheme would create 1.5 million square feet of shopping space, as well as hotels, restaurants, cinemas and apartments.

Agreeing to this plan, which was six times bigger than the experts advised, demanded courage. Once it was in place, however, we were able to plan a lot more. A new conference centre on the waterfront with hotels, a new museum and huge apartment towers. An entire new office quarter. Altogether £4 billion of investment was ploughed into less than one square mile, the majority of it privately financed, the rest public investment in major infrastructure.[16] Overall, we envisaged rebuilding almost a quarter of the entire city centre, the greatest and most extensive redevelopment in Liverpool's history, even in the boom years. For the first time in decades, the future looked bigger and brighter than the past. You could feel the pride and confidence flood back into the city and its people.

A bold vision, audacious goals, a plan. One step was missing: achieving it. Innumerable 'great plans' for cities, firms, institutions and governments have been unveiled with a great fanfare, only to gather dust on the shelf as people decide they are all too difficult to make happen. What is required is an imperative – an immovable event by which point the project must be completed, thereby demanding clear decisions and action. Liverpool pulled off a masterstroke. By winning the competition to become the European Capital of Culture for 2008, they created a big event that put huge pressure on everyone to get things done by then. This would be a year-round celebration of the city's rich culture, attracting people from all over the world. And they did it.

Everything was built, on time, on budget. The new development provided a shiny new setting for the old architectural gems. The capital of culture was a huge success: in that year, Liverpool was the fourth most popular destination for holidaymakers in the UK.[17] The city was catapulted from 15th to 5th in the UK's league table of shopping destinations.[18] And the broader economy benefited. After years of bumping along the bottom of every economic table, Liverpool became the fastest growing metropolitan area in the UK.

There is, of course, much more to do but the city has regained its confidence. Having tasted ambition, it has something to build on. Its reputation as a city to work and invest in has been transformed, strengthening its case for inward investment. In a myriad of ways, it has begun to reconnect with the outside world.

Looking back, it seems incredible to think that a commercial city, once the hub of world trade, whose impressive waterfront the builders of Shanghai copied, became so isolated, insular and unconfident. That, sadly, is what failure can do to any organisation, community – or, come to that, individual. The revival of Liverpool shows that you should never let your future be a prisoner of your past. Its revival has lessons for everyone about bold plans, timing, risk and, above all, courage.

Such demand for ambition – and courage – provokes the usual pleas from those in an organisation. 'I haven't the time to do anything else.' 'I can't take on any more.' But people, and organisations, are always capable of doing more than they think. Later, I will explain how to make that possible. But one thing is clear: you need determination – and perseverance – to realise those ambitions. The Victorian writer and thinker Samuel Smiles said of Napoleon that his favourite maxim was 'The truest wisdom is a resolute determination'.

> He was told that the Alps stood in the way of his armies – 'there shall be no Alps', he said, and the road across the Simplon was constructed through a district formerly almost inaccessible. 'Impossible' said he, 'is a word only to be found in the dictionary of fools'.[19]

Such resolution and determination are critical to make courageous aims a reality – so long as, in the drive to achieve something, you do not forget your values.

4 Values

Strong values underpin successful businesses. They give managers a sheet anchor, something that holds their position and keeps them from being smashed against the rocks when caught in a storm. Values govern how a business behaves, what it sees as important, what it does when faced with a problem.

People often look back on the 1950s and early 1960s, before the days of miniskirts and Flower Power, as a golden age. Not in my book. I remember it as a period when background mattered more than merit, when many people suffered from poverty of ambition.

There was, though, one good thing about that period that was lost during the 1960s: a set of values that governed good behaviour. Respect for others, integrity, perseverance, a clear sense of right and wrong – these values were drummed into me thanks to my Catholic upbringing. In the rush to break down class barriers and end stifling traditions, such values were lost – and replaced by moral relativism, a sense that anything goes. In our wish to end discrimination, we began to tolerate everything.

This matters to business just as much as to society as a whole. Strong values underpin successful businesses. They give managers a sheet anchor, something that holds their position and keeps them from being smashed against the rocks when caught in a storm. How to react to a competitor's surprise initiative, whether to sack an employee, whether to invest in a particular venture: the answer to difficult questions, the stuff of sleepless nights, can be found if one remains true to a set of clear, eternal values. More than that, being true to these values enables trust and confidence to take root, binding employee to employee, employee to employer, and customer to a company. This inspires employees to follow the management, to go the extra mile, to help their colleagues, while building loyalty among customers.

People's behaviour is swayed more by emotion, their gut reaction, than by reason. Those emotions are often driven and underpinned by values, such as rewarding people who do the right thing, showing respect for others, selflessly helping those in need. There may be rational arguments as to why such values matter, but most people will probably say 'because my gut tells me it's the right thing to do'.

Drew Westen, in his book *The Political Brain*, berates politicians who have 'an irrational commitment to rationality'.[1] He says 'If you think about voters as calculating machines who add up the utility of your positions on "the issues", you will invariably find yourself scouring the polls for your principles. And as soon as voters perceive you turning to opinion polls, instead of your internal polls – your emotions, and particularly your moral emotions – they will see you as weak, waffling, pandering and unprincipled. And they will be right.'[2] Westen then argues that voters do not debate policies that have no 'emotional implications' for themselves or their families: 'from the standpoint of research of neuroscience, the more purely "rational" an appeal, the less it is likely to activate the emotion circuits that regulate voting behaviour'. Hence the political adage 'Persuade with reason, motivate with emotion.'

Successful politicians have always understood this – business leaders less so. Yet employees and customers are driven as much by emotion as by reason, and their attitudes are shaped by their experiences of, and feelings towards, a brand or business. This is why values are so important. They govern how a business behaves, what it sees as important, what it does when faced with a problem – everything from how it handles the need to cut costs to what a shop assistant does when asked by a customer 'Where's the ketchup?'

Given all that, it is odd that analysts and boffins who pore over companies' performance do not pay more attention to corporate values. True, it is difficult to put a figure on a 'good value', let alone try to measure a company's adherence to its values. Nevertheless, you only need to walk into a reception area, or a store or showroom, to get a feel for whether the company has values that respect its employees or try to earn the trust of its customers.

Some managers are cynical about writing down an organisation's values. Everyone shares the same values, the argument goes, so why bother articulating them for your organisation? While it may be true that people do share many common values, when you write down what you and your team care most about, you are likely to be creating something unique for your company or organisation. (When John Lennon was asked how he composed such different records, he replied he didn't know as he always set out to make a new record exactly the same as the one before.)

Companies usually fail when they lose sight of their values and start to make decisions solely on the basis of short-term gain and profit. They take risks and will even bet the whole company – everyone's jobs, pensions, livelihoods, the lot – on a single decision. Unless the company is facing annihilation, there is never any case for that. A company with values – a sense of right and wrong, a wish to treat its employees decently – would never take such a gamble.

I did not always think that the words 'business' and 'values' belonged together. Brought up in a socialist household, from an early age I associated 'business' with dark satanic mills run by ruthless bosses, devoid of any values. Even by the end of my business degree, which had been tinged with a socialist antipathy towards profit and the market, I was still a little wary of what business entailed. And that explains, in part, why I was drawn to the Co-operative Society at the outset of my career.

The Co-op's roots were in the workers' movement, in the days before socialism. Its founders, and those who worked for it when I joined, had a strong belief in democracy and social justice. Owned and run by its members, it attracted very well-meaning, compassionate people, motivated by a wish to do their bit to help those less fortunate in society. It was all very laudable – but the ends (democracy and social justice) began to dictate the means of achieving these goals. The Co-op was managed as a democracy. Taking a decision took an age as everyone had a say, so no one was really in charge. What's more, even though it had been set up with the noble intention to serve every customer, irrespective of their means, the customer's voice actually got lost in the babble of views and debate. No one was quite sure what the organisation was there to do. Was it to give work to people, or improve society, or win customers, or make a profit? A basic question, but one that was never answered. I quickly learnt that values matter not just in terms of what you want to achieve, but how you set about achieving your goals. Without a clear process (about which more later) strong values and noble ambitions remain just words.

From the charm, glacial pace and traditional English tea party atmosphere of the Co-op, in 1979 I went to the Wild West – Tesco. Having begun life as a market stall in the hurly-burly of London's East End, Tesco was run by its founder, Jack Cohen, with intuition, flair and a dictatorial stamp – all of which you could still feel in the Tesco I joined. Competitive, aggressive and overly formal (many of the managers had been in the Army), most of Tesco's people had come from backgrounds like mine. To get on, you had to rely on your own efforts, drive and determination. It was each man – and it was generally just men – for himself. In a company with a clear structure and rules of behaviour that may just about work. But in those days Tesco had little of either.

The management structure had been created by power struggles between colleagues (if they called each other that). It was brutal, tough, uncultured – but full of energy and drive. Adding to the tension was the company's underperformance. People felt under pressure – but alone. To let off steam, their safety valve was their voice: shouting at people was routine. With little structure or sense of civil behaviour, the environment was unpredictable and volatile. One minute you could find yourself in a grown-up meeting with the senior managers, the next you could feel as though you were in a school playground as someone was teased for how they walked or spoke.

I am sure that Tesco was not unlike other businesses of that era, but I was shocked, bewildered and scared by all this. Having been to university, I expected something more cerebral, mature and rational. Above all, I expected better manners. I had been warned that I would be eaten alive – and after only a day in the job I felt jaws snapping around me. I faced a choice: kill or be killed.

So I changed, became combative, pushy and aggressive, not afraid to step on people's toes. On a good day I was the funny northern bloke who kept asking for things. On a bad day I was the irritating northern bloke who kept asking for things. And there were more bad days than good ones – two of which are seared on my mind.

Aged 23, I presented to the senior directors some ideas on how we might improve our health and beauty range. It was my first major project at Tesco, and I had to talk about it in front of the entire senior team – about 60 people in all. Hardly the stuff of high politics, or so I thought. When I finished, the insults began.

'You're really out of your depth here, Leahy.'

'You haven't the first idea what the hell you are talking about. I've been doing this job 15 years and you come in here telling me what to do. Just who do you think you are?'

'Are you trying to tell me how to do my job?'

I did not have the courage to say 'So why aren't you doing it?'

Four years later, at a company conference in 1983, I gave a speech on the need for excellent customer service and swiftly discovered that, so far as many were concerned, marketing was nothing more than a data-crunching backwater, far removed from the front line. Once again, the brickbats flew. 'What right have you to talk about the customer?' 'Are you lecturing us?'

By the time I became Chief Executive in 1997, Tesco had already begun to change. More women were working in the business. The warmth of success had thawed icy relationships. But there were still constant turf wars which exhausted people. An air of machismo and a dog-eat-dog atmosphere stifled ideas and new thinking. It seemed essential to me that people should be more valued and respected.

I concluded we must codify Tesco's values. My predecessor had been a big figure, and well liked: the business needed to know what I stood for. I also wanted to instil in Tesco a clear sense of values that sprang from our staff, and their commitment to the customer. Values written on high and passed down like tablets of stone would not live on the shop floor. Tesco's values had to be Tesco's creation.

So we took the tens of thousands of people who worked for us, organised them into groups of 30 or 40 people and asked them, over the course of a year, two simple questions. What does Tesco stand for? What would you like it to stand for? We collated their answers, and then they – not the senior management – fashioned and tinkered with them. Words and phrases were rejected by the staff: 'taking risks' was deleted, for example, as it made people feel insecure. And in the end, out popped two core values.

Our first value, 'No one tries harder for customers', summed up Tesco's employees' description of – and pride in – Tesco. Our second – 'Treat people how we like to be treated' – reflected the kind of place they wanted to work in. Beneath each of these core values the staff inserted others which expressed and unpacked its meaning.

Under 'No one tries harder for customers' they wrote:

- Understand customers better than anyone.
- Be energetic, be innovative and be first for customers.
- Use our strengths to deliver unbeatable value to our customers.
- Look after our people so that they can look after our customers.

Beneath 'Treat people how we like to be treated' they wrote:

- All retailers, there's one team . . . The Tesco Team.
- Trust and respect each other.
- Strive to do our very best.
- Give support to each other and praise more than criticise.
- Ask more than tell and share knowledge so that it can be used.
- Enjoy work, celebrate success and learn from experience.

Simple and powerful, these sentences gave our team not merely a guide for behaviour, but also a sense of equity and confidence. They knew what behaviour they could expect of other colleagues. And these values were Tesco values. After years of struggling to be like Sainsbury or Marks and Spencer, we had finally the confidence to say 'This is us, this is how we behave.' The values spoke to our sense of – and certainly my belief in – meritocracy: of treating people the same, irrespective of their background.

When we unveiled them, we had expected that some people would shrug their shoulders and dismiss the values as just words. The reaction we received was the opposite. Some of the old guard – and they generally were the old guard – baulked, as they saw this as a cultural revolution. It was. Out went the machismo, the shouting and the laddish behaviour, and in came a more sharing, possibly more feminine culture. And that, it seemed, was not for them, and off some of them went.

Creating the values was, though, the easy part. The hard part was living them. The phrase 'living corporate values' has the air of creating a cult about it. However, I see it not as a cult but as a culture, revolving around the customer and built on manners and decency. It's not founded on, say, playing endless rounds of golf with colleagues (in any case, I can't play golf) but on behaviour towards those around you. To create that culture, leadership is critical. A team needs to be told 'This is important' by the leader. And they need to see the leader not merely talking about values, but using them and making decisions on the basis of them.

You cannot create a culture based on values overnight. Indeed, the process is never-ending and relentless. Wherever I went, I would talk about the values. Fourteen years of speeches, presentations, pep talks, away days, conferences – be it a 50-minute speech or two minutes of remarks, I always referred to them. That bored me to death – but only by repeating simple things, time and again, do you drive the message home: 'This matters'. These values had to live in the hearts and minds of the men and women who have to implement our strategy: every man, every woman, no matter what they did. And looking back to my first years as CEO, out of all the things I did, communicating our values and our strategy to our teams in our stores and operations had perhaps the greatest benefit.

To help a team in any organisation understand what is expected of them – how they should behave, what the purpose of the organisation is and how they fit in – you cannot rely on a memo or an email, nor can you take the easy option of sending round a DVD to be played. Nothing beats a face-to-face talk. I stress the word 'talk': not high-flown rhetoric, full of gushing phrases and big words, but a simple chat, explaining what you are there to do, how you are going to achieve it, and why each and every person listening has an important role to play.

Even today, when new technology provides so many different ways to communicate, face-to-face communication is every bit as important as it was in the days before email and Facebook, perhaps even more so. In the middle of a blizzard of information – be it from TV, Twitter, blogs, emails, the radio or even the dear old newspapers – it is difficult to communicate with people and, even if you do get their passing attention via just one of these media, your message is likely to be devalued, to put it mildly. To cut through all the verbiage, something more is needed, something which will add emotion and authenticity. That is why talking to someone face to face is so important.

A leader cannot delegate this role to another. People want to see you, the leader – to look at how you behave, and whether your actions really match your words. In an instant, they can tell whether the person before them understands the problems they face, has a plan to overcome them and believes that those challenges can be overcome. In a flash, they can decide whether they trust you (of which more later). And at the most basic level, it says something about you as their leader that you have come to see them personally – it shows that you know they matter.

Slim understood the need for everyone, not just the frontline soldiers, to know the importance of their role:

> It is harder for the man working on the road far behind, the clerk checking stores in a dump, the headquarters telephone operator monotonously plugging through his calls, the sweeper carrying out his menial tasks, the quartermaster's orderly issuing bootlaces in a reinforcement camp – it is hard for these and a thousand others to see that they too matter. Yet every

> one of the half million in the army – and it was many more later – had to be made to see where his task fitted into the whole, to realise what depended on it, and to feel pride and satisfaction in doing it well.[3]

So for the first few months after he took command of the Fourteenth Army, Slim gave three or four pep talks a day to his men. He felt 'more like a parliamentary candidate' than a soldier.

George MacDonald Fraser, author of the Flashman novels and the James Bond film *Octopussy*, fought as an infantryman in Burma under Slim. (He was apparently made a lance corporal four times, but was reduced to the ranks three times for minor offences, one of them involving the loss of a tea urn.) In his memoirs of that campaign, he wrote:

> The biggest boost to morale was the burly man who came to talk to the assembled battalion . . . it was unforgettable. Slim was like that: the only man I've ever seen who had a force that came out of him, a strength of personality that I have puzzled over ever since, for there was no apparent reason for it . . . He knew how to make an entrance, or rather he probably didn't, it came naturally . . . no fanfare, no announcement, simply walking on stage . . . there was no exhortation or ringing clichés, no jokes or self-conscious use of barrack room slang . . . he was telling us informally what would be, in the reflective way of intimate conversation. And we believed every word of it – and it all came true . . . He had the head of a general with the heart of a private soldier . . . He thought, he *knew*, at our level; it was that, and the sheer certainty that was built into every line of him, that gave Fourteenth Army its overwhelming confidence; what he promised, that he would surely do.[4]

This description is testimony to Slim's genius and insight into how humans think. 'We played on this very human desire of every man to feel himself and his work important,' he later wrote. Thanks in large part to the effort he put into communicating directly with the troops, 'they felt they shared directly in the triumphs . . . and that its success and its honour were in their hands as much as anybody's'.[5]

Tesco is a big business – hundreds of thousands of staff, thousands of managers. Just as Slim's plans depended on thousands of men and women doing a multitude of tasks – soldiers, airmen, mechanics, drivers, cooks and so on – working together to meet a common goal, so did I depend on thousands of people, doing everything from stocking shelves to marketing, buying stores to cleaning them, all working together to win customer loyalty. You can have the slickest advertising, the best products, the smartest stores – but the power of these things is lessened if a customer is not looked after by a member of staff when they visit the store. It is that experience – of being pleasantly surprised by some small helpful gesture – that makes the brand special, and builds loyalty between it and the customer.

We had big plans, and bold objectives, but we knew we could not succeed if we did not take everyone along with us. I also knew that we would hit rough, stormy weather on our voyage: I wanted everyone to be on board, not just in body, but in mind. I could only achieve that by going to see our team, and discussing with them not just what we were trying to achieve, but the values that underpinned our goals. And so I decided to take the message to our staff with what we called Town Meetings.

We started with our store managers, the bedrock of any retail business, and those of similar seniority in the rest of the organisation. There were about 3,000 at that time, so we split them up into groups of around 200, and set out on the road to meet them.

We tried to keep the atmosphere personal and informal. The staff would sit around tables, each seating about ten, and I would stand in the middle. Presentations were deliberately kept short and impromptu as we didn't want an overproduced affair, but an authentic one. Most of the time was reserved for questions and answers. No matter how brilliant the speaker, monologues switch people off – maybe not at first, but certainly once they realise that is all the communication is going to entail. I wanted to be part of a conversation, not give a lecture. If our managers left the event feeling that they had been lectured at and that their views were irrelevant to me and my team, the event would not have just been a failure, it would also have damaged relations between them and us. Every question from the staff demanded a serious answer. They had to know that we respected their views and what they did, and they had to *feel* it.

These meetings served another purpose. They allowed our teams to get the measure of me and to look me in the eye. I was keen that as many of them as possible should meet me before they read about me in the media – so I kept a relatively low profile, much to some journalists' frustration. (Interestingly, Slim had no PR department, much to his relief. 'A commander, if he is wise, will see that his own troops know him before the press and other cymbal clashers get busy with his publicity. All that can be most helpful afterwards.')[6]

The first Town Meetings exhausted me. I felt the curious, inquisitive gaze of my entire leadership team sizing me up, noticing and analysing the slightest mannerism or phrase. I didn't worry so much about the fact that I am not a charismatic speaker. What bothered me more was that I would be opening right up at these meetings, revealing not just a lot about my ambitions for the business but the kind of person I am. If that person was not someone whom those thousands of managers wanted to follow, I would be sunk. Unsettling though it was, I soon learnt there was no other way about it but to be completely honest. You have to let people feel they know you and to decide whether you are a person they can trust. A Town Meeting was the best way of letting them make that judgement. Slim wrote that only two things mattered about his talks: 'first to know what you were talking about; and second, and most important, to believe it yourself'.[7] Fortunately, I could do both.

We then asked our managers to tell their own staff about the meeting and what we would be trying to do. We never told them what to say: that was up to them. This may sound like an unlikely way of getting thousands of staff onto the same wavelength. Usually, the 'internal communications' department at a company's headquarters produces presentations and piles of bumf for managers to dole out to their teams. That would have defeated the entire purpose of the exercise. Our teams had to express, in their own words, what we were trying to achieve: it had to be their plan, not ours. And this worked well. Whenever people from outside visited Tesco, they always commented that, no matter who they spoke to, at whatever level, Tesco staff always seemed to know and feel part of the big picture. The Town Meetings began to paint the canvas.

Town Meetings improved communications not just between managers in head office and stores, but within the stores themselves. As managers found them useful, they were much more prepared to take the time to talk to their own people, helping to spread the habit of face-to-face communication and visible leadership. Each day in stores, depots and offices, managers would brief their team leaders who, in turn, briefed their teams. We called them Team Five meetings – because they only took five minutes and so they could be done standing up. Those five minutes made a big difference, as everyone then knew what was going on and that they had a part to play. Even in the age of instant communication, it takes a manager longer than five minutes to compose a bad email.

As the business grew, Town Meetings took place all over the world, from Birmingham to Budapest to Bangkok. Inevitably each Town Meeting differed a little according to national culture. In some of the Asian countries, where respect, courtesy and deference are part of good manners, it was difficult to get the informality people in the UK came to expect. Our local teams tailored the meetings to address this and put staff at ease.

By the end of my 14 years as CEO, I had seen every one of our managers face to face in a Town Meeting – that is 10,000 people in all. Many of them had been there at the first meetings we had, and by the end it felt as if we had been on the journey together. We could all remember the ups and downs, the mistakes and the excitement, the risks we took as we tried to find our way forward. This gave us not merely a sense of perspective, but also a feeling of belonging and ownership: that everyone's hard work, no matter what they had done, had helped us achieve something special. And that, in itself, helps enrich a person's sense of contribution. An ambition shared at one meeting has, years later, become a reality, not just a big part of our business but of our customers' lives. Whether it was Express stores or our expansion into Asia, everyone began to take pride in what we had done. 'I was there, I was part of that.'

Acting on your values

One of the company values at Tesco was 'Treat people how we like to be treated', as I mentioned earlier. An almost universal code of respect towards others, recognised in some form in every culture and religion, it is relatively simple to see how to live by this value on a day-to-day basis. (Making sure your actions live up to your words is quite another thing, though.) Basic good manners, treating everyone as equals, praising as well as criticising, listening as well as lecturing: these things build a person's confidence and sense of worth, and create a place of work where ideas, problems and success are all shared.

I knew that 'Treat people how we like to be treated', like any value, should not simply govern how you behave towards others. For a value to mean anything to the business, it must be the first benchmark against which any big decision is judged, and must guide the business itself. Only if a team sees that the management practises what it preaches will they listen and change their behaviour. This is far easier said than done, especially when you are making a major decision on something of real significance in which there are competing, legitimate commercial concerns, some of which conflict with the values. Like politicians, managers have good intentions but tend to lose sight of them when financial and other pressures come into play – one reason being that there are many well-developed financial measures to help one make long-term decisions but few of these are based on cultural values. That is a pity, because financial judgements made in a wider context, and based on clear values, generally lead to a better material outcome in the long term.

All this became apparent to me during the slow, sure and – to me – tragic demise of the company pension scheme. Pensions: the very word can provoke a yawn and a gentle lowering of the eyelids. To anyone under the age of 35, retirement still seems a lifetime away, and therefore pensions are a subject for another day (or decade). For anyone approaching retirement, their pension – and the subject more generally – understandably sits centre stage. Yet to everyone, whether they have just started work or are nearing their retirement party, how their employer helps them prepare for old age says a lot about that employer. Just as you can judge a society's values by how it treats its old people, you can judge a company's values by how it helps people for life after retirement.

Given that Tesco aspired to 'treat people how we like to be treated', our pension scheme had to meet our employees' expectations of what fair 'treatment' would be. By 2000 our scheme – like so many others – faced a serious problem. Set up in the 1970s, it was a defined benefit final salary scheme: pensioners would receive in pension a percentage of their salary at the time of retirement from Tesco. As with many British companies, booming investment returns and relatively low employee contributions made the scheme not just a good benefit, but an ideal way for our employees to save. They contributed, Tesco chipped in and the company managed the fund. Such schemes became the norm – the baseline expectation of what 'Treat people how we like to be treated' probably meant to our employees.

The success of these schemes provoked their demise. Many schemes had a surplus of assets over liabilities. Successive governments were therefore keen to limit the tax relief the schemes enjoyed, so they placed restrictions on the amount of surplus a scheme could have. This meant – bizarrely – that it became more tax-efficient to reduce contributions to limit the surplus.

Then, just at the height of the schemes' popularity in the mid-1990s, when companies and members had stopped contributing to the schemes, a number of problems began to emerge. People were living longer – which meant the funds would have to pay out more to members than the actuaries had estimated. (When the Tesco scheme began in the 1970s members lived 11 years into retirement: today it is more than 20 years). Low inflation meant pension schemes' liabilities – the pensions that the scheme would have to pay out in years to come – cost more to fund. This happened at the same time as stock markets underperformed their long-term average for nearly a decade, depressing investment returns for pension funds. Adding to the schemes' woes, the Government changed the tax regime, making them much less tax-efficient. They also introduced a raft of legislation to protect people's pensions (after a number of pension scandals), which made pensions much more costly to provide. Any one of these developments would have posed a significant challenge to a pension scheme. Taken all together they brought into question the viability of pensions as a company benefit.

What I expected would happen – and what was needed – was a debate about long-term savings. Instead, the defined benefit company pension scheme, which had been so lauded, was suddenly friendless. A trickle of companies announced the closure of defined benefit schemes, replacing them with defined contribution schemes or, in some cases, no scheme at all. And that trickle soon became a flood.

A defined contribution scheme shifts the liability from the company (usually an experienced investor and administrator) to an individual who generally has little experience of investment or administrating a pension. If managed by the individual who is paying into their own pension, advisers' fees can eat up 30 to 50 per cent of an uncertain return. So one consequence of the move to this type of scheme was a decline in the value of a pension. Another was a decline in employee loyalty, as people came to feel that the company they worked for no longer cared about their retirement.

Tesco, the largest private employer in the UK, was affected by these challenges like everyone else. Our advisers said that we should follow the herd and join the stampede for the exit. The board did not agree. We decided instead to modify our defined benefit scheme from one based on an employee's final salary to one based on the salary earned over the employee's career. The scheme member would still have a defined benefit at retirement, but the cost to the employer would be both more predictable and, in some cases, slightly lower.

We took a different path from most other companies, for several reasons. All Tesco's staff had always automatically enrolled into our pension scheme, so the vast majority of staff were members. Our pensions, therefore, were not a perk for a few senior employees, but something in which everyone had a stake and an interest. Furthermore, on our board sat both long-serving executives (who had grown up in the company and readily identified with the employees) and independent directors: they all understood that the Tesco pension benefit was one of a number of long-term benefits that allowed relatively low-paid staff to share in the company's success. Consequently, the board always recognised pensions as part of a wider culture which rewarded staff loyalty, and contributed to high staff morale and commitment – all vital to the success of the Tesco brand.

Above all, we felt the shift from a defined benefit to a defined contribution scheme grated with our values. It was too big a shift of responsibility from management to our employees, many of whom had little experience of long-term saving outside of the company schemes. That said, we also knew we needed to change: we could not continue as we were. So we approached the problem, admittedly a serious one, like any other business problem in the belief that if it was addressed head-on, it could be managed.

We shared the problem with our staff. We gave annual updates on the cost of providing a pension and asked staff to meet their share of the increase. Some senior staff contributed more than their share, because they trusted that the company was doing the best it could and they could see it was better than the alternative.

The problems and the closure of so many other schemes helped us in one sense. Whereas before employees may have taken the benefit for granted, now they certainly knew its value and were as determined as we were to see if we could manage our way through the problem. Offering a good pension became more of a competitive advantage in employment than ever before. It confirmed that our values meant something as Tesco followed its own path when it would have been easy to follow others.

We managed our pensions better, so that the cost of administering them actually dropped over time. We gave the subject much more attention. We employed better people to manage pensions and were able to run our scheme with very good returns (and with some of the lowest administration costs in the industry). We also continued to invest in equities, which may carry some risks but also give a higher return. Business is about risk, and a pension scheme is just another business risk. The expectation that you attempt to remove risk by investing in nil-risk assets is counter-intuitive. Poor return on the most 'risk averse' pension funds has resulted in the greatest risk of all becoming a reality – the closure of the fund.

Tesco today is responsible for more than 20 per cent of all members of open defined schemes in the UK private sector – a remarkable ratio for a business that employs about one per cent of the private sector workforce. A Tesco employee will retire on a pension which is two and a half times larger than that of someone who has made similar payments to a defined contribution scheme. Had we taken a different course, I doubt I could have looked an employee in the eye and said 'We live our values.' The decision was difficult, the financial costs in the short term ran into hundreds of millions of pounds, but it was the right thing to do.

Different cultures, shared values

How our values changed Tesco's culture is, though, only half the story. The values transformed our relationships with our customers, too. Hamish Pringle and William Gordon, in their book *Brand Manners*, unpick that relationship. They say a transaction involves four different dimensions. There is the rational experience – what goes on: 'It's even better than I expected.' Then the emotional experience – how we feel: 'I would like to do that again.' The political experience – why it is right for us: 'Was this a good deal for me?' And finally the spiritual experience – where it leads us to – or 'whither': 'I feel better off as a person for that – and the world may be benefiting too.'[8]

A powerful brand has values that appeal to customers in each of these dimensions – and those values have to live in the customer's experience of the brand. Our values had to be Tesco, pure and simple – the way we work, the way we manage. It was not enough simply to agree on the values – we had to live them, to mobilise tens of thousands of staff to live them, day in, day out, so that every time a customer came into contact with the Tesco brand, that experience provoked a positive rational *and* emotional response.

Encouraging people to behave in a certain way grates with the wish to give people more freedom and control so that they can grow in confidence and take initiative. Successful organisations know where the balance lies. They focus on what matters, and set clear expectations as to what is and is not acceptable behaviour, be it in terms of relationships between staff or with customers. Staff are given the freedom to take the initiative when handling customers, so they can respond quickly to customer demand. And then management support the team to deliver, through training and nurturing talent.

What did all this mean on Tesco's shop floor? It was summed up in those three words: 'Every Little Helps'. I have always seen them as a way of talking to customers about our values. Our internal value of 'No one tries harder for customers' is explained through the idea of 'Every Little Helps' – Tesco doing lots of little but important things to make shopping that bit easier for customers, from price to quality to innovations. These small things matter to customers on an emotional level, not just a rational one. An 'easy' shopping trip is more than just one that saves time: it saves energy, hassle and a 'bad experience'.

As 'Every Little Helps' became more well known, it reinforced in our staff's minds the core value of 'No one tries harder for customers'. There was less of a need for tedious rules and regulations, as the simple sentences of our values summed up a guide to behaviour and decisions that governed most situations. A manager in Hungary would not need to ring head office to ask whether he should change a format or buy a new brand of shampoo: whatever the customers wanted, they should get. If someone in Korea had spoken offensively to a colleague, the manager would not need some lengthy process to explain why that was wrong: the values said it all.

The values bound the business together. They were universal. No matter what their creed or race might be, people agreed with them.

That said, even though values are universal, that does not mean managers can simply jet in from their home country and tell the staff 'Here are our values, now live them.' Universal values cannot be applied blindly, without awareness of cultural differences. How a company's culture and values travel and are transplanted from one part of the world to the other is far from straightforward. Many firms never replicate the strength of their home market in other parts of the world even though they are a successful business. They soon find that cultural differences – which never appear on business plans for international expansion – matter enormously. Thousands of employees are selling goods and services to millions of customers, all of whose experience, tastes and values are shaped by their own local cultures and background.

Out of all the markets and sectors that are susceptible to local tastes and cultures, selling food must be top of the list. You are what you eat: your tastes, culture and background are, in some way, reflected in what you eat, and how you prepare it. Sunday lunch for the family, a quick snack for one in the microwave, an elaborate dinner party: food retailing is shaped by local tastes. This may explain why there are only a dozen or so multinational food retailers: Carrefour, Metro, Ahold, Aldi, Lidl and Schwarz, Jusco (of Japan), Delhaize, Casino, Walmart, Costco, and of course Tesco. These are the few firms who have made a sustained effort in multiple countries.

Tesco was a relative latecomer. While Carrefour had been operating outside France since the 1970s, Tesco had by the mid-1990s no overseas experience other than two relative failures – one in Ireland in the 1980s and another with a small French business sold in 1997.

The UK accounts for just three per cent of the world's GDP.[9] No matter how great your success in that market, it will never be enough to become – let alone remain – a world-leading company if you ignore what is going on in the rest of the world. So when I became CEO I felt compelled to try again to become an international retailer. Recognising we were late, in 1996 we drew up a list of countries which had not yet developed strong local retailers and yet whose prospects looked promising. Two immediate groups emerged: the former communist countries of central Europe, which were just emerging as consumer markets; and the Asian Tiger economies, whose growth had been built on manufacturing exports but who were now becoming consumer markets themselves. In Asia we focused on Korea, Thailand, Malaysia and Taiwan. The bigger countries – China, India and Japan – came much later.

South Korea was the biggest of all these markets. The prospect of a British supermarket retailer, with little or no experience outside its home market, investing in South Korea, must be one of the most extreme tests of cultural transfer anyone could possibly contemplate.

Korea has a long and proud history. Surrounded and often challenged by its much larger neighbours China and Japan, it has fought to maintain its independence and unique character to the point of isolation at times. Its recent history has been remarkable. Separated from North Korea after the Korean War, South Korea was left devastated and starving. It was, by some estimates, the second poorest country in the world. By an almost superhuman effort of collective national will, the South Korean economy was rebuilt on manufacturing exports led by family-controlled enterprises, following the pattern of economic growth in neighbouring Japan.

By the late 1990s, although a developed country with a successful liberal democracy, Korea was little understood in the West. Despite the rapid growth in consumers there had been relatively little foreign direct investment. Even hugely experienced multinationals, such as Nestlé or Unilever, had made little impression there. Formal and informal barriers to foreign investment protected domestic operators until they could compete against multinationals. On the rare occasions when those barriers were overcome, the foreign investor encountered feisty local competition and strong social norms supporting local companies over foreign intruders. We were advised more than once that South Korea was too tough a nut to crack and we should look elsewhere.

The Asian financial crisis of 1997 hit South Korea particularly hard. The country's large family enterprises had become too indebted and overstretched and the IMF had to be called in, a move that caused intense national shame. Those companies that had become overstretched were told by the government to focus on their core markets and divest where they had become over-ambitious. Foreign investors were encouraged to buy what the Korean companies put up for sale.

Arguably the greatest of these Korean companies was the Samsung Corporation. It had a presence in everything – textiles, construction, electronics, vehicle manufacture, banking. The company had correctly identified modern retailing as a strategic growth area thanks to the rise of the new Korean consumer, and they decided to create a retail business from scratch. The omens were good. After all, the Koreans had turned fishing villages into the world's largest shipbuilding yards in under 20 years. Samsung's ambition was matched only by their drive. They scoured the world for talent, taking the best from America, Europe and Japan. They then developed a high-end department store format and a hypermarket format which they called Homeplus. They had opened one type of each format when the 1997 financial crisis struck. Now they quietly began to look for foreign partners for the fledgling retail business so that they could concentrate on electronics, construction and finance.

When SH Lee, head of Samsung's retail business, considered

which of the world's best retailers might be suitable partners, Tesco was not on his list – although Sainsbury was. We heard about this and approached him. We may have started out slightly on the back foot, but we made it clear that we were prepared to take a risk on Korea when others were holding back, and so, after various discussions, we became Samsung's chosen partner and bought 80 per cent of their Korean retail business. It proved that not only do the best opportunities come at difficult times, but friendships made in difficult times are likely to endure: you have already shown your trust in each other.

Although Tesco acquired an 80 per cent economic interest, this was still a joint venture. Samsung's continued presence was vital to us. We had little experience of joint ventures and no experience of one with Korea. It's not surprising, therefore, that lots of experienced people advised us that the whole enterprise was a bad idea and would be inviting years of conflict for control. As it turned out, they were utterly wrong: the joint venture proved a perfect set up because it made sure that we were collaborating with a Korean business culture rather than taking the more conventional route of imposing our familiar western business culture. We hired academic experts in joint ventures and learnt all we could about how to make it a success.

What we learnt was simple. Be trustworthy, respect the other partner, agree a common objective, identify your complementary strengths and bring those to the joint venture. Of all these, trust was the most important. Western businesses have a tendency to be less trusting of people and places with which they are unfamiliar – Asia being a prime example. This can undermine any relationship, especially in Asia where this virtue is highly valued and is usually reciprocated in full measure. Respect is similarly highly prized, as is the humility required to listen and learn.

The Korean management team responded well to the trust

we placed in them and the respect we gave them. They wanted to create a world-class retail business which would become the leading example of modern retail in South Korea. All we had to do was to agree to that, back them and help them. We were always coaching rather than controlling. There were inevitable bumps in the road. When we replaced their new IT system with our own, for example, it proved a blow to their pride and prestige, but by then allowing them to improve the new system they immediately felt that they were contributing to the group and trust was established again.

Many of the Korean general managers we took on were of a higher calibre than the retail industry in the West is able to attract. However, they were not experienced retailers so we encouraged them to use customer research and to focus more on the consumer. Clubcard was launched early on to provide the data to make this possible. This helped us to improve products and services and begin to create our own brands. By introducing good retail processes, retail productivity was improved. Central logistics were built to link the supply base to stores and improve economy of scale.

The store format, designed by the Koreans, was a mini-shopping centre built over three floors containing a hypermarket, a food court and smaller shops (many of them boutiques), with three or four floors of car parking above or below it. Such a design – of vertical buildings on small land plots – reflected the limited availability of land in mountainous Korea, where well over half the population lives in high-rise apartments in densely packed urban conurbations.[10] (The Seoul National Capital Area is the world's second largest metropolitan area with 25 million residents – more than half of South Korea's population. Although the city of Seoul itself accounts for only 0.6 per cent of the entire country's land area, it generates 21 per cent of South Korea's GDP.)[11]

We made relatively few changes to this well-planned format except to straighten shopping aisles, make product displays more powerful and research sites better (to improve new stores' locations). We also introduced our popular Express convenience stores which were ideal for the dense high-rise catchments. Finally, we began the process of establishing a global systems platform to run our operations behind the scenes.

None of these changes was easy, and they could not be imposed. Our values – especially to 'treat people how we like to be treated' – guided us: we had to share information, work as a team and listen as much as lecture. If you give the local teams leadership and authority you cannot run the risk of undermining them at every turn with your own views. Instead we had to show that any change we felt they should implement would make things work better.

Gradually, as trust grew, the proud Korean team recognised that Tesco possessed some useful skills in retailing and could offer some advice and guidance, particularly in systems and sourcing. They also liked to take anything we offered and improve on it. But we were always careful that they should come to their own conclusion that our approach to some particular issue or problem was better than theirs – and that our solution was the best in the world (for they would settle for nothing less). In fact, of course, Head Office was not always right, the UK was not always best. Every department or function really did need to demonstrate that their way of doing things was world class or they would really struggle to get it adopted. Instead of a parent–child relationship developing, the Koreans came to describe the relationship between Tesco and them as more like that between an older and a younger brother.

We too learnt a great deal from the Korean approach to life. Put simply, the British management of Tesco had always respected people as customers, pure and simple. After all, our core value was 'No one tries harder for customers'. The Koreans, however, viewed people as both customers and citizens in one. The individual and the collective were indivisible. This attitude came from the huge collective effort required to rebuild Korea where the individual had to be subsumed by the collective need.

The sense that the customer was also a citizen manifested itself in our stores. In every Homeplus shopping centre there was an extra floor on top of the three retail floors. This was given over to the Culture Centre, a community education centre built, fitted out and operated by Homeplus.

When a Homeplus store opened, local people were invited to become members of the Culture Centre. Thousands of people signed up for the annual programme of classes, some for adults, others for children: English language, computer, ballet, painting, child rearing, craftwork. In a typical store there would be a total of 400 classes per quarter with 10,000 local participants. By 2011, there were 110 centres around the country.

Homeplus therefore saw its role as serving the whole person – customer, citizen, community member. When we asked our Korean colleagues the business rationale for this activity, they fell silent. It was just what one did, so natural that it was human nature.

We realised, of course, that Homeplus's Culture Centre would be difficult to replicate in Britain or the USA. The Koreans have an insatiable desire for educational attainment and self-improvement. About 15 per cent of the average household spending is on education – almost as much as is spent on food.[12] Competition for educational attainment is so high that Korea must be the one country in the world where the government has asked families, in effect, to stop taking education so seriously and spend less money on it.[13]

This is partly related to the workforce's profile. Although a fully developed and sophisticated liberal democracy, South Korea is still socially conservative in some things, one being the status of women in the workplace. After marriage, it is expected that women give up work. Although this custom is slowly changing, there are many women who have time on their hands and a thirst for learning – both for themselves and their children.

That said, we realised that the values embodied in Homeplus were not unique to Korea. Even in the individualist West, people wanted to know what Tesco was contributing to their community, as well as what we did for them as individual consumers. We therefore made a fundamental change to our whole strategy and way of doing business. Up until this point, our Steering Wheel – the method by which we set out targets and navigated towards them (which is discussed in Chapter 6) – contained just four segments: Customer, Operations, People and Finance. Now, we added a fifth Community segment, which became our strategic plan for how we would contribute to the wider community. We put it right at the heart of our business, ensuring that we would apply the same strict disciplines and measures to our community contributions as we did to other business areas. Sustainability, education, diet and health and support for the local community now went high on our list of priorities – themes common to Tesco throughout the world, even if the details varied from country to country.

The Homeplus business in Korea has gone from strength to strength. From just two stores, it has grown to over 450 stores. It has steadily increased its share of the market: Homeplus is now the number two hypermarket retailer in South Korea and, in 2012, is challenging to be number one. That growth has taught us that cultural transfer is not easy, especially in retailing, but has underscored its importance. When you invest overseas, you have to bring your company values with you. They are the essence of your business, so you cannot leave them at home. But you have to apply those values with care and sensitivity, building a culture around them that reflects local traditions. Most important of all, your company culture has to be open enough to evolve organically, absorbing the experiences of new countries and cultures and being strengthened by them, but all the while anchored to your values.

Using values to transform organisations

Values have become part of the wallpaper of every corporate communication, plastered up by well-paid consultants who devise the values and then walk away, leaving the management to 'implement' them. Organisations that behave like this fail to understand that values are critical to success. Without them, a company has no soul, no guiding compass. Clear values set a framework for good behaviour, a sense of discipline and an environment in which people feel confident and secure.

This applies to the public sector just as much as the private one. The public sector is steeped in values. Thousands of public servants have a vocation, a calling. Rarely, though, does one get the sense that these dedicated professionals' values are driving the organisations in which they work. All too often, large bureaucracies have suffocated these values with targets, diktats and orders from on high.

Consider education. Schools, like companies, are usually judged on their quantifiable performance: exam results, truancy, the number of students who go on to university. Those raw figures cannot reflect what may underpin them: the values and ethos of a school, something you can only judge with personal experience. Yet look at schools that have been turned around and, more often than not, it is a new set of values that has driven success.

Mossbourne Academy is a state school in Hackney, one of the most deprived parts of London. The Academy is new, built on the site of a school that was often described as the worst school in the country. Many of its children come from deprived backgrounds, most are from ethnic minorities – and a fair chunk have parents for whom English is not the first language. The school is in a tough neighbourhood: gangs, knife crime and drugs are on its doorstep. Despite all this, Mossbourne has outstanding academic results, its pupils often winning places at some of the best universities in the country.

Clearly the school's former headmaster Sir Michael Wilshaw was inspirational, and I suspect he had good teachers too. Yet the striking thing about the school is its clear values and discipline. Pupils begin each lesson by reciting a mantra, which combines both a sense of purpose and code of behaviour: 'I aspire to maintain an inquiring mind, a calm disposition and an attentive ear so that in this class and in all classes I can fulfil my true potential.'[14] Those who misbehave are given an hour's detention that same day after school: serious misdemeanours are punished by a three-hour detention on a Saturday morning. All pupils are required to wear a school uniform, with straight ties. Pupils are sent home if their hair is too short or too long, or if they are wearing the wrong type of shoes. All teachers are called 'Sir' or 'Miss', and when a teacher enters the classroom, the entire class stands up.

Discipline – a subject I will touch on later – reflects respect not just for authority, but for others. It creates a secure, stable environment in which the students can learn. 'A lot of our children come from unstructured, chaotic backgrounds,' said Sir Michael. 'We need to build more structure into their lives, not less. Schools that are imprecise about discipline end up with a huge amount of confusion, with staff taking different views about what is acceptable.'

And that brings me back to where I began. Clear values give people that structure – be it at work or at school. People know where they stand, and what to expect from others – be they colleagues, classmates or customers. That creates a stable environment, one which nurtures trust, and one in which it makes it easier to get things done, the subject to which I now turn.

5 Act

Intention is never enough. Plans mean nothing if they are not effectively enacted.

'Why is it so difficult to get things done around here?' politicians often moan. Making a speech, winning an election, launching a policy paper – all that is one thing: turning honeyed words into reality is quite another. Business managers may not make speeches, nor run for election, but many share that frustration. 'We decided to launch this initiative a month ago. Why has nothing happened?' They think that making a decision to do something or change something – a decision that may involve uncomfortable discussion and debate – is the hard part. It may be hard, but it's harder still to get something done.

Organisations that reverberate to the cries of chaos and confusion suffer from a variety of ailments. The worst is a lack of clear purpose and strategy, manifesting itself in people frantically 'doing something' as they labour under the delusion that activity equals progress. Almost as bad is deciding on a core purpose that is completely misguided. Then there are the 'too many chiefs' organisations, run by no one because everyone is in charge. Finally, there are organisations in which the management focuses entirely on building processes and structures to create a product or service – not on fulfilling a broad, core purpose that delivers value for customers – and so they forget that great products and services seldom create great business; great businesses create great products and services.

Intention is never enough. Plans mean nothing if they are not effectively enacted. In the 1920s Herbert Austin, founder of the Austin Motor Company, tried to copy Henry Ford's approach to car manufacturing by building an assembly line. The problem was that Austin's workers were paid by the number of cars they made – 'piece rate'. Workers focused on completing as many cars as possible, whatever speed the production line ran at. An Austin worker recalled:

> You had so much time for doing a job. If you were on ordinary time you'd get two pounds a week and then you'd have to go quicker and quicker to get more. So the assembly line would start at time and a quarter . . . and then it would go up to time and a half, or three pounds a week. [Management] would speed it up as we got used to it . . . to double time. And when it got to double time, they'd stop. No more, no faster. And what we used to do, we'd have a real good go, we'd pick the bodies up . . . and jump the pegs [to move the cars along faster than the assembly line] and we'd make it up to double time and a half, which was about five pounds a week, and this is a lot of money in them days.[1]

A great plan, but lousy implementation.

I agree with Sam Walton, the founder of Walmart, who once said 'I have always had the soul of an operator, somebody who wants to make things work well, and then better, and then the best they possibly can.'[2] If you consistently focus on how your plans are implemented, the quality of service will improve. And successful implementation depends on five key things: a clear decision, a simple process, defined roles, robust systems and discipline.

Turning words into actions

I have always attached great importance to how decisions are made, and ensuring that people respect and act according to those decisions once made. Whether it is an organisation of 500,000 people or 50, if people start questioning a decision after it has been taken and saying 'I don't agree, I'm not going to do that', chaos will ensue. Structured decision-making and disciplined implementation are therefore absolutely critical. This is not just good management: it builds trust in an organisation. After all, most people are not present when decisions are made that affect their working lives – be they nurses or checkout staff. They need to know that a just, fair and reasoned process is in place, and that their interests have been represented. They also need to know what is expected of them. Victims of opaque decision-making swiftly become demoralised, uncertain as to how decisions are made and convinced that they cannot make a contribution or influence an outcome.

Making a decision may involve agonising debate, yet the elements that actually inform a good decision are quite straightforward. You start by getting the facts and researching the issue under discussion. Next, you get together all the key people who will be responsible for putting a plan into practice and discuss it with them. This serves several purposes. Those people obviously may have a valuable contribution to make. Consultation may help people respect the decision – 'I may not agree with it, but at least I had a say' – which can make them feel committed to act on it. By the same token, consultation will also help people understand what the consequences would be if nothing was done. But at some point, the manager has to say 'enough', stop the discussion and make a decision – 'We will do it.'

The decision has to be made formally, openly and transparently, not out of the corner of the mouth or via a coded email. It is amazing how many people can leave a badly run meeting unsure if anything was decided. That decision then needs to be communicated consistently around the organisation, and a process to review progress put in place. This will create a sense of responsibility, an acknowledgement that achieving the goal will be rewarded.

At this point, the team also needs to know that mistakes will inevitably be made in implementing the plan or project. The leader needs to make it clear that, if a mistake is made, the project will be stopped, lessons will be learnt by everyone, and then it will start again. There will be no recriminations, no blame game – these kill the chances of people taking initiative or coming up with new ideas.

So much for the decision. You then have to write down what sequence of events and actions are required to turn it into a reality: the process. This sounds pedantic – and it is – but the danger is that if you don't do this managers and their teams will say 'We know what we need to do', without any common agreement as to what is required. Result: confusion the next day as lots of people land up doing the same thing or tasks completely unrelated to the project in hand.

This basic discipline of clarifying the process is alien to many organisations. It is seen as boring – which it can be. It is also regarded as 'obvious', and so is swiftly pushed aside by something else viewed incorrectly as 'more important'. When bureaucracy is involved, the problems are compounded. People have particular responsibilities and specialisms, which means they cannot build a process from start to finish: they don't have the full picture but they nevertheless hate to admit this, worried that they might then lose influence.

Writing down the process overcomes this problem. And it's essential that the focus is on the process – the simple steps it will take to achieve your goals. If the approach is to ask 'Which departments or teams will be involved?', the process is unlikely to be simple. For example, getting a carton of milk onto a shelf and then into the customer's basket will inevitably include IT, transport and operations – but if you think in terms of 'How do I involve IT?', the process will become confused. By thinking like this, problems or issues can be created that may not have any relevance to or bearing on the passage of the milk carton from the dairy to the checkout. It's much better to trace the journey of the carton right from the beginning to its final destination, rooting the process firmly in practical steps. Once you've done that, you can then work out who will be responsible for each part of its journey.

This means that detail does matter. A tale recounted by Samuel Smiles suggests Michelangelo would agree. Michelangelo was explaining to a visitor at his studio what he had been doing to the statue since the visitor's previous visit. 'I have retouched this part – polished that – softened this feature – brought out that muscle – given some expression to this lip, and more energy to that limb.' 'But these are trifles,' remarked the visitor. 'It may be so,' replied the sculptor, 'but recollect that trifles make perfection, and perfection is no trifle.'[3] Details can certainly bog leaders and managers down – as the cliché goes, they must be able to see the wood for the trees. However, when drawing up a process, a leader must be sure – and needs to check – that there is one person who is responsible for understanding the wood, trees, branches and twigs of the entire system being designed, and that person leads the project.

I learnt the hard way that the plan does not have to be absolutely perfect in all details. If you aim for perfection at the start of creating a new process, your ambitions may never see the light of day. You have to accept that there will be some trial and error. Because of this you must also avoid doing too much, all at once. Try pouring water down a pipe: too quick and you spill some, too little and you are there for ages. The same applies to processes: you need to ensure you stretch a team, but not so much that they make so many mistakes that they lose confidence and feel the enterprise is a non-starter. Some mistakes, though, are inevitable.

Once you've written down the process you need quickly to establish the roles that need to be filled. What exactly does this person need to do? And how should they relate to other people in the process? What is the job description, the job role? If you don't do that you end up with people undertaking pointless tasks or – at the opposite end of the spectrum – claiming 'We're currently too busy doing this to do that.'

Each year, millions of pounds and thousands of hours are wasted on job design, job measurement, job valuation – ignoring what the organisation actually does on a day-to-day basis. Managers point to smart 'organograms', charting who is doing what, unaware that the actual tasks being performed by those people may bear little relation to their 'job description' – often because no one has made the effort to clarify what specific roles people are meant to undertake. The danger of this is that people end up having little idea how their work contributes to the progress of the company overall – how they 'fit in'. They soon get bored, they see another job that looks interesting and they subtly start modifying their own role accordingly. All this corrodes an organisation's structure, and its morale.

Such organisations unwittingly see 'human resources' as a form of welfare that shuffles people from one task to another because their managers dare not dismiss them, or to assuage their concerns about status: 'Is my job bigger than his?' 'Am I more important than him?' Honest conversations are avoided in the interests of being nice. It's an attitude that does no one any favours. If people are to feel fulfilled in their work, they need to know how they are contributing to the company's progress.

Organisations around the world are guilty of this sort of poor management, English companies particularly so. The English are very bad at being completely straight with people. They like to start sentences with 'I'm sorry' or 'Would you mind terribly if . . .?' I don't hold with this. I have always tried to be straight with people, as I believe that honesty and openness pays off. So instead of beating about the bush, I told people at Tesco in simple terms about their role, and I attempted to address their frustrations as candidly as possible. 'I know you like Fred's job, but this is your job. Some day you may well do Fred's job but today you are doing this one. You have to learn certain things before you can do Fred's job and this is one of them. It may at times be boring, and repetitive, but it's important if we are to achieve our goals.'

To ensure that this directness was transmitted throughout the company, I reshaped the human resources department, took it off the board and out of its silo, and integrated it into Tesco's operations. Some worried that by changing the role of the HR department, we were signalling that we were downgrading the importance of people. It was the reverse. Managing people is too important to be given to one department to handle: it is the essence of a company, the responsibility of all our managers. Managers who are leaders do not subcontract management of their staff to human resources. HR is vital, but not when it is operating in isolation from the rest of the business. Furthermore, this change also ensured that our management did not think about people in terms of abstract structures, but in terms of the work they undertook and the roles they fulfilled.

By giving people a clear sense of their role and how it relates to the company's goals, you can push power down the management ladder: everyone knows what they are responsible for, and they know how to achieve it. And the more you push power down the ladder, the more dynamic the company becomes and the fewer layers of management it needs. This may seem obvious, but it's remarkable how few organisations work in this way.

Far more common is the large, centralised enterprise with numerous layers of management down which orders are given, while information and requests for permission to act in certain ways are passed back up. This traditional structure, which you find in everything from banks to public services, suffers from a multitude of weaknesses.

First of all, it strips those at the bottom of the ladder, who deal with customers (or citizens), of any sense of initiative and professional responsibility. They may be the people who have first-hand experience of a particular problem and so know how to solve it, but they are not given the authority to do so. Instead, the issue is passed to those higher up, who often have no first-hand experience of the problem.

This is unsatisfactory in itself but it also has other consequences. It allows head office to take the plaudits for progress, while condemning those out in the sticks either to get no sense of ownership of success or the blame for failure. This could not be more wrong. As Frederick Reichheld has pointed out, 'one successful approach to sustained value creation is built on relatively autonomous individuals and small teams sharing the benefits of their own productivity growth'.[4] In a large bureaucracy which tries to control everything, that sense of owning success is impossible.

Another problem with organisations that indulge in layers of management is that they can create career structures that distort the allocation of talent. Grand titles and a seat at headquarters may give people a sense of worth, but it also sucks good people into offices distant from the scene of the action: where the company deals with its customers. Moreover, a plush HQ, full of brainy people developing strategy, can quickly become a hornet's nest of cliques and political rivalry, as people lose focus on the customer – be it the mum doing her weekly shop, or the patient in need of an operation. Management turns inwards, focusing on its own concerns and what people see around them.

At Tesco we created a clear, very flat structure of just six layers of management between me and the checkout assistant. This helped us all, from the board down, keep our finger on the pulse – or rather the shop floor – which is where the value is created. We stopped middle management becoming a barrier between the senior management and the stores: the board was, quite literally, in the shops much of the time. We resisted being trapped in a gilded cage, fed by middle management.

And Tesco's head office is anything but gilded. The unglamorous New Tesco House – 'new' is stretching it a bit, as it was built in the 1970s – is on an industrial estate in Cheshunt, about 20 miles from central London. I kept a very tight rein on the number of people based there. Small head offices have to be focused: the team does not have the time to worry about issues that are not priorities.

As Tesco grew, rather than creating new layers of management I would remove entire functions and broaden the responsibility of operational, general management. I used to challenge why new jobs in the back office (any new role that was not in our stores or depots) had to be created, particularly one with 'planner' in the title – a job description that contains the word 'planning' is not one focused on doing. Instead, I would urge people to break problems or challenges down into smaller steps, smaller tasks and smaller teams – and see if they could therefore be handled by our existing personnel. I would urge them to start with a clean sheet of paper, and ask themselves, on a regular basis, how things could be done differently. My thinking was that the fewer jobs and functions, the less opportunity there was for people to get in each other's way.

Increased scale requires more resource, more specialisation and more complexity. For example, as we expanded Tesco's offer into clothing, we had to bring in hundreds of specialists in fashion, design, buying and merchandising. However, we did this sparingly: no organisation should carelessly employ more people unless it can be absolutely justified commercially, and there is no one in the existing team who can fulfil the need.

People were encouraged to make decisions themselves and take the initiative: when something was referred up to head office that was not a priority, I would tend to send it back to where it came from, suggesting to the sender that they did what they thought best.

In my experience, complicated structures cause more problems than they solve. The best ones are simple and lean, and designed to serve people in the front line, not control them. They ensure the quick and effective execution of clear, simple processes. And when a process works, it's deeply satisfying for everyone. When I walked around a store that was really humming, where the stock was full and there was a sense of bustle, I could feel the staff's satisfaction and pride in their store. By the same token, I knew that when attention was not paid to process, failure quickly set in and frustration was the result. Imagine something as simple as a toiletries fixture in Tesco that hasn't been filled because the product hasn't arrived, or the delivery is late. That's a failure of process, one that can be avoided if you are clear in your own mind and with your staff about precisely what it is you want them to do.

Tough love

Discipline is a word that people dislike using for fear of being seen as harsh, ruthless, uncaring. Discipline implies our liberty has been curtailed, which unsurprisingly most people dislike. But discipline matters in any organisation, just as it does in society as a whole.

Without a sense of discipline and order, confusion creeps in. Processes are left undone or done late. People start to do someone else's job – or nothing at all. Unchecked, little by little, the organisation begins to decay. The individuals with the strongest personality begin to impose their will on others. Common, shared aims and values are replaced by factions vying for power. As the organisation fragments, it ceases to function and deliver for those it serves. Talented people leave, failures mount and the organisation falls into a vicious circle of decline.

Military leaders understand this best of all, as their lives – and those of their men and women – depend on it. In a pithy lecture on discipline, Viscount Slim wrote:

> True discipline is not someone shouting orders at others. That is dictatorship, not discipline. The voluntary, reasoned discipline accepted by free, intelligent men and women is another thing . . . Even in an Army it is not merely a question of giving orders; there is more to a soldier's discipline than blind obedience. To take men into your confidence is not a new technique invented in the last war.[5]

Slim then talked of the importance of every man and woman knowing the ultimate purpose of the enterprise – a point made earlier. 'The essence of industrial discipline,' Slim wrote, is 'to know what you work for and to love what you know'.[6]

I'm only too aware, though, that however powerful the rallying cry may be, managers have to contend on occasion with the recalcitrant employee who turns up late, who leaves jobs half done, who says 'I'll do better next time' but never does. They shun the 'voluntary, reasoned discipline' that Slim extols. The question, then, is how do you deal with them?

The Irishman in me says 'I would never have started from here in the first place.' This means picking up on small failures before they become big ones, and before an 'I can get away with it' culture begins to spread. Again, this is easier said than done, but it begins by not letting seemingly trivial details or practices slip. 'The air of efficiency' is not something you can fake. Dirty floors, unemptied bins, untidy warehouses: however efficient the organisation may claim to be, such an environment will not encourage people to be efficient. Once again, this observation has an old vintage. Samuel Smiles wrote:

> Attention, application, accuracy, method, punctuality, and despatch are the principal qualities required for the efficient conduct of business of any sort. These, at first sight, may appear to be small matters; and yet they are of essential importance to human happiness, well-being, and usefulness. They are the little things it is true; but human life is made up of comparative trifles. It is the repetition of little acts which constitutes not only the sum of human character, but which determines the character of nations.[7]

When faced with shoddy process or inaction, nothing beats a face-to-face chat with the person responsible, asking them to talk through what they did and getting them to understand the problem. As I will explain later, shouting, abuse and male machismo is completely counterproductive – and a sign of weakness in a leader.

The moment that you worry about something being wrong, that is usually the time to act. The danger is that because the decision requires uncomfortable conversations, your brain starts to find excuses not to act. The longer you prevaricate, the bigger a problem can become. What might have been solved by a simple intervention – and perhaps a difficult conversation – then needs to be tackled by disciplining, moving or even firing an employee.

The guide in these situations is simple. If you want your decision to be fair, reasonable and just, you must stick to your values. That decision – to restructure a department, or dismiss someone, for example – may give you a reputation for being tough. Yet if that reputation is based on your unremitting focus on the truth, and people see you act according to the values you espouse, that is no bad thing for a manager: your integrity will grow.

This brings me to the question of how tough a manager should be. In *The Prince,* Machiavelli advised Lorenzo de' Medici that, while it is 'far better' for a prince 'to be feared than loved if you cannot be both', the prince must avoid being hated:

> Fear is quite compatible with an absence of hatred; and the prince can always avoid hatred if he abstains from the property of his subjects and citizens and from their women. If, even so, it proves necessary to execute someone, this is to be done only when there is proper justification and manifest reason for it.[8]

The 15th-century Florentine Republic and 21st-century Tesco may not share much in common: Tesco does not practise capital punishment, and the CEO cannot confiscate his employees' property, let alone 'their women'. Yet the notion that you can manage a modern organisation by fear alone is an appalling one – fashionable though it is for CEOs to be seen on TV screaming at people. Fear suffocates ideas, and breeds resentment. Fear is no guarantee that processes will be stuck to, or jobs completed. Fear results in bad decisions, as people try to please their manager rather than do what is right.

You can both be feared and loved – you might call it a form of 'tough love'. Tough action must have 'proper justification and manifest reason for it', as Machiavelli says. Most of the time, that action does not entail shouting at an employee 'You're fired!', but simply expressing disapproval – which may be nothing more than a stern look.

One of the commonest challenges any manager faces is when an employee does not turn up for work, day after day, for no apparent reason. As I travelled around our stores in the early 2000s, I began to notice something I hadn't seen before: absence from work was creeping up. Looking into this, I found it was not just a problem for Tesco. In fact, we were suffering less than most, and considerably less than in the public services. Once I dug a little deeper I realised that this new pattern of behaviour was largely due to an important change in employment legislation which had been introduced with little comment. Before the change, if you were off sick, you had to go straight to the doctor and receive a sick note in order to be paid. The changes allowed you to certify yourself as 'sick' for up to three days, and still be paid.

Absence, which had never been above four per cent, quickly crept up to seven per cent. In some stores and depots it reached as high as ten per cent – which meant that some members of staff were off for more than one month every year. Our stores and depots are among the busiest in the world. If a member of staff does not show up, customers queue for longer at checkouts and shelves begin to empty. So in the worst cases this threatened an entire store's operation. As the problem was growing so fast we risked falling into a dangerous spiral: those who turned up for work came under huge pressure thanks to their absent colleagues and, seeing that their colleagues were 'getting away with it', they were beginning to wonder why they should not 'throw a sickie' too.

'Throwing a sickie': I could not believe my ears when that term was bandied about by the media as if it was the latest fashion, and you were behind the times if you didn't 'throw one' after a heavy night out on the town. I was brought up to believe that paid work is a contract and people should fulfil their part of the bargain. Using a legal loophole to claim to be sick was, in my eyes, an abuse of the trust that employers placed in employees. Furthermore, people of my generation did not take work for granted: we knew what unemployment meant. When I started work at the end of the 1970s, the UK was haemorrhaging manufacturing jobs and unemployment was on its relentless climb towards the unheard-of level of 3 million. If you were lucky enough to get a job, you valued it.

During the long boom that began in the early 1990s, the job market began to change for the better. Services took off, and soon made up four-fifths of the economy. By the start of this century there was actually a labour shortage. While this was good news, one consequence was that some people did not value having a job in quite the same way as before. There were so many jobs around that, if you lost yours, you could walk straight into another one. Little wonder, therefore, that such a blasé attitude to holding down a job began to seep into popular culture.

This trend was beginning to undermine our business. We had to act, but carefully. The large majority of staff were not doing anything wrong. Draconian action would risk breaking the trust between the company and our employees which underpinned so much of our success. That trust rested on management fulfilling its responsibility to make the workplace a good, satisfying place to be.

People are generally reasonable in what they expect from work. In my experience they ask for just four things: to have an interesting role, to be treated with respect, to have a chance to get on and a boss who helps. We built our whole way of managing around trying to offer these things as well as better pay and benefits. Faced with rising absenteeism, we realised that we needed to do more. We gave extra support to stores where absence rates were high – more help on personnel management and recruitment. We put more management support into night shifts in particular. Yet that wasn't enough. So we did what we always do when we don't have the answer about a staff issue: we spoke to our staff.

That simple act of communication began to unlock the problem. Our staff gave us lots of practical advice. They didn't like the higher rates of absenteeism either. It affected them directly. After all, they were the ones who had to make up the shortfall in staff all the time. They agreed with us that the increase in absence was a problem, that it often wasn't due to genuine sickness and that we should do something about it. However, as we talked, they let us into their lives. Like so many of our customers, our staff were feeling the stress and strains of juggling work and family. There were problems with childcare or appointments that sometimes made it difficult to get to work.

These were genuine cases which deserved our help, not a bureaucratic, inflexible 'sort it out yourself' answer. We decided to work with anyone who had a real problem to move their shift to another time so they could be off to do what they needed, and make up lost hours at a more suitable time. For a lot of staff we made permanent changes to their working arrangements to suit them better.

We started a system of 'planned absence', in which staff notified us in advance that they would be off for a particular shift, giving management the chance to plan ahead. We asked staff always to phone a manager the day they were off and explain what the problem was. When people returned to work we always had an interview with them so we could properly understand the reason for an absence. We were careful never to confuse unexplained absence with genuine illness, and we were more supportive of the long-term sick, staying in touch with people who were off for a long time and helping out where we could. When people felt ready, we would bring them back to work on any duties they could cope with, and let them work part time if they wished. A lot of people who have been off for a long time lose confidence and never come back to work, so this kind of contact and support was really helpful.

In short, we bent over backwards to show that we were willing to help those who had genuine reasons to be off work. This was not easy for us: our managers had to be very determined to come up with arrangements that were fair to everyone. But all this effort built trust, and earned our staff's support to be firm with the minority who abused the system. That did mean disciplining some people, yet more often than not those people who were unwilling to accept the responsibility of turning up for work resigned.

Such an approach encapsulated the words 'tough love'. We were behind those who wanted to work hard and accept their responsibilities – but came down hard on those who refused. We prepared the ground so that employees felt that what we were doing was fair and reasonable and, indeed, what they would themselves do in a similar situation. By treating people how we like to be treated, we created a strong team.

Strategy in action

Process, roles, discipline – these are things that irritate people who are in a hurry to see their bold, revolutionary idea become reality. Bursting with ideas, desperate to change the world, they brush aside what they actually need to do to achieve their goals. It's an understandable fault, but it is a fault nevertheless. At Tesco, whenever we had a great new idea or wanted to launch a major initiative, we focused forensically not just on what we wanted to do but on how we were actually going to achieve it. And perhaps one of the best examples of an audacious, well-executed plan was the launch of Tesco.com, today the world's largest online food business.

Tesco.com had an unusual beginning way back in 1995. This was the very dawn of the internet – before the dot.com bubble had grown and burst, before Google, iTunes, Facebook and Twitter had become household names, and certainly before the internet offered anything much of real interest to the consumer. I had been invited to visit an exhibition called 'Smart Store', put on by Andersen Consulting (now Accenture) and dedicated to 'the shop of the future'. My reaction to the invitation was typical of a lot of executives. I was very busy, I had seen this kind of exhibition before and had always been slightly disappointed, and so I was tempted to give it a miss.

However, as I knew one or two of the Andersen people and the exhibition was only down the road, after work one day I suggested to Tim Mason that we go along. All credit to the consulting firm, they put on a good show. We spent a worthwhile hour wandering around several 'space age' presentations about the retail industry that sought to predict what life would be far into the future. Nevertheless, like the other retailers, as we wandered around our minds were mainly preoccupied with yesterday's sales and whether tomorrow's sales would be any better. The long term was next month, the very long term Christmas, and anything beyond that – well, it did not really matter.

The final exhibit was a mock-up of a domestic kitchen. On the kitchen counter there was a computer. This seemed rather incongruous in 1995, when only 25 per cent of homes actually had home computers, and those computers that were around were bulky and unwieldy.[9] 'What's that doing there?' I asked. 'One day housewives will order their food from their kitchen using a computer,' replied the intrepid consultant.

At this point the other retailers all fell about laughing, and began to run through all the reasons why this would never happen in their lifetime. How would they 'transmit' an individual order (email was not even part of everyday language)? How would they even know what to order? And what would you do with the order, even if the customer managed to get it through to you? You'd have to select the items required and then find a way of getting it to their house; since the average family's food shopping weighs 100 pounds, you could hardly stick a stamp on it and post it. What about fresh food – some of it, like bread, lasting only a few hours in peak condition? How could anyone possibly work out how to get that to a customer? True, since time immemorial, wealthy people had been able to get others to shop for them, but that would never work for 'ordinary' people. And even if you could work through all those problems and technically make it work, the costs would be ridiculously high.

Such were the objections, and I think Tim and I joined in the mockery. But on the way out, no longer part of the crowd, we turned and said to each other at the same time 'Even so, it would be good if you could do it – customers would love it.' It was half in jest, but the germ of an idea had taken hold. That evening I suspect all the other retailers drove home, secure in the knowledge there would never be a home shopping service. After all, everyone had agreed it was impossible. Within a year, Tesco.com had launched.

The idea was utterly compelling to us. We were convinced this innovation would be loved by customers because of the novelty and – above all – the convenience it would offer, so we had no choice but to do all we could to make it possible, to overcome all the well-known obstacles and make a profitable business. We had no special insight or any particular technological skills; we simply had a different mentality. Tesco existed to make lives easier for customers – that is how we saw ourselves, not as a retailer for whom distant social innovations brought by the computer were either of no relevance or a threat to be resisted. If this new technology offered the prospect, however slight, of a time-saving innovation in peoples' lives, then we were interested.

I suspect a lot of retailers were afraid of the internet, and hid their fear in the hope that the internet would never take off. They did not research its potential because they were frightened they might find that this technological innovation would make their business model obsolete – the nightmare that keeps all CEOs awake at night. There was certainly a lot of discussion that a home shopping service would simply eat up the customers who used existing stores.

We shared some of these concerns, but we nevertheless decided to go ahead. For a start, we knew that the worries being expressed were speculation, not fact. If we actually did something, we'd be able to find out for ourselves – and be the first to move into this new world. We also trusted the customer. If the internet was going to take their lives in a different direction, who were we to stop it? We should accept what was happening and follow the customer, even if that meant huge challenges and changes for our company. And the challenge was certainly huge. Building an internet service meant creating a new process from scratch: supplying stock, giving customers a chance to buy via the internet, getting the goods to them – we were at square one.

The next decision we had to take was how to begin: should we draw up a big plan or just press ahead with a simple start-up to pilot the idea? I decided we needed to get going quickly and therefore we should start in a modest way, which did not even need the board's approval.

We decided to start with a simple process which we would develop as we went along. This was, after all, wholly new terrain for us. Exploring it was to be an exhilarating experience: we were inventing an entirely new form of retailing, an opportunity few people have. We knew that we would have to change many things, and that change would be quicker and easier if we kept our process flexible and simple to begin with, tightening it up only as it became clearer how it would work best. It also made sense, we thought, to use assets we already had. Our name was well known – so why invent a new one? We should start with customers we knew or those whom we could attract for little cost. Our stores, obviously, were close to where people live so they were not a bad place from which to pick customer orders off the shelves. Best of all the staff were experienced. They knew a lot about products, customers and systems and could be easily trained. Actually, it was more like the staff training us than the other way round. Once they knew what we were trying to do they used their common sense and experience to come up with myriad improvements and solutions to problems.

We created a small team led by an energetic store manager, Gary Sargeant, and set out to create an e-commerce service from our existing infrastructure of stores, systems and people. It was a very simple process. We put up a list of products on the computer, and customers could transmit an order by phone, fax or computer. The order was sent to one of a few trial stores where it was picked from the shelves, put into a van and delivered. There was no great invention in that, but at least we were under way. We had a service and were operating. More importantly, we had the beginnings of a process. We were starting to learn all the things we would have to do, and all the improvements we would have to make for this enterprise to be profitable.

The source of business would be critical in determining whether breakeven could ever be reached. Our early experience gave us hope. Thanks to Clubcard, we could see how much of our business was entirely new custom and how much was coming from people who usually shopped in our stores. We found that 66 per cent of the business was new – either new customers or new spend from existing customers. There was enough new business there to make a profit if we could make all of the other bits work.

The wisdom of our entire approach and process was soon to be challenged. The possibilities of the internet had fired the imagination of the world. Madness took hold, creating the dot.com boom. Set up a company, call it a '.com' and, it seemed, the value of that company would magically double, triple and just keep on rising.

Webvan was one such start-up. Its idea was to reinvent home shopping from scratch. Their entire process was built around the concept of not having any stores. Instead, customers would order direct from a purpose-built warehouse where their order would be automatically picked and dispatched. Everything was to be specially designed for this new model of doing business. Interestingly, George Shaheen, the head of Andersen Consulting which had staged the Smart Store, left that company to become the CEO of Webvan. In the dot.com frenzy, Webvan raised $375 million in an initial public offering, valuing the business at $6 billion at the end of the first day of trading[10] (about 35 per cent of Tesco's entire value at that time) – even though they had been in operation for just five months in the San Francisco area alone, and just 10,000 people had signed up for the service.[11] They were able to invest all this money in infrastructure for the new business, telling investors they would make grocery retailing on the high street obsolete.

Reading the Webvan prospectus, endorsed by prestigious investment banks, I was incredulous. I had no idea how they could begin to make such claims. This 'new retailing', however, caught many people's imagination. This made Tesco's investors sceptical of our methods – even though our processes were simpler, and our customer base more robust than Webvan's. Whenever we spoke about our e-commerce business we were told we were doing it the wrong way, it would never work and that Webvan was much better. However much progress we made, and however much more money Webvan lost, conventional wisdom remained the same – even though Webvan was gambling everything and we were gambling only what we could afford.

The controversy was resolved before too long. Webvan went bust. Sainsbury, who had imitated the Webvan approach, was also forced to give up. It had proved simply too expensive to rebuild food distribution from scratch without an existing base of customers. The upfront costs were crippling, and the idea demanded so much capital that, in the relatively low margin industry of retailing, I don't think Webvan's business model could ever have been the competitive killer that was envisaged. The return on its capital was just too low.

Webvan's failure taught us an invaluable lesson. When creating a new offer, the critical aim – and basic building-block of success – is to win custom, not to create a perfect process. The search for perfection never ends: the company that seeks perfection from the word go usually lands up staking its entire existence on the quest. Much better to get cracking by creating a simple process that you can build on and perfect it as you go along.

Within two years of Tesco.com's launch, we were beginning to make good progress, and as more and more people gained access to the internet, we dropped the phone and fax as a source of orders. We had no real idea what demand would be like, but it quickly outstripped our most optimistic hopes. Customers were so delighted with the convenience offered by the new service that they were incredibly forgiving of mistakes – and there were plenty. Easter eggs for fresh eggs, cream of mushroom soup for mushrooms, cat food for dog food.

We knew customers would give us some time to iron out teething problems – but not long. What was a marvellous innovation for a customer today would be regarded as 'normal service' tomorrow – so we had to refine the process to make it perform as well as possible. It was simple maths. If each step is 100 per cent reliable then after, say, five steps in the chain you still have

100 per cent reliability. But if you are only 98 per cent accurate, the impact of that inaccuracy is magnified each step of the way. After five steps you're down to 88 per cent – the process quickly degrades.

As Tesco.com became established, we realised just how wrong 'conventional wisdom' can be. Everyone had initially assumed that a typical customer would be a cash-rich, time-poor professional. It turned out that the customer base was much wider than this – Tesco.com was used by all income groups, and was particularly attractive to housebound people: the old, people with a temporary or long-term ailment, mums with babies or toddlers who needed constant supervision. New types of shopping behaviour appeared: sons and daughters were ordering remotely for delivery to their elderly parents, small businesses (like children's crèches) used the service, as did small hotels. People mastered the online process by the end of their second shop: a week's shop took 15 minutes compared with up to a couple of hours for a conventional shop (including travel to and from the store). Clubcard data revealed that, while a store might stock 40,000 food items, people actually chose from a much narrower repertoire themselves, often just 300–500 products over the course of a year. By providing a list of a customer's own shopping, their 'favourites', we could dramatically speed up the time it took to order. The delivery charge was £5, so customers tended to place bigger orders to defray the average cost and they quickly worked out that, if you added a 'cost' for the use of the car and the time a shopping trip took, it was in fact very good value.

Another bit of received wisdom was that shoppers would use the service just to buy non-perishable items – nappies, detergent, toothpaste and so on – as they would not trust the retailer to deliver fresh food. Anyway, surely customers like to inspect fruit, vegetables and almost anything with a sell-by date before they buy it? Wrong again. The contents of an online shopping basket were pretty similar to that of a traditional in-store one – which showed that our customers trusted our staff enough to select fresh goods on their behalf. In fact, we trained specialist staff to pick perishable foods for shoppers, and amended existing processes to meet the special challenges of selling fresh food online: for example, we had to coordinate the baking of bread with the picking of bread to fulfil Tesco.com orders, so that customers received it as fresh as possible.

These first few years were a classic example of learning on the job, and the benefits of starting a big project with small, careful first steps. Using the information we had gained about how customers behaved online, we rapidly reworked our deliberately loose process, gradually firming it up and turning it into a stable system as new patterns of behaviour became more certain and predictable.

Tesco.com also taught us a lot about our existing business. The data told us which order was picked from which shelf in which store at what time, making us the first retailer in the world to get a real-time picture of the true availability of our products, as opposed to a theoretical measure of availability calculated by our computers. This data did not make pleasant reading. We had spent a lot on ordering systems and logistics, which were reckoned to be the most sophisticated in our industry. (They had to be: UK stores are up to four times busier than US stores.) Our computer systems made a calculation of our availability at 98 per cent – a good performance given the demands on our stores. As Tesco.com grew, we found that true availability was nearer 92 per cent.

Shocked by this finding, we completely rebuilt our supply chain, warehouses, ordering and replenishment systems. This took several years, but by the end of it our actual, true availability over 40,000 products in store really was 98 per cent. This, in turn, taught us a lot about rebuilding work processes, training people in clear roles within those processes, and writing simple computer systems to scale and replicate the work flows. Our confidence in our data meant we were able to develop a world-leading replenishment system that delivered the product for the shelf at precisely the right time. This made the whole store easier to restock. It also meant our perishable food was delivered much quicker and therefore fresher to our shelves, which gave it a longer shelf-life when customers took it home. Better still, our computers could now map the exact location of every product on every shelf in every store, cutting the time it took our teams to pick goods off a store's shelves for an online order. We turned this into an 'app', allowing customers to go into a store and identify the precise location of any given product.

There were some other great, unforeseen consequences for the business. Tesco.com was a school for talent. Young executives – Carolyn Bradley, Ken Towle, John Browett and Laura Wade-Gery – gained hands-on experience of operations, seeing for themselves the importance of building robust processes and having the independence to take initiative and innovate. All went on to do big jobs in Tesco and other companies.

Many new roles were created in-store as well – home delivery driver, in-store order picker, order dispatcher and so on. All of these carried a lot of responsibility, as some of these people went into people's homes, each one an ambassador for Tesco. Such personal contact with a customer meant they could make or break the customer's loyalty to the company.

In a final, perhaps slightly ironic twist, we have gradually been opening stores to supply online shoppers only. With no checkouts or car parks, these stores resemble what the Webvan distribution centres might have become had they focused on winning customers rather than creating the perfect distribution system. Fortunately, thanks to their established customer base, these Tesco stores immediately became profitable.

Today, Tesco.com is the world's largest online food business – profitable, fast-growing and rapidly expanding to countries as diverse as South Korea, the Czech Republic and Ireland. Seventeen years after it was created, sales were around £3 billion. Three and a half million British households, almost 14 per cent of the total, have used online food shopping in the last three months – benefiting from a revolution led by Tesco.

The story of Tesco.com shows what happens when a small team of people take an idea, make a decision to turn it into reality, and then build simple systems and processes to do so. It is not a story of one person creating a perfect, new distribution system on a drawing board, but one of constant change and improvement. Above all, it is a story that shows the critical importance of focusing on process – even if that means starting small and growing slowly.

How not to do it

As the Tesco.com experience shows, turning a simple idea into reality demands clarity of vision, a simple process, clear roles and a willingness to learn from mistakes. Every organisation makes costly mistakes when it tries to change how it operates. The successful organisations are those which learn from their mistakes. In the private sector, failure to learn ultimately results in failure overall, as shareholders take fright at the prospect of more of their money being wasted. The company goes bankrupt, and may enter business textbooks as a case study in how not to do things. Such market discipline obviously does not exist in companies that are deemed too 'big to fail' (such as large banks and state sponsored industries) and much of the public sector. In government organisations, often the worst that happens is an inquiry by a group of officials or politicians, some uncomfortable media coverage, possibly the resignation of a minister and then – well, not much. The money is written off, and government goes on. To that extent – unfair though this may seem – it's often the public sector that affords the most telling examples of poor ideas, badly executed.

In Britain there have been numerous examples of wasteful spending on botched projects. One such is FiReControl, launched by the Department for Communities and Local Government in 2004. Its purpose was to improve national resilience, efficiency and technology by replacing the control room functions of 46 local Fire and Rescue Services in England with a network of nine purpose-built regional control centres using a national computer system. The original estimate to complete the project was £120 million.[12] Following a series of delays and complications, the project was terminated in December 2010. None of the original objectives had been met. The minimum cost to the taxpayer: £469 million.[13] The Department estimated that the total cost of completing the project would have been £635 million – more than five times the original estimate.[14]

'In hindsight,' the project's director later told a Parliamentary Committee, 'if we had not ever started the project, then that would have been possibly the best course of action'[15] – to which millions of taxpayers would no doubt cry 'too true'. Criticising people's actions after the event is easy. You never have the benefit of hindsight when you are in the middle of a project. Business people should also beware of lecturing the public sector, which has different priorities, incentives and accountabilities from the private sector. Fire control centres, for example, have a vital and very particular role to fulfil, dealing with the sort of emergencies you don't see in business very often.

Yet as I read the report on the failure of the FiReControl, I could not help thinking that it represented a novel way of illustrating how best to approach the creation and development of new systems. Novel in that, if you did the exact opposite at every stage of the FiReControl project, you would come pretty close to an ideal approach.

When embarking on any project that demands change, you need to know what the problem is. In the case of FiReControl, the original 46 centres were stand-alone: they couldn't talk to each other. That is a theoretical problem, but was there real evidence for its actually being a practical problem – in other words, how often did the various centres really need to talk to each other? And even if there were actual problems to be solved, from the outset this plan seemed a large hammer to crack a small nut. There are only 1,400 controllers. So the project, even before everything went wrong, planned to spend about £85,000 per controller so that they could talk to each other. That alone should have rung alarm bells (no pun intended).

Arguably, then, the project itself was misguided. Leaving that aside, though, there was the question of implementation. As I've already said, it is always best to ask the operators (the managers and staff who actually do the job) to write down the processes involved. Should things then go wrong, you will be able to locate the cause of a problem, isolate it, make a change and then identify any knock-on effects. You also need to make sure that any changes to existing processes are reflected in changes to people's roles – after all, they will be joining up the dots. If they don't understand their role, nothing will work.

In the FiReControl project, no real attempt appears to have been made to understand what staff were already doing and absolutely no attempt was made to prepare them for their new roles.[16] Every one of the 46 centres had a completely different way of doing things, but it seems that this was not all written down so that it could be clarified and streamlined into a new approach.[17] All that is clear is that the operators were not really consulted about the proposed project.

Compounding this problem was lack of responsibility and accountability. Operators – the managers of the process – must be responsible.[18] They may well need to bring in experts, but it is their job, their process and it must be their system. No one appears to have been fully responsible and accountable for the FiReControl project, least of all the fire controllers who were to operate the new system. Instead, there was a heavy reliance on outside experts and consultants.

FiReControl was, it seems, also cursed by the notion that this was a 'new challenge'. Every leader likes to think their organisation is unique, their problems have not been seen before, and therefore the new system they are creating will be truly radical – hence the need to use 'experts'. However, while it may be comforting to think that your organisation is different, and that the challenge has never been encountered before, in reality it is rare to find a genuinely new problem and even rarer to find a problem that requires an entirely new system. Most problems have been faced before – and usually by someone already in the business. Therefore nearly every solution to a system's problems should be 'off the shelf', as there is usually a perfectly adequate system already in existence which can be adapted as necessary. If not, the 'experts' should be able to help – but that doesn't involve a shift in accountability: the process owner must always remain accountable.

Some things that a management team may undertake will be genuinely innovative: they may, for example, want a proprietary system to give their organisation competitive advantage. This will, however, also be a rare occurrence. Beware of the in-house IT team which wants everything bespoke, managers who would rather a system be changed than change their own behaviour, and consultants who make more money on bespoke, complex solutions than providing standard, off-the-shelf product installations.

If an organisation really has to do something for the first time, the trick is to make sure the change is incremental and begins with small steps, so that the mistakes you will inevitably make won't destroy the organisation (be it public or private) entirely. The greater the cost, the greater the caution required. An organisation that embarks on a £120 million project that has never been done before should proceed with extreme care.

Tesco often ventured into new territory, but cautiously, usually one step at a time. When developing a new system – especially a complex one – we learnt the importance of setting clear milestones to measure progress and performance, breaking projects into bite-sized chunks and stating clearly what needs to be achieved, by what date and at what cost. Those milestones are there for a reason. The temptation is, of course, to ignore them if a date or target has been missed, as people fear failure. Instead, when something goes wrong (as it invariably will) the project should be halted and not started again until the cause of the failure is known and addressed. As a rule of thumb, anyone who gives you a price for something and comes back within a couple of years, without progress but saying the price has almost trebled (as happened with the FiReControl project),[19] does not properly know what they are doing and must not be allowed to carry on.

Finally, the implementation of a new system matters as much as the system's development, and requires just as much preparation as designing the new process itself. Communication is critical: everyone needs to know precisely what is expected of them, and why. We cannot fault the FiReControl project on implementation: it never got that far.

Obviously I do not know all the ins and outs of the FiReControl debacle. Rather than trying to apportion blame, I would like to think that the Government – and the wider world – has learnt from these costly errors. And that brings me to a confession. I am immediately struck by the mistakes made in the FiReControl project because I have made a number of them myself – from missed systems deadlines to costly write-offs. When projects fail, they generally do so because those commissioning them have not thought through what they want the new system to do, nor have they written down a clear process. And I have certainly been guilty of that.

What was sad about the FiReControl experience was the cost of the mistakes. £469 million was written off, comfortably more than what Tesco spends on all its IT each year, worldwide. Sadly, this figure pales against the cost of the botched project to computerise NHS patients' medical records. Originally estimated to cost £6.2 billion, after nine years the project was cancelled – by which time it had cost £12.7 billion.[20]

Boring detail, big growth

In British culture, there is little that is regarded as glamorous about designing processes, roles and systems that work properly. We are a nation of thinkers – 'doing' is seen as a little grubby, unsophisticated and boring. This means not nearly enough talent is focused on how to implement decisions successfully. Companies that have recognised this – and I would boast that Tesco is one – have been rewarded in a myriad of ways.

A company that can act successfully can grow fast. Processes can be scaled up: once a process is properly defined, you can build IT systems to perform part or all of it – faster, more reliably and for less. You can enjoy a dramatic improvement in performance by removing pinch points and bottlenecks: by minimising waste, you do more with less. A process can be based in one country, but serve another. For example, Tesco has no back office or administration in North America. Fresh and Easy stores are run entirely on processes out of India on standard platforms.

Processes can also be copied from one country to the next, and improved to make them better still. This does not mean you sell the same products everywhere. Quite the reverse. The beauty of a standard process that works well is that you can sell different products around the world, but efficiently everywhere.

A few decades ago Ford tried to develop a 'world car' that would look the same all over the world. However, all the components they used were locally manufactured, so although it looked the same it was completely local in its composition. What Ford realised over time – and what Volkswagen do so brilliantly – is that you can create a common platform for manufacturing a car that looks different all over the world. It is designed for the demands and cultures of local markets, but it has common components beneath the bonnet. The bits that you don't see are common everywhere, while the bits that matter to you are local.

The same applies to retailing. The first global retailers (like Toys R Us) tried to make everything – brands, formats, ranges – look the same around the world. They soon discovered that all retail must be tailored for the local customer. Tesco has a simple doctrine: local, but global. We create local stores that look completely different depending on the continent but run them on global operating systems. Our common platform is called, suitably enough, 'Tesco in a box'. These are core work processes (the company's hidden wiring and plumbing, completely unseen by its customers) which have been turned into systems and are then used across the group – such as ordering, finance, replenishment, merchandising, customer data handling. These systems enable local managers to tailor what their stores offer to meet local tastes, while still benefiting from Tesco's scale as a global operation.

Good processes in all types of organisation should be capable of being applied universally. When that happens, a company benefits from higher productivity. Immeasurable benefits are just as important. When a team acts as one, efficiently and effectively, everyone enjoys the satisfaction of a job well done and the morale of the business rises. Instead of having to placate people frustrated by inefficiency and delay, managers have time to think ahead, to spot mistakes before they become a problem, and to focus on new opportunities. Far from being a straitjacket which constrains individuals, good processes and systems allow people to complete work in a satisfying way, liberating them to do new things.

Again, this is not a new thought. Samuel Smiles wrote 'An economical use of time is the true mode of securing leisure: it enables us to get through business and carry it forward instead of being driven by it. On the other hand, the miscalculation of time involves us in perpetual hurry, confusion, and difficulties; and life becomes a mere shuffle of expedients, usually followed by disaster.'[21]

Sadly, too few people heed his words. Processes, job roles, systems, discipline – none of it is glamorous, but all of it critical to successful action, and creating the freedom and potential to grow. Growth brings its own challenges – which brings me on to the need for balance.

6 Balance

A balanced organisation is one in which everyone moves forward together, steered in the right direction, without being overrun by the juggernaut of bureaucracy.

To act effectively, it's not only essential that each person should know what their job is; it's also essential that the very different departments and groups involved come together to achieve the goal. How do you ensure that your big decision is translated into action by the many tasks, some very small, that these thousands of people do, day in, day out? How do you unite all parts of the organisation, creating teams and knitting them together? How does the management actually steer the organisation towards its goals?

Take Slim's approach, for example. While galvanising the loyalty of individual solders and marshalling them to focus on achieving one objective – the destruction of the enemy – he also forged the army and air force into one weapon, breaking down service loyalties and the 'silo mentality'. Describing the Fourteenth Army's crossing of the Irrawaddy River, Slim wrote of the importance of the sappers who built the roads, the lorry drivers who used them and the mechanics who serviced the lorries, working as one, slick team. 'They identified themselves utterly with the troops ahead; they were and they felt themselves to be a part, and a vital part, of the team. They had the pride and bearing of fighting men, for they were one with them'.[1]

The challenge for any large organisation is to create not merely that sense of camaraderie, of moving together as one, but a framework in which each person and every team can perform their roles as they best see fit. It is a framework that encourages initiative and innovation, it makes people take responsibility for their actions, but above all it measures and directs their progress so that the priorities of one part of the organisation do not conflict with another. This is a balanced organisation, in which everyone moves forward together, steered in the right direction, without being overrun by the juggernaut of bureaucracy.

'Bureaucratic' is one of the worst insults you can throw at someone – you're slow, unresponsive, wedded to rules and regulations. For the humans inside a bureaucratic organisation, work can quickly become a rather confused, isolated and unsettling experience. They feel trapped by a structure which controls rather than serves them. It is difficult for any one individual to sense the purpose and direction of the whole enterprise. Their world closes in, becoming confined to what they can see and influence.

As their world shrinks to what they can measure and control, people become detached from the higher or wider goals of the institution and defend their own interests fiercely and increasingly at the expense of everyone else. Individual departments gradually – and unwittingly – reinterpret targets to suit how they like to operate. Over time, as measures of performance across the organisation drift apart, it becomes difficult to get a clear picture of overall performance or to coordinate parts of the organisation. People increasingly don't really know how they are doing or what difference they make – indeed whether anyone else would notice if they weren't there. They come not to trust other departments. Insecurity, bordering on paranoia, sets in, which prevents people innovating, showing initiative or following what they know is the right course of action.

And so arrives the day when, at a meeting, you realise that everyone around the table has a completely different take on the problem under discussion. They have become so detached from the organisation that they have even developed their own systems for measuring performance and have created their own version of reality. Then the organisation really is in trouble: it has become fragmented, unbalanced and impossible to move forward.

By the time I became CEO, I had seen enough of the dangers of bureaucracy to know that Tesco needed a means to unite the company, connect big decisions to small actions, and allow the leadership to steer the entire organisation at speed to reach our goals. Growth could not depend on me, or my board directors, or everyone sitting in Tesco headquarters issuing directives. We could set the strategy, the goals of the business, but we had to trust our teams across the country – and later the world – to do what they thought best to meet them. The management had to focus on the wood, and let our teams in countries around the world grow the trees. This meant creating a culture where people could take responsibility for their actions and dare to try something new – rather than constantly covering their backs. We had to let go, accept that mistakes would be made, and not try to micromanage decisions taken by those on the ground.

Around the time I became CEO I read *The Balanced Scorecard* by Robert Kaplan and David Norton. They realised that many businesses – Tesco included – judged progress against things like lower costs, quality and response times. The problem was that these indicators measured the performance of existing processes, and did not reflect progress against strategic aims. Nor could conventional analysis account for intangible assets, such as innovation, customer loyalty and staff skills. Worse, companies whose actions reflected short-term aims might meet their targets, but the company would be destroyed in the long run. For example, a company can increase prices or cut back on quality of service, which will boost its profits in the short term, but destroy customer loyalty in the long run. Such companies are not 'identifying the processes that were truly strategic: those that must be performed exceptionally well for an organisation to succeed'.[2] Action and strategy, in other words, become unbalanced.

So Kaplan and Norton developed the 'balanced scorecard', which reflected – in their words – 'the balance provided between short- and long-term objectives, between financial and non-financial measures, between lagging and leading indicators, and between external and internal performance indicators'.[3] Put another way, the scorecard measures the outcome of past events and indicators that will drive future performance. More than this, a balanced scorecard's purpose is 'to articulate the strategy of the business, to communicate the strategy of the business, and to help align individual, organizational and cross-departmental initiatives to achieve a common goal'.[4] Everyone then knows what to do, why, and how it fits in with the rest of the business.

Today, a 'balanced scorecard' is familiar jargon to many businesses. Back in 1997 people probably thought I was talking about cricket. But I liked the idea, and I commissioned Bill Gordon, a management consultant, to think how it might be applied to Tesco. My instruction was that I wanted to give all our teams a tool to steer their part of the business – but at the same time make sure that all parts remained connected, so the business could move forward in a balanced way.

He took my instructions literally – and came back with a Steering Wheel. The wheel was divided into four parts: Customer, Operations, People and Finance – to which we later added Community. Each of these was underpinned by several commitments, reflecting what our staff, customers and shareholders wanted us to do better. Some would be common to any business – 'grow sales' or 'keep staff absence to a minimum'. Others were unique to retailing, relevant to people on our shop floors, be they staff or customers. 'The aisles are clear.' 'I can get what I want.' 'I don't queue.' Attached to each segment was a target for the year. This target would change every 12 months, and would be measured and reported weekly to the business. It would be reviewed by the Executive Committee quarterly to assess progress. A simple traffic-light signal would show whether the store, or team, was on track to reach their target (a green light) or underperforming (a red light).

From the very first moment I could see the power of this simple device. As Kaplan and Norton promised, this tool helped us to clarify our vision and strategy; to communicate and link our strategic objectives and targets; to plan and set clear targets; and to improve feedback and learning from the shop floor.[5] The very act of creating the Steering Wheel forced the senior management team to agree not just broad-brush strategic statements, but what delivering them would mean in practice. We did not end management by turf war or the silo mentality ('Yes, I know there's a problem, but it's so and so's problem to sort out'), but the Steering Wheel nevertheless brought a new discipline and consensus to managing business, day in, day out.

Above all, though, the Steering Wheel was practical and simple. Most 'management tools' are ignored by employees, tucked away in a corporate report or pinned to a noticeboard in a dark corner of the company canteen. They don't drive a business any more than a car manual drives a car. Our Steering Wheel, though, could be applied to each and every part of the business, every division and every store. Each segment of the wheel measured performance of about four or five activities, so each wheel would only have 20 measures. But as you drilled down, each of these measures could go into still more detail, which eventually linked it to the individual targets and performance of stores – and then, at a lower level still, the teams within that store.

In that way, simple summaries of big targets were directly linked to the day-to-day work of thousands of people. All our teams, wherever they worked, would be able to see at a glance how well their store or operation was performing. Clear, transparent, accountable – but above all balanced. Every part of the business had targets to work towards, but no target would undermine or destabilise another part of the operation.

Best of all, the Steering Wheel helped us manage change in a balanced way. Successful retailers spot a new trend or demand well before it can be called 'fashionable' – indeed, the most successful retailer creates the fashion, and rides the waves of a trend. That gives companies – again quoting Kaplan and Norton – 'the ability to manage successfully a multi-year product development process or to develop a capability to reach entirely new categories of customers' which 'may be more critical for future economic performance than managing existing operations efficiently, consistently and responsively'.[6] The Steering Wheel helped us implement such changes, some of which took years and involved many different processes, across the entire business – new ways to design stores, creating new ranges of products, new methods to restock stores.

This tool became the way – the only way – we managed our stores as we grew. It allowed us to honour our dictum of being 'global but local' and to preserve our heritage of starting life as a street stall in the East End of London. I did not sit in Cheshunt, fashioning Steering Wheels for stores in Poland or Korea – that was left to the teams on the ground. Every store, anywhere in the world, has its Steering Wheel, tailored by local management teams to reflect local culture and custom. Everyone in the business, wherever they work, knows exactly what their team is meant to achieve. Across the world, we would use the same indicators for performance, but set different targets appropriate to the local market: for example, we measured queue length everywhere, but would set slightly different targets to reflect how busy stores were in each market.

This level of accountability also gave us a means of measuring progress, enabling us to gauge whether our strategy was working, from the company as a whole down to each individual store. Better still, we could identify and then unravel the conundrum that managers sometimes face: although an objective has been met (such as increasing availability or lowering costs), the desired outcome (such as increased sales per store) has failed to materialise.

You would think measuring things in business would be relatively easy. In one sense, it is. A lot of business consists of activities repeated over and over again. Indeed, you want it that way. If you create as many reliable processes as possible the outcome is more predictable. All that should lend itself to measurement. Data now is cheap to collect and interrogate and there are often standard measures to follow in areas such as finance.

Yet, time and again, measuring things causes problems for organisations. Quite often a target is chosen to guide a business towards a desired outcome, but when you hit that target you do not get the outcome you want. For example, you might think that the number of people waiting in a checkout queue is a good way to measure satisfaction with the speed of checkout service. A target is therefore set to cut the number of people waiting at a checkout. It transpires, though, that even though fewer people are waiting in line, there is no increase in satisfaction with the service at the checkout. Why? Because what matters to customers is not the length of the queue, but the time it takes to queue.

It's also possible to create two measures that conflict. At one point, for example, we focused both on cutting the numbers of customers queuing, and on getting cashiers to input more information at the tills (data such as the age of the customer or whether they had coupons), which slowed the process down.

This is a problem that any organisation encounters when it tries to set a target. The National Health Service in England is overflowing with cases of the undesired outcomes that 'performance targets' have on clinical care. For example, the Department of Health focused for years on speed of response as a measure of performance of the ambulance service, rather than on clinical outcomes for patients. An official report into the consequences of this target found that 'The 8-minute response target, intended for the most seriously ill patients, is one of the most demanding in the world. However, without more direct measures of patient outcomes, its application has skewed ambulance trusts' approach to performance measurement and management. This has led to such practices as sending more vehicles than necessary to meet the target, leaving extra vehicles to be stood down. The target is also applied to a much wider group of patients than intended.'[7] Another example comes from the world of planning controls. Responding to complaints that it took too long for local councils to agree or reject planning applications, the Government set a time limit for councils to come a decision. To ensure that they met the target, councils began to reject applications almost out of hand.

And, of course, you have to allow for the fact that sometimes the best measure of something may not be the obvious one. My father-in-law, Herbert Blank, had first-hand experience of this. He sold industrial laundry machines for hotels, restaurants, hospitals and other institutions. At the time their unique competitive advantage was an invisible marking system, which ensured that individual items never went missing in the laundry. Herbert sold these machines around the world, and took one to a trade fair in the Soviet Union in the early 1960s. Herbert's stand was visited by none other than Nikita Khrushchev, First Secretary of the Communist Party. Khrushchev thought the USSR could overtake the USA in science and technology, so he was on the lookout for new innovations. He was attracted by Herbert's machine, made some unkind remarks along the lines of 'If it can get Molotov's underpants clean it truly is a remarkable invention', and said it was just the kind of technology the Soviet Union should have.

My father-in-law was delighted. Now it was just a question of finding someone to authorise the purchase. He had done his homework and worked out who in the hierarchy had the official authority. This person was tracked down, but no, he couldn't authorise it. Herbert tried his subordinate, then his boss, all to no avail. After a month spent scouring the official system a friend suggested he look at a different hierarchy. 'Find out which of them gets the most visits to the Black Sea resorts: he is likely to be the person with the most power.' So Herbert researched Black Sea holidays and discovered that there was little correlation between officials who went there most often and the official hierarchy. He eventually tracked down the person with the most holidays – and he duly authorised the purchase of Herbert's laundry machine for the Soviet Union. The measure of power in the Soviet Union, it turned out, was not the obvious one.

At Tesco we always found the most reliable measures – if not always the easiest to ascertain – were those which described what the customer wanted. The measures that could cause trouble were those that managers found easy to implement (usually something that happened anyway, as a by-product of another process) but that did not always reflect what customers wanted. A good example comes from the unpromising-sounding area of computerised book stock records – in other words, the record of whether a product is available. Easy to produce and a very accurate internal measure, a computerised book stock record can tell you immediately that a product is in the store.

Unfortunately, what it can't do is inform you whether that means that it's actually on the shelf or still sitting in the storeroom. We only realised this when we tried to speed up our efforts at restocking stores overnight. According to our official records we were doing well. However, we hadn't allowed for the fact that we weren't actually giving our teams long enough to do the job. The result: products were certainly somewhere in store, but inaccessible to the people who wanted to buy them. So as far as the customer was concerned, they were out of stock.

The lesson we learnt from this was that we needed to establish broad measures for customer satisfaction to make sure we avoided coming up with ones that conflicted with each other or could not be correlated. When it came to ensuring availability, for example, our measure was that customers would agree with the statement 'I can get what I want'. This ensured that we avoided a common mistake in retailing: putting out the widest possible range but in the process both overcrowding shelves and not focusing on the availability of particular, key brands. Getting the balance right shapes how customers respond to the statement 'I can get what I want'. Above all, our measure recognises the reality that the perfect combination of range and availability is subjective and personal to each shopper.

We used similar simple measures for other aspects of customer satisfaction. We found that if a customer agreed with the statement 'The aisles are clear', they were not merely saying that they did not find boxes cluttering up the aisles, but that they found the simple shop design easy to use. Similarly 'The prices are good' was the only reliable guide to prices and price marketing. 'I don't queue' covered everything to do with checkouts and waiting around the store. 'The staff are great' obviously told us about service in all its forms. We developed lots of more precise measures, but our performance against these major statements of customer experience were the only ones that really mattered, and they ensured that everyone in the business understood the shopping experience – from price to service – that customers wanted.

Keeping both feet on the ground

A balanced organisation is one whose senior managers have both feet on the ground: they don't get carried away by their ambition, they always remember that plans and initiatives have to be practical if they are to work, and they are relentless in their wish to keep close to the action. I liked to think of Tesco as having the body of a global business, but the heart of the small one that Jack Cohen founded. Balancing such a company took effort.

One activity, above all, helped us balance the organisation. It broke down the silos that had grown up between departments, so that everyone could see how Tesco looked and operated overall, not just from their own unique perspective. It ensured that everyone gained a better sense of where they fitted in, how their contribution made a difference and the impact of their decisions and actions on other departments. It allowed them to balance their own contribution and measures against the contribution and measures of other parts of the company. Best of all, it enabled them to learn how relatively small adjustments to the way they measured and managed themselves could make a much greater contribution to the effective performance of departments elsewhere in the organisation. This magical device was called TWIST: Tesco Week In Store Together. (For a very powerful idea it is a rather lame title, I admit.)

TWIST came about after I had been grappling with the problem of bureaucracy for some time. Even though senior managers spent a lot of time on Tesco's shop floor – I spent around two days a week out in the shops and the depots – I was conscious that we suffered the same problems as every other organisation: people get tied to their desks and bogged down by their own workload, whether imagined or real. I was also aware that I was a visitor to the shops for a short period, no more than a few hours in each store, sometimes less. That fleeting visit meant I never actually did the jobs that most of our half a million employees performed day in, day out – working on checkouts, filling shelves, working in the warehouse and so on. Neither I, nor any of my colleagues in senior management, could possibly truly understand during a short visit what challenges our teams on the ground faced, or how a new initiative was panning out in practice. To get under the skin of the business, the senior management – indeed, all management – had to commit more time to being on the front line.

So I gave myself a challenge. I would work for one week every year as a general assistant doing every job in the store. Checkouts, shelf-filling, back room, pricing, customer queries, working on counters – you name it, I would do it. I then said to my top managers (over 3,000 people, including store managers) that before I 'TWISTed' again in a year's time, I would like them to do their first week. It was a simple contract between us: if I would do it then so would they – and they did.

I picked my store (a large superstore at Royston in Hertfordshire) and phoned the manager on Friday to tell him he would have a new member of staff on Monday. I didn't want him to have too much time to worry about what was about to happen (though, admittedly, he had the weekend to get through) nor did I want the store, in its well-meaning way, to have time to cushion things for me.

I learnt more in that week than any other week that year. For example, I had previously had little knowledge of all the hours of the Tesco day, even though it's a 24-hour business. Now I did. I came to appreciate the jobs people did (from the sheer hard work of completely filling up the shelves overnight to the knowledge needed to handle the complex myriad of customer enquiries on the service desk). It also gave others the opportunity to see how bad I was at some tasks. I was particularly slow on the checkouts. I remember one patient customer saying 'You're not very good but you tried very hard and I think you'll go far in Tesco.'

By the end of the week, although I was heartened to have found that the business was fundamentally sound, I had learnt a lot about what was going wrong – things you could only see by actually doing them, not by watching or visiting. I had plenty of ideas to take back to head office, but that was not ultimately the point of the exercise: what really mattered were the 3,000 managers who would TWIST after me. Their first-hand experience – one year's TWIST for them amounted to about one person spending 60 years on the shop floor – was a revelation for the entire company. Managers found that it transformed how they looked at their own job. They understood how important it was to think through the impact of their actions and decisions on others. By experiencing life on the shop floor, they realised how they fitted into the company as a whole. What to a specialist might seem a small decision – such as the design of a staff uniform, a merchandise plan or a staff rota – could actually change the way that hundreds or thousands of people work. That is hard to understand when you are sitting in a remote office, but you appreciate it when you witness it at first hand. One consequence, therefore, was that everyone who went on TWIST felt a greater sense of self-worth, as they could see the impact of the decisions they took.

Various 'team TWISTs' were developed, involving everyone who had anything to do with a particular department (bakery or clothing, for example): they would work together so they could quickly fix anything they found that had gone awry. When, for instance, we discovered that our directors could not fill shelves as swiftly as they had estimated, we changed the number of staff allocated to our stores' fruit and vegetable departments. Even the Executive Committee for the UK took over the running of a store for a week (I won't say whether the turnover went up or down). All in all, by getting our managers to see things from the shop floor, it enabled us to balance the business.

Short term vs long term

'The essence of all military planning is timing. A brilliant plan wrongly timed, put into operation too early or too late, is at the best a lame thing and at the worst may be a disaster', wrote Slim.[8] The same is true in business. A balanced business does not simply move forward as one: it moves at the right time, at the right pace. Some may think that they are more controlled by events and the actions of others than by their own deliberate decisions – especially in today's fast-moving world. To accept this is to be governed by your in-box, what the competition does or the vagaries of the world economy. Yes, the actions of others shape the world in which a company competes and an organisation operates. But good leaders, and good business people, sniff out the opportunity to take the initiative, and decide when and how to act. All this is done deliberately – and after deliberation. Getting the timing right is very much part of balancing a business successfully. How do you do that?

Sadly there is no universal truth, but two things are critical: to make a decision yourself, and to choose the time at which you do so. Decisions to act should not be set by external events or clamour, the noises off. 'Doing nothing is not an option', managers are often told. To remain balanced, to avoid a headlong rush into a new venture, doing nothing may be precisely the thing to do. The challenge you face may not be clear, or the solution may elude you. When you do get a clearer picture, it may also become apparent that the solution to the problem will take a long time to implement properly. The overriding lesson I learnt was that the bigger the challenge, the bigger the decision, and the more essential it therefore is to wait until you are ready to make it – and only to move when you are ready to take the entire organisation with you.

Wherever possible at Tesco, we would start slowly and cautiously so the inevitable mistakes were small. When we had enough experience on the ground, we would try to build up the investment – sometimes placing some pretty large bets on a country or sector, but always willing to be patient. Tesco would spend almost three years researching a new country to get the entry route and entry timing right. When we moved into banking it was clear that to build a bank based around our own customers would take a generation. We were prepared to wait that long because going faster would mean taking an unnecessarily large risk. (Those organisations who felt they had to create banking business quickly were usually the ones who got into most trouble in the financial crisis of 2007–8. Time pressurised them into taking too much risk.)

Most decisions that most managers take are not on this order of magnitude. As a general rule, therefore, making quick decisions is a good habit to get into, so long as those decisions are based on sufficient information and insight and don't involve large-scale risk. Being first can catch your competition off guard, gets you noticed and can give you a good reputation as an innovator, a trendsetter not a fashion follower. Being first can announce your arrival into a new sector. Some years ago we pioneered the removal of lead from petrol with the campaign 'on lead we lead', which helped us to increase our share of petrol retailing. Likewise, when we opened terminals for the UK's National Lottery on every till, and when we were the first to enable mobile phone top-up at every till, we dramatically increased our share in a new sector with an early innovation. All this supports the thought that 'speed kills' – being first to move, you throw your opponent off balance.

The problem with this race to be first, though, is that it can hide a different motive: to do something to plug a short-term need, to get through a week or a month, to make a budget or beat the same period last year. This throws a company off balance, as it leads to management by impulse and expediency: everyone intends to think and act long term – but next time. 'Lord, let me think long term – but not yet.' Next time comes, the pressures are still the same and another short-term solution is chosen: a discount to bribe a customer to switch to you, or a reduction in service to save on costs to make a budget. Before long the company is trapped into that way of thinking. The long term simply becomes a series of short-term decisions one after the other. The quick decision or quick action which was intended to save time ends up wasting months or even years. A good manager will call 'halt', whatever the apparent consequences of delay, and take enough time to understand properly what the underlying issues are and what fundamental change is needed to provide a lasting solution.

Perversely, even if you think you are acting according to your plan, and you have evidence and data to support your plan, you can sometimes be too early if you move first. In 1990 we felt consumers were changing their shopping habits and looking for healthier foods that had fewer additives and were kinder to the environment. We developed products that were Lean, Clean and Green. Look at the market 20 years later and this might appear to have been a trendsetting, far-sighted move: lean, clean and green are all big drivers of custom. However, we were a decade too early. What we had spotted was a real trend, but not well established enough to withstand the recession of the early 1990s.

Balanced organisations take decisions smoothly, not in a knee-jerk fashion. Their managers understand that time is a dimension of management: they know that you can make choices as to when to act, not just how to act, and they differentiate between decisions that need to be taken in the short term and those which demand longer deliberation. Our Steering Wheel always contained projects ready for immediate implementation, and projects that were to be prepared and implemented the following year.

Of course, for many organisations, setting long-term goals may seem something of a luxury, as they are constantly under pressure to deliver in the short term. Public companies, for example, have to take account of many different interest groups – from employees to shareholders to politicians and the media – many of whom expect immediate, visible success and are fiercely critical if it is not regularly delivered. In Tesco's case, many fund managers are only really interested in how the company's shares perform against a particular benchmark. If the company makes a strategic move, all that matters is whether its stock price will go up or down on the day. (There are, of course, exceptions to this – such as the investment company Berkshire Hathaway.) I was CEO of Tesco for 14 years. During that time, thanks to the efforts of everyone who worked there, the company did well and the share price reflected that. It was a good stock to own through the whole period and some funds gained (as did I). Yet the entire shareholding of Tesco was bought and sold eight times in that period. (That rate of turnover is low by market standards: the average company's issued shares are bought and sold every eight months.)

Yet the long term matters most. You only have to look at the best private family companies to realise just how important long-term thinking is for a business – and, come to that, any balanced organisation. After all, these are the enterprises that actually tend to do better (in terms of sustained economic return) than public companies, despite the obvious disadvantages of a more limited access to capital, problems of succession and recruiting leaders from a much smaller pool of talent.

Family-owned companies can balance long-term plans against short-term needs. Planning for the long term obviously runs in a family's DNA: they think in terms of generations, not annual reporting cycles. Plans are based on the timescale that is needed to achieve a goal, not an artificial timescale driven by a need to please the stock markets. The Duke of Westminster (one of the richest men in England) once told me his family firm began when William the Conqueror sent the Duke's forebears up to Chester to subdue the troublesome Welsh after the Norman Conquest in 1066. They have been in business ever since. So when others complain of how difficult a particular business cycle is, he gently points out that at the last count his firm has survived around 200 recessions and 50 wars.

Without institutional investors breathing down their necks, these companies do not face the same pressure to announce earnings growth every quarter. They can move swiftly to take on competition and postpone earnings growth to protect their long-term position. Look at China's nimble-footed, fast-growing family companies, which are prepared to reinvent their business model several times over as competition or technology changes.

Even when family companies are listed on public markets they still outperform. The owners' experience of the business makes for more confident, balanced decisions, with more of a feel for what really matters for the company. The best family businesses follow the good practice of public company governance and work hard to ensure that the next generation gets plenty of business experience outside the family firm to bring in fresh ideas. On top of that, family firms are more likely to have a guiding set of principles to which they adhere even if they become unfashionable. This clarity of purpose, consistently applied, allows value to accrue and multiply over long periods of time. All these things are preconditions, if not guarantees, of superior business performance. And they all add a sense of balance.

I met and worked with many family-owned businesses at Tesco and saw many of the ownership qualities which create good businesses at first hand. One company is worth a special mention: Tata.

Tesco spent a long time considering who would make the best partner for our planned investment in India. Two factors complicated things – challenges that remain to this day. First, direct foreign investment in retail is not allowed there: only indirect investment via wholesaling, logistics and so on. Second, India will undoubtedly become a huge consumer market in time, but it's not there yet. The size of the country is matched by the size of the challenges it faces. Tesco therefore needed to be patient, and it needed a partner who felt the same way.

The partner we chose was the Tata Group or, to be precise, its retail subsidiary called Trent. One of India's most respected companies – if not the most respected – Tata has been around for 100 years. With business interests in IT, steel, automotive and consumer goods, it is still family-controlled: the group is led by Ratan Tata, while Trent Retail was managed by his half-brother

Noel Tata. Both Ratan and Noel are personally charming, experienced and generous business partners – a solid rock on which to build a relationship. Over and above that, we found that Tata had very high ethical and professional standards. Their talented team shared our sense of timing: quick, even impatient on tactics, but long term and patient on strategy, making sure we grew on solid foundations. Although it is still early days for Tesco in India, together with Tata our Star Bazaar retail brand is growing rapidly.

Knowing Tata, I was fascinated to watch their acquisition of Jaguar Land Rover from Ford Motors. Ford and Tata, both outstanding companies, have very different philosophies. Ford is probably the best-known name in cars, having made motoring affordable and pioneered global car manufacturing. Tata Motors aspires to be the company that makes motoring affordable in the developing world, but I think even Ratan Tata would agree that it will be some time before they can claim the same imprint on the world of motoring as Ford.

The intriguing question is what does Tata think they can do that Ford could not? The answer appears to lie in Tata's different style of management and culture, which reflects its ownership. Ford are methodical, process-driven, objective and hierarchical – all understandable attributes in a global, capital-intensive business. Tata wants more passion. Ratan Tata's father owned one of the first Jaguar XK120s in India and Ratan is a car enthusiast and a lover of good design. Tata have not tried to hide this enthusiasm of the owner for the business behind a veil of dispassionate corporate oversight. They believe a luxury brand needs emotion, and who better to provide it than the proprietor? So they have subjective belief as well as objective analysis, inspiration as well as method, entrepreneurial management as well as hierarchy. They have encouraged the management to be bold and have backed them with hard cash, billions for new models, at a speed which requires conviction as much as an investment case.

We tried to preserve this sort of passion and long-term approach at Tesco, and we were helped in this by the nature of its senior figures. Tesco's management used to be very much a family affair, as I have already described. By the time I was appointed to the board, the family had gone, but the sense of belonging to an enterprise that thought and acted with an eye on the long term was very much still in evidence. We tried to get the best of both types of ownership: the transparency and good governance of a public company blended with the long-term perspective of a family company. Most of us had given our entire careers to the organisation – my Executive Committee had an average of well over 20 years with Tesco – and were in it for the long haul. We were completely committed to the strategy, our staff and the firm – and that sense of devotion bred a sense of the Tesco family. We were able to balance the short-term pressures we faced from some investors with the long-term aims of the company.

The words 'long term' ran like a thread through many decisions we took. For example, starting in a new country takes ten years to build the store network and probably another ten years to create a leading consumer brand: we set up shop in more than ten countries. Or consider our stores. Investing in property is a long-term decision looking forward 30 years: we built and own more than 70 per cent of our property. Above all, we never ceased trying to run the company according to a clear set of values, and never lost sight of our core purpose: to create value for customers to earn their lifetime loyalty. To build lifetime loyalty, you need to have a long-term perspective – and that comes from balanced management.

'Real time', balanced scorecards, Steering Wheels, multi-year product development: this is the language of corporations. Translated into simple terms, Tesco's growth depended on our implementing a strategy throughout the entire business, checking that the strategy was working at all levels, and then moving on to the next stage of growth. For that, we did not simply need to work together – we needed a balanced approach. And we needed something else too: a simple approach to the way we did business.

7 Simple

Change in any fast-moving, fast-growing company is not easy. My solution is quite simple: to make things simple. Simplicity is the knife that cuts through the tangled spaghetti of life's problems.

Each day, our world becomes more complex. Organisations grow larger, technology becomes more powerful, networks between companies, nations and people become more entangled. Across the developing world, the rise of the 'megacities', combined with the digital revolution, mean that ever more people are leading busy, hectic lives in congested environments. Climate change, a company's IT system, balancing work and family life: the challenges we face – be it as a nation, as a company or as individuals – seem to become forever more complicated.

That's not helped by people being bombarded with information and choice while leading busier lives. A weekday edition of the *New York Times* contains more information than the average person was likely to come across in a lifetime in 17th-century England.[1] A typical supermarket in the UK today stocks 40,000 products; in the 1950s it was just 2,000.

Nor are we making life easier for ourselves. As organisations – governments in particular – grow in size, so too do their bureaucracies and processes. In the National Health Service (which grew in just 50 years to become Europe's largest employer) the total number of staff rose by 30 per cent between 1999 and 2009, but the number of managers rose by 84 per cent.[2] Bureaucracy has a tendency to dissipate know-how, as empires and fiefdoms are created, each jealously guarding their own territory and expertise. This makes implementing change – and making things simple – more difficult. In England, nine government departments spend more than 50 per cent of their budget through 'arm's-length' or devolved bodies. An official report found that, when required to cut spending, 'departments are less well placed to make the long-term changes needed, partly because of gaps in their understanding of costs and risks. From our reviews to date, departments have not yet developed new lower-cost operating models. Departments cannot achieve long-term value for money until they identify and implement new ways of securing their objectives with a permanently lower cost base.'[3]

And as governments and all types of organisations grow, so too do the mountains of paperwork and missives they spew out. There are more than 21,000 regulations and Statutory Instruments currently on the statute books in Britain: the cumulative cost to business of regulations introduced since 1998 is estimated to stand at nearly £90 billion.[4] Tax is another example: the UK tax code doubled in length – to 11,520 pages – between 1997 and 2009.[5]

Meanwhile, the speed of change is only going to accelerate thanks to the power of the microchip. According to 'Moore's Law', the number of transistors that can be placed inexpensively on an integrated circuit doubles approximately every two years. This has a direct impact on the power of many digital electronic devices – such as processing speeds and a computer's memory – which is growing at almost exponential rates.

If all this leaves you wanting to shout 'Stop the world, I want to get off!', I sympathise. Individuals want to lead easier, simpler lives as the demands on their time increase. Companies and governments who offer that will succeed – those who don't will fail. Red tape, long-winded decision-making processes: these cost companies their profit, and cost politicians people's votes. The imperative is to be able to change, and change fast, to meet new demands, challenges and the impact of new technology. Change in any fast-moving, fast-growing organisation is not easy to achieve. My solution is quite simple: to make things simple.

A simple aim brings focus to what people do. A simple proposition is easy for people to understand. Simple acts take less time to learn and less time to do and cost less. Simple systems take less time to establish, are easy to change and are actually more satisfying for the people who work with them every day. Simplicity is the knife that cuts through the tangled spaghetti of life's problems.

The most powerful ideas and solutions to problems are incredibly simple. Truly influential leaders understand this – they know that simplicity is power. '*Liberté*, *égalité*, *fraternité*'. 'I think therefore I am.' 'From each according to his ability, to each according to his need.' 'No taxation without representation.' These are simple thoughts which encapsulate complex ideas. Distilling them took time and hard work, but each became a powerful (and sometimes destructive) force.

Simplicity, however, is something that people frown on. One reason is that 'simple' gets confused with 'simplistic'. Our culture tends to instil in us a sense that a complex understanding of life is a sign of intelligence. We look up to people who use long words, jargon and sophisticated terms, perhaps in the hope that they have the answers to all these hideously complex challenges we face.

Simple also gets confused with easy. Simple thoughts and ideas are not easy to create. As Edward de Bono, who has written an engaging book on simplicity, put it, 'Simplicity is not easy'. Mark Twain once received a telegram from a publisher: NEED 2-PAGE SHORT STORY TWO DAYS. Twain replied: NO CAN DO 2 PAGES TWO DAYS. CAN DO 30 PAGES 2 DAYS. NEED 30 DAYS TO DO 2 PAGES.

Twain's reply reflects the pain that writers (myself included) feel when trying to express complex thoughts in simple English. It is demanding, challenging and takes time. Shortly after the Second World War Sir Ernest Gowers was commissioned to write a guide to writing simple English for the British Civil

Service. *The Complete Plain Words* is essential reading for any manager who wants to communicate more effectively. Gowers wrote that 'writing is an instrument for conveying ideas from one mind to another; the writers' job is to make the readers apprehend the meaning readily and precisely.' The fault of jargon, or sloppy writing, he observed 'is not that it is unscholarly, but that it is inefficient. It wastes time: the time of the readers because they have to puzzle over what should be plain, and the time of the writers because they may to have write again to explain their meaning. A job that needed to be done only once has had to be done twice because it was bungled the first time.' The Gowers 'golden rule' is to 'pick those words that convey to the reader the meaning of the writing and to use them and them only'.[6] Less is more.

Making things simple, however, threatens people. Simplicity forces people to strip out unnecessary processes – which can lead to cutting jobs or, at the very least, having uncomfortable conversations with staff (and especially vested interests) to tell them to change how they work. And simplicity brings in its wake transparency and accountability: chaos and bureaucratic processes create hiding places for inefficiency, idleness, under-performance. Complex process can leave a muddled chain of command: no one is quite sure who is responsible for what.

Lack of attention to simplicity has allowed processes in organisations worldwide to fur up. You can track how sclerosis sets in. The objective of a process is never completely clear: no one writes down what steps need to be taken, and by whom (as I set out in Chapter 5). So everyone sets about doing what they think will best achieve the goal. Then someone tries to improve efficiency not by going back to first principles and asking 'What are we trying to achieve?', but by immediately writing down in gobbledygook the existing process, which complicates things still more.

When trying to achieve something new, or overcome a new challenge, people usually add new processes to their workload, rather than asking 'What can we stop doing?' or 'Can we change the system to achieve a new goal, while keeping the system simple?' A very simple idea, which can underpin the mission of an entire organisation, becomes confused. Like a Christmas tree, the more baubles and decorations that are hung upon it, the less you can see its original, simple form.

Simplicity in practice

Apply these observations to retailers and you can see why simplicity is so important. Consider how many thousands of products a supermarket sells, and the logistics required to make sure that the store has ketchup, ice cream, razor blades, tomatoes, shampoo – anything and everything you would expect from a store, when you want it. Each one has to be packaged up, delivered, unpacked, and put on shelves. Think about the store's customers. Each one is different. No two shopping baskets are full of exactly the same things. How does the store attract different people, with different tastes and different budgets? And then there is the competition. Competitors are going to be after the same customers. They will price goods differently. How do you compete and differentiate yourself from them? And finally there is the need to change – responding not just to long-term trends, such as the emergence of social media, but to short-term fashions or the impact of a sudden spell of cold weather.

Soon after I was appointed CEO I became very aware that Tesco was finding it difficult to grapple with these challenges. Its systems were becoming too complicated. Simple tasks had become cluttered up by new additions and plans. We were finding it hard to turn decisions into action as we were running hundreds of projects all at the same time. It was clear, therefore, that we needed to do some weeding and pruning, to stop people doing what was unnecessary and bring more focus and simplicity to everything we did.

My wish for a new culture of simplicity was lapped up by the team, partly because the notion runs in Tesco's blood. When Jack Cohen set up his market stall in London's East End he didn't have the time, resources or space for complicated processes. Being small-scale forced him to focus, to cut out waste and to simplify. We took this to heart, creating a guiding principle to make our processes 'Better, Simpler, Cheaper'. Every change, every innovation had to pass a test: the change had to make the store better for customers but, at the same time, cheaper for Tesco and simpler for the staff to operate.

In our drive to 'keep shopping simple' for customers, we took out all the frills in the building and in the design and layout of equipment. Within a few years, we had reduced the cost of building a store from £230 to £150 per square foot, and were creating better stores which customers and staff preferred. Simpler construction materials and techniques meant stores were built in less than half the time and for less money. Standardised and simplified equipment meant we saved twice; through bulk buying and through a simpler specification. Space was saved in stores because, as we simplified our replenishment systems, we had less spare stock.

The greatest benefits, though, came from simplifying processes for staff. At the back of my mind was a simple test to check whether what we were asking people to do was truly simple. The ABC test (yes, simple to remember) stood for 'Simple is Achievable, brings Benefit and is Clear'.

Achievable – people said 'I can do this new process correctly first time': they had the right skills, and were given all the necessary resources, to do what was required of them. Benefit – the process helped us achieve our aims, or fixed something that was broken. Clear – it was easy to remember and explain to others, and people did not need a manual to understand what was asked of them.

This was also a means to turn simplification into a habit. We could have elevated 'simple' to become a value. This would have had its merits: if simplicity is seen as something to be treasured, a trait that people admire and an aim that the organisation cherishes, everyone in an organisation might begin to think in terms of simplifying processes, or finding simple answers to problems. But as Dr de Bono also wisely remarked: 'Much more important than simplicity as a value is simplicity as a habit. This means that simplicity becomes an automatic part of the design process whenever thinking is used. Values can be ignored but habits cannot be ignored.'[7]

Once a new simple process has become a habit, people will ask 'It's so simple, why did we not think of this ages ago?' The answer to that conundrum is almost certainly that no one thought to ask the right people the question 'Can you make this process more simple?' Many companies employ strategists or blue-sky thinkers to simplify systems. Sitting in their offices, far from the scene of the action, these experts usually have little first-hand experience of a process. It is always far better to ask the people on the front line, who perform tasks each day, how to simplify things. Everyone who works in Tesco is now encouraged to suggest ways to make their work easier. If their idea is picked up and implemented, that person is given a Values Award, recognition of the contribution that they have made. This has generated thousands of ideas. Consider some very basic items.

First, a bottle of water. Not that long ago, bottles of water were carefully stacked by suppliers in lorries, unpacked at the back of stores, taken on trolleys into the stores and then put on the shelves. That meant they were handled several times. It was labour-intensive – and time is money.

Nowadays, suppliers put bottles straight onto pallets on wheels, which are then lifted onto lorries, and subsequently unloaded and pulled straight into stores. When the pallets are empty, supermarkets send them back to the suppliers, who fill them up again. You may think that is incredibly obvious. But to make it happen, the whole supply chain needed to change: to enable bottles to be placed on pallets, and the pallets onto lorries, the layout of factories had to change, and the lorries' capacity had to be adapted so the pallets could fit.

A similar mindset was applied to our handling of apples. We had a code for apples which was tapped in to the till. The trouble was that different types of apple had different codes. So our checkout teams had to use pictures to work out what type of apple the customer had selected. This took time. Then one of our team noticed that the suppliers stuck tiny numbers on the apples, a different number denoting a different type of apple. Why couldn't we simply programme our checkout systems with these numbers? So simple, so obvious. We did it. We saved customers' time, and our money.

Similarly, sandwiches. The sandwiches we sold used to have a bar code tucked away on the back of the pack so as not to spoil the design of the label. However, when sandwiches were reduced in price because they were nearing the end of their shelf life, we had to put stickers on the front for the customer and on the back to correct the bar code. This meant that someone had to label both sides and the checkout assistant had to look at both sides. Tesco sells about one million sandwiches a day, so the need to examine a pack closely took up a lot of our staff's time – and meant customers waited longer. Someone on the shop floor noticed this, and suggested that we put the price and the bar code together on the front of the pack. The saving: half a million pounds.

New technology can, of course, help simplify processes, but only if you are clear about precisely what outcome you want to achieve. During my time as CEO, the savings Tesco made – largely in terms of hours taken to achieve an aim – were immense. For example, in the UK between 2008 and 2011, by improving the scanning processes and systems at our checkouts, we saved 18,000 hours per week; by introducing handheld devices and computers on the shop floor to manage stock, we saved 3,500 hours per week; by introducing 'Pay at the Pump' for those purchasing petrol, we saved 2,300 hours per week; and by introducing self-service tills, we saved 21,000 hours per week. Four initiatives; more than 40,000 hours saved (admittedly, though, each one demanded considerable initial investment). These examples are dwarfed, however, by the time we saved by putting products into display trays that can be slotted straight onto shelves: 43,000 hours per week – or, put another way, 2,236,000 hours per year. All this by making one process more simple.

And that brings me to the humble plastic tray, one of the best examples of how a simple idea can transform an entire system – in this case, the supply chain of fruit and vegetables.

Delivered daily by the farmer to wholesale markets, bought fresh each day by the greengrocer and lovingly displayed in a shop or on a stall – fruit and veg sum up people's ideal of food shopping: fresh, healthy, available. For decades, however, there was a gulf between the ideal and reality. Growing up in Liverpool in the 1960s, I found that the fruit and veg sold by our local greengrocer was usually expensive and generally poor quality: a limp lettuce, a few bruised apples, and certainly no avocado or exotic fruits.

At that time, the supply chain was not a chain at all. The consumer and the farmer were unconnected. With no clear idea what to produce, famers simply produced what they could, sent it to market and hoped for the best. They didn't know what would sell or how much they would receive for what they provided. Their livelihoods were either feast or famine. Produce was either in short supply and expensive, or over-abundant and too cheap to guarantee the farmer a return. In both cases it was poorly packaged, of low quality – and still relatively expensive.

Another consequence was that fruit and vegetables did not play a big part in most people's diets. When I joined Tesco, the sales of butter equalled our entire sales of fruit and vegetables. Today, fruit and vegetables probably outsell butter by forty to one. The demand for fruit and veg has gone up year after year – I do not remember a single year of decline in the past 30 years. The same applies to developing markets – India being a good example: as soon as a supply chain is created which can get fruit and vegetables to consumers in good condition and at low cost, demand takes off.

This rapid growth soon began to strain both our supply chain and the stores. A busy store today might turn over £300,000 in fruit and vegetables in a week. Although this might be about 10 to 15 per cent of that store's sales, it could easily account for 30 per cent of the physical number of cases delivered. In such stores, that could mean nearly 40,000 cases needed to be delivered every week. The fruit and veg section of a store can sometimes be quite a tight, small area – not much more than 100 feet by 40 feet. So on a hectic day, staff might need to unload several thousand cases into that space while customers do their shopping.

Furthermore, handling fruit and some vegetables in and out of different cases – in the field, the pack house, the warehouse and the store – not only took time and got in the way of customers but had a tendency to damage delicate produce. That caused wastage and meant that we needed 100,000 tonnes of cardboard cases each year to protect the goods we were moving around, jettisoning the packaging the moment the produce reached the store.

And then, a member of staff (we're not sure who) came up with a simple solution: to design plastic cases that would be robust enough to protect perishable fruit and vegetables from the moment they were picked or harvested – and be reusable. We therefore designed stackable trays that could be fitted onto a specially designed trolley: a stack of ten of them could be moved around a warehouse and – critically – straight onto a shop floor by one member of staff (not a whole team) with little effort. The cost of renting the tray for one trip was a lot less than the cost of a new cardboard box, so farmers and shippers saved money – and so, unsurprisingly, they helped us design the system. The box was standardised, so that all the handling equipment on the farm, in the pack house, in the warehouse, on lorries and in stores could be designed to handle this one type of unit efficiently – instead of the dozens of different case dimensions that the industry had used previously. This meant that the product, once packed into the tray, would never have to be handled again until selected by the customer. Waste was cut; quality was improved.

We took this simple idea and applied it right up the supply chain. For example, a lettuce farmer developed mobile pack houses that actually went out into the fields: the lettuce was picked and packed into the tray on the spot. It was shipped to our depots the same day and was on sale the next day.

Meanwhile, we redesigned our display fixtures in store to accommodate the tray system. They became a simple metal frame which the trays slotted into either singly or in stacks depending on the volume. These trays had bar codes which allowed them to be tracked on their journey and (crucially) sent to the correct stores. The system meant that staff could handle a vast increase in volume relatively easily. Little extra store space was needed because replenishment was so quick and simple. Despite the speed and volume, the product was better protected and fresher than ever. It was good for the environment because of the hundreds of thousands of tons of cardboard that were saved. It reduced distribution costs and costs for the farmers in materials and damage.

Better, Simpler, Cheaper. Better for customers: lower prices, better availability, better quality and better freshness. Simpler for staff: a uniform system, quicker and easier to handle and move and replenish. Cheaper for Tesco and suppliers and farmers: less waste, lower materials cost, lower shipping costs and better labour productivity. The system was so successful it was copied by all the supermarket chains in the UK, increasing the economic and environmental benefits. Tesco has taken it to other parts of the world. No doubt some will miss the pyramid of oranges carefully built on a market stall. Something has been lost but, thanks to this simple thought, much more has been gained.

Simple ideas, big innovations

A focus on simplicity can not only improve processes, it can also help a business to innovate successfully. Most businesses struggle with innovation. They assume that innovation must by its very nature be complex – the most unhelpful phrase in innovation is 'it can't be that simple' – and so they slip into tortuous and overly complicated thinking without even realising it. If they do realise it, they think such complexity must be inevitable.

Judging from my experience, I would say that the genesis of the best innovations comes from looking at the world around you, making a simple observation, and drawing a straightforward conclusion from what you see. The insight does not have to be startlingly original – more often than not it is simply seeing facts in a new way, connecting disparate events or applying what is already known to a new context.

The great engineer Isambard Kingdom Brunel took his inspiration for how to bore a tunnel under the Thames from the tiny shipworm:

> He saw how the little creature perforated the wood with its well-armed head, first in one direction and then in another, till the archway was complete, and then daubed over the roof and sides with a kind of varnish; and by copying this work exactly on a large scale, Brunel was at length enabled to construct his shield and accomplish his great engineering work.[8]

Many of the best business insights are those which spot a new trend. To see the future, look around you now. Those things that will shape society in five or even ten years' time almost certainly exist in some form already, although maybe not in their final form. The rise of China, digital information, the popularity of talent shows, the growing number of old people: these trends are hardly state secrets or difficult to spot. Successful societies and businesses do not merely identify such trends but understand that they bring in their wake new needs and opportunities, and then act accordingly.

A new observation can become a simple idea at the heart of an innovation, providing clarity of purpose that drives that idea through the many stages of development and into reality. Without that simplicity, innovation can easily become hesitant, bogged down by uncertainty and lacking a clear direction. The development of Tesco Express is a good example.

Tesco Express are convenience stores. When our first Express opened in 1996, it was an unexpected development for the company because Tesco had spent the previous 20 years moving away from small-store retailing on the high street. There are around 1,500 'high streets' in Britain and, unsurprisingly, that is where the Tesco business began growing rapidly in the 1960s and 1970s. When the supermarket format was imported from the USA, British retailers faced an obvious problem: space. In most British cities and towns buildings were crowded together. It was difficult and costly to expand by buying up neighbouring properties.

Why was there pressure for a bigger store? The economies of scale in retailing are hard to pin down. Most people assume that the greatest economy comes from a retailer buying in bulk products from suppliers. Bulk purchasing certainly matters, though not as much as is conventionally assumed. In fact, the best economy of scale comes from bigger stores. Offering a wider range of products under one roof at low prices attracts more custom. This drives down costs, which in turn enables retailers to cut prices still further, driving volume higher still. So begins a virtuous circle, based on bigger stores and reinforced by bulk purchasing.

As the industry began to realise that bigger meant better, Tesco left the high street in search of larger sites in the suburbs for bigger stores, which could offer more of a range of goods and parking for the growing number of car owners. But this move came at a price. To fund the acquisition and construction of these stores, we had to sell off our high-street units. In time, however, what started out as a necessity became part of Tesco's mindset: we were a business that sold small stores to build large ones. As the brand improved its image, so this mentality was reinforced. Small stores, it was felt, represented the downmarket past; big stores were our shining new future. Like many other retailers in Britain and further afield, we were not going back to small stores. Big was beautiful.

The creation of Express, and the complete reversal in strategy and thinking that followed, highlights two common characteristics of innovation: accident and inquisitiveness.

We were looking at something quite different, the cash-and-carry sector, when we stumbled across the insight that spawned Express stores. The cash-and-carry sector, being wholesale suppliers to other businesses, is obviously not 'retail' as most people would define the word. Indeed, most cash-and-carry outlets are not usually permitted to sell to ordinary shoppers. In 1995, however, we were beginning to hear that the main cash-and-carry company was subtly shifting its position to go after retail customers. In other words, it was becoming our competitor. One morning, therefore, I visited a cash-and-carry outlet near London's Wembley Stadium with John Gildersleeve, our Buying Director, so we could see for ourselves what was happening.

From one perspective, our trip was pretty pointless. We could not see any significant changes in what the cash and carry was offering. It looked like business as usual. I was about to forget the whole thing when, as we walked through the car park, I noticed how busy it was. There were scores of little white vans filling up with a mix of products and goods that could only be for small, high-street convenience stores. Presumably, these stores must have been doing tidy business if they were keeping the cash and carry so busy. And this was a puzzle. Conventional retail thinking – supported by market data – said the convenience store sector was in terminal decline. The market share of the stores was small and getting smaller. All the talk was of the closure of hundreds, if not thousands of these small stores.

I asked John to have a quiet word with one or two of his suppliers who also served cash-and-carry stores to see how they were doing. He came back with surprising news. Our suppliers were doing very nicely in this sector. Far from struggling, convenience stores were thriving.

Now that this area of retail had our attention, we had to explain the apparent contradiction between what we were beginning to see with our eyes and what the market data was telling us. Britain in the mid-1990s was coming out of recession. As people became richer, the industry assumed that customers would return to their 'normal' old habits of one-stop shopping which had been such a feature of the late 1980s. People had jobs, disposable income and cars and there were plenty of new things to buy. Furthermore, our big stores were indeed doing well. All the signs pointed to a return to 'life as normal'.

But clearly life was not returning to 'normal'. Something else was going on. To find out, we turned to the best source of wisdom and advice: the customer. Customers told us that although the economy was growing again, the world had moved on dramatically since the late 1980s. In particular, their lives were getting busier and more complicated, giving them less time to plan. Everyone was affected to some degree, particularly the young and especially young men. The same person was behaving like two different consumers: sometimes planning a full weekly shop at their favourite retailer and watching every penny, sometimes – in emergencies – shopping at a nearby store and not particularly caring about the price. We asked customers what they thought of the stores they used for convenience. 'Not much' was their answer – but the desire for convenience overrode other considerations. Conventional wisdom was (as is so often demonstrably the case) wrong: convenience stores had a future. Customers never fail to surprise.

All this led me to a simple conclusion. If shoppers would not come to Tesco's big stores, then Tesco would have to come to them. We had to stop thinking that we were in the business of opening big stores and closing small ones. Big was still beautiful, but small could be just as attractive. That simple thought meant adapting our strategy purely to deliver economies of scale from large stores: we now needed to find a way to serve customers in small local stores as well. The poor choice and high prices of convenience stores would not be acceptable from Tesco. If we were going to enter this market we had to reverse the economies of scale: the 'big store' offer of high quality, good choice and service at low prices had to be turned into a small store package.

The simplest way to discover how big a challenge we faced was to create one convenience store and see how close we could get to offering what the customer wanted. Clearly we had to cram everything that customers expected from our other stores into a much smaller one. This forced us to strip what we offered – and how we operated – down to the barest essentials. Everything had to be made very simple.

We set ourselves a straightforward brief: to open a convenience store of 3,000 square feet, offering no more than 3,000 products, the mix of which would allow a customer to do their entire weekly shop from the store. In other words, it was to be a small food supermarket rather than a Japanese-style 'distress convenience store' that you would go to when you ran out of milk or bread. The prices could be no more than three per cent higher than the superstores. These, I should point out, were high hurdles. At the time, local convenience stores were anywhere between 10 to 20 per cent more expensive than typical supermarkets. What's more, they tended to avoid carrying a wide range of fresh foods because wastage was high in relation to the low volumes being sold.

A store that was 3,000 square feet, sold 3,000 types of product and had prices no more than three per cent higher than those found in our typical stores: this may have been an arbitrary target, but it was a very simple and clear idea. We quickly learnt that such simplicity helped the team achieve our aim, as it forced everyone to think in a disciplined way and gave them a framework in which to build new systems.

The first prototype Express store was on a petrol forecourt in Barnes, west London. Although it was not that profitable, sales were very good and customers liked it. It showed enough potential to encourage us to open some more stores, which we duly did. Small stores do not cost much so it was easy to open them in different places and to learn by doing it. As we moved into different neighbourhoods, however, we found that the stores' performance was much too varied, and the whole model was not robust enough to roll out on a large scale. We could see that each local neighbourhood was subtly different, with its own microculture of tastes, needs and behaviour. So we needed to find an easy way to tailor each store to its market to maximise its potential, without making the whole format too complicated to roll out.

When faced with a problem like this, it is best to do whatever is simple and easy and see if that helps you overcome it. Thanks to Clubcard, we had masses of data about customers in each neighbourhood. This blessing, however, was also a curse: we had so much information that there was a danger that we could easily be overwhelmed by it and paralysed by the search for perfection. Instead, we decided to create a simple matrix based on differences in income and the type of neighbourhood – high or low income, village or housing estate and so on.

To stand any chance of being profitable and offering all that customers needed, the Express format also had to plug into the Tesco systems so that it could benefit from our infrastructure. Many of the products we sold were unsuitable, or the way they were transported or packaged was over-engineered or too complex for a small store: cases were too large, marketing materials were too big to be displayed in small stores, shelving was too high. Back-office functions, like personnel policies or ordering systems, were also too complex. So we stripped everything down to the most simple, essential element, and took out what was not vital. Dozens of operating manuals were binned. We also automated a lot of decision-making, particularly around ordering and replenishment.

The range of products to be sold in an Express store was initially selected from what we sold in our existing stores. Express's turnover was tiny, so our buyers were reluctant to devote much time and attention to it, as it made no material difference to our overall turnover. So we turned things upside down, and asked buyers to regard the 3,000 products in an Express store not as an afterthought, but as the first and most important products in their categories. Instead of a hand-me-down range of cast-offs, the buyers gradually built a customised range for Express which, in turn, actually strengthened the structure and appeal of the ranges we sold in our larger stores.

With this careful rebuilding of the model, we produced something which was recognisably Tesco, able to benefit from the economics of Tesco's network, and simple and robust enough to be operated by small teams in multiple locations on relatively low volumes. On top of that, we were able to meet the challenge of fresh food supply with some innovations in packaging and distribution and changes to our ordering systems. For example, Express's customers wanted to buy individual, large pieces of fruit, whereas customers in larger stores wanted to buy a number of smaller pieces of fruit: we had to adapt the supply chain, making special purchases for Express stores. We developed vacuum packaging for fresh fish and meat: given that the volume of sales in Express stores were lower than in other stores, this allowed these products to stay fresh for longer. We designed smaller vehicles (which could be easily parked in tight spots) to deliver produce to Express stores; these could carry refrigerated food as well as other produce, cutting out the need for multiple deliveries. All this learning meant that we were able to roll out the format confident that it could be adapted to meet the needs of different locations, and to produce a robust profit.

With its remarkable combination of low prices and exceptional choice, combined with quick service in a convenient location, Express quickly became our most popular format with customers. Eighty per cent of customers walked to the stores, the catchment radius of each store typically being about half a mile. Staff liked it too. Being a neighbourhood store, the staff could get to know their customers. Most of the staff lived locally too, so they could walk to work. Above all they enjoyed the variety of the work, the ability to make a clear, tangible difference and the team spirit. Small stores rely on teamwork: everyone has to be able to cover for everyone else. An Express's manager was literally running a small business, and had to be capable of turning their hand to everything – from customer relations to cash management to security to marketing. Reflecting the fact that more was demanded of these staff, and because there is such a clear link between a team member's contribution and the branch performance, for the first time we linked pay to a store's performance. Express stores became a breeding ground for talent because of the responsibility managers were given.

Tesco Express went into the most depressed high streets, the toughest council estates, remote villages, university campuses. It gave a new lease of life to the high street. It benefited other local traders, who gained from the increased footfall. All in all, the stores were good for society. Good for the environment, good for employment, good for people's diets – as we were able to offer fresh fruit and vegetables at affordable prices, not the soggy lettuce and bruised apples that I remember from childhood.

Not everyone was happy. Some people thought Tesco should not invade what they saw as the preserve of small retailers, and they argued that there were already 'enough' Tesco stores. Although loud, these protests were the views of a minority who could afford – both in terms of money and time – to shop at existing convenience stores or supermarkets. Most people, short of time and on tight budgets, could see the benefits of Express stores.

Gradually, Express stores have been introduced into every country where Tesco operates. The model has had to be carefully refined to tailor it to the local market and the particular features of each country's convenience sector. The thousands of Tesco Expresses all over the world now generate sales running into billions of pounds. Highly profitable, the convenience format is the fastest growing after e-commerce. As societies become more urban, and people the world over lead busier lives, the format is bound to expand. And all from a simple idea that came to us in a car park in Wembley.

Simplicity defies convention

Simple things often have the most profound effect on our lives. The paper clip, the rubber band, the Post-it note, the drinks carton: the world may have become digital, but these things have endured. Inventing something simple, however, can be very hard for companies. Simple inventions are often revolutionary: they break all the rules and defy the status quo. How a company is structured, how it thinks, its supply chains – a truly radical invention tramples on all these things and says 'This is the future.'

Henry Ford's account of making the Model T Ford shows

that the best innovations are those which are simple – both in their design and, crucially, their manufacture:

> The important feature of the new model . . . was its simplicity. There were but four constructional units in the car – the power plant, the frame, the front axle, and the rear axle. All of these were easily accessible and they were designed so that no special skill would be required for their repair or replacement. I believed then, although I said very little about it because of the novelty of the idea, that it ought to be possible to have parts so simple and so inexpensive that the menace of expensive hand repair work would be entirely eliminated. The parts could be made so cheaply that it would be less expensive to buy new ones than to have old ones repaired. They could be carried in hardware shops just as nails or bolts are carried. I thought it was up to me as the designer to make the car so completely simple that no one could fail to understand it. That works both ways and applies to everything. The less complex an article, the easier it is to make, the cheaper it may be sold, and therefore the greater number may be sold.[9]

Corporate culture can stifle such innovation. 'Head office cannot see the point' of research; a new process would 'run counter to targets'; a new idea was 'noted' – but nothing was done. Bold, simple ideas are diluted, so as to make an innovation more familiar, more like 'business as usual', which is usually fatal to an invention. This makes the story of Nespresso, created by one of the world's largest global companies Nestlé, all the more remarkable.

Like Tesco, Nestlé is large but nimble. I have worked with the company for 20 years, and I admire its approach to business and innovation. Together Nestlé and Tesco conduct over one billion pounds worth of business every year across numerous brands and a growing number of countries. Nestlé – which is perhaps best known for its global brands like Nescafé and Milo – spends one billion euros a year on research into nutrition so as to keep a sharp, competitive edge. With a keen sense of the local nature of markets, they seem to have struck the right balance between decision-making at the centre and in individual markets. In every country in which they operate, their teams have considerable autonomy, and they are happy to maintain strong local brands.

Nestlé set themselves a tough challenge: to simplify and miniaturise the coffee-making process, so anyone could enjoy a great cup of coffee. For a large, global company, whose entire manufacturing processes and supply networks reflected the conventional way people made and drank coffee, this demanded radical, simple thinking.

Coffee has been in our kitchens and cafés for centuries. The art of coffee-making reached its zenith in Italy, where a machine was developed to force hot water through the ground coffee under pressure, removing the bitterness and capturing the aroma. Once that was developed, progress stopped. For generations coffee-making remained a messy, long-winded process: grinding coffee beans, pouring and storing grains, fiddling around with filters, disposing of the grains.

Way back in 1976, Nestlé came up with the answer: a pod of coffee which was placed in a special machine that forced hot water under pressure through it. The end result: fresh coffee but no grinding of beans or cleaning of filters. Ten years of continuous development followed (Nespresso is now protected by no fewer than 1,700 patents),[10] and the product was finally launched in the (then) booming Japanese market to supply gourmet coffee to restaurants, not direct to customers. The result? Indifference. Less than half the machines made were sold.

The company could – and, some would argue, probably should – have given up, but they pressed on. Now they tried the office sector, enjoying a little more success but still hampered by the brand's premium positioning. And then they decided to market direct to the consumer, setting up a membership club for those who really wanted a top-quality cup of coffee. The old supply chain, of various manufacturers selling machinery and coffee, was replaced with just one: Nespresso. It sold you the machine and the coffee – plus service for the machine: one brand, one supply chain, a one-stop shop. The coffee may have been more expensive than the instant variety, but it was nevertheless a fraction of the price that you would expect to pay in a coffee shop.

Now Nestlé needed a completely new marketing channel to service the consumer directly. Nespresso was created as a separate company within Nestlé to preserve its distinctive identity. Everything about the 'club' had a sense of exclusivity – the machine's design, the pods, the advertising. Stories about Michelin-starred restaurants serving Nespresso helped build the brand's cachet. Interestingly, its sister brand Dolce Gusto took a different route, operating through traditional retail outlets like Tesco – and seeing a similar success to Nespresso. (Nestlé has seen its profits froth thanks to Nespresso: the company does not separate out profits, but a former executive reportedly puts gross margins for Nespresso at about 85 per cent, compared with 40 to 50 per cent for other filtered coffee brands.[11] Between 2006 and 2010, sales of Nespresso are estimated to have tripled, exceeding $3 billion.)[12]

And what sustained the company through all the years it took to reinvent their market and their way of doing business was clarity of purpose. It was a simple idea that broke with tradition – and transformed the way people make coffee.

Of course, simplification can be taken too far. As you simplify a process, you may stop adding value: just as a picture may be less rich without detail, so too might a process. Clearly this is a question of judgement. In the USA, when we launched our Fresh and Easy stores, we initially went too far in simplifying the range of products that our stores sold – and eventually reintroduced over a thousand products. But all too often the risk of 'oversimplification' is used by those who are fearful of simplicity as an excuse not to change at all.

And, finally, simple means keeping things short and to the point, and knowing when to shut up. The Duke of Wellington once told a Member of Parliament 'Don't quote Latin: say what you have to say, and then sit down.' He was quite right. Simplicity is a force for good, and is a stepping stone to creating lean organisations.

8 Lean

Sustainable consumption depends on desiring goods and services that use fewer natural resources. By thinking lean, we can go green – and do more, for less.

Lean is a word that has spawned a whole industry in management consultancy. 'Lean production' and 'lean manufacturing' are systems in which waste of all kinds (processes, material, time) is eliminated in a relentless, continuous drive to create more value. The lean producer's motto is 'less is more': less input for more output.

To do more for less, to make something become better at the same time as becoming cheaper, sounds impossible. The default setting – 'conventional wisdom' – is to think you can make something better, but only if you spend more money on it; or you can make something cheaper, but only if you take something away and make it not quite as good as before. The popular understanding of productivity reflects this thinking. Productivity is defined as output from input. What productive value you create as output from the resource depends on what you put in (such as labour, capital or energy). People assume from this that you can increase output with more input or, if you reduce input, output is likely to be affected.

This thinking has become part of accepted wisdom in many societies. It explains why the reform of public services always seems to get bogged down in political tit for tat. When one side says we need to spend less, the other side says that means things will get worse. This is nonsense.

Consider two examples from the British public sector. First, building new schools. In 2003, a £45 billion plan was launched to rebuild or refurbish every secondary school in England, making it the Government's single largest capital programme in any area. It was a monumental task, and by 2010 just eight per cent of the planned renewal had been achieved.[1] Meanwhile, the cost of the scheme had risen to £55 billion. After much political huffing and puffing, the scheme was cancelled.

A review exposed a litany of problems. For example, the goal of the entire programme was to deliver 'educational transformation'. The review was unable to find a definition as to what this meant: definitions ranged from 'providing fit-for-purpose learning environments to a more dramatic goal of producing iconic school buildings that were "truly world class"'.[2] Mountains of paperwork – about 3,700 pages of guidance and contracts – drove up costs: this process could cost up to £11 million before a school's construction had even begun.[3] And the procurement of buildings started 'with a sum of money rather than with a specification', designs were 'far too bespoke', and there was 'no evidence of an effective way of learning from mistakes (or successes)'.[4] By setting clearer goals, cutting out the bureaucracy and using standardised drawings and specifications, the review concluded that both time and money – up to 30 per cent of the current cost – could be saved 'while also improving the quality of the finished product'.[5]

Another example comes from the welfare system. In England there are estimated to be 120,000 'troubled families', suffering from serious problems – including parents not working, mental health problems and children not in school – and causing serious problems, such as crime and antisocial behaviour. Successive governments have launched expensive initiatives and plans to help these families, involving numerous agencies. Each agency has traditionally worked in its own silo, with its own agenda, bureaucracy and aims, sometimes duplicating and (worse) conflicting with others. The result has been that each family might have contact with up to 20 local agencies. Unsurprisingly, this approach now carries a large price tag. These families, who make up less than one per cent of the population,[6] cost taxpayers £9 billion overall. £8 billion of this is spent on reacting to these families' problems and the trouble they cause, with just £1 billion being spent on trying to turn around their lives in a targeted, positive way.[7] The cost to local services is, on average, a staggering £330,000 per family, per year.[8] High spending – and no improvement in results.

At last, the Government has worked out that one integrated approach would cost much less – the local services' bill falling to £14,000 per family[9] – and deliver better results. For example, one family in Salford (in northern England) required 250 interventions in one year including 58 police call-outs and five arrests; five 999 visits to Accident and Emergency; two injunctions; and a Council Tax arrears summons. Thanks to this new approach, the £200,000 cost was cut by two-thirds.[10]

You can save money without harming what is delivered. You can improve what is delivered without necessarily spending more money. By addressing pinch points and bottlenecks in the system, so that all processes are aligned and waste is minimised, you can transform productivity. Not only is it possible to get the same output from less input, but you can get dramatically more output from less input. You can make services and products better and cheaper at the same time by having a clearer idea of what outputs your customer values most, and by simplifying and aligning the processes that are intended to deliver them.

These insights lie at the heart of 'lean thinking', for which we have to thank two car companies and a supermarket chain. Henry Ford established the mass assembly manufacturing line, enabling quality and quantity of production to be increased while the cost to consumer was cut. Ford understood how waste eroded human effort:

> A farmer doing his chores will walk up and down a rickety ladder a dozen times. He will carry water for years instead of putting in a few lengths of pipe. His whole idea, when there is

> extra work to do, is to hire extra men. He thinks of putting money into improvements as an expense . . . It is waste motion – waste effort – that makes farm prices high and profits low.[11]

Ford saw the benefits of making parts (and the processes to fit them) as simple as possible, allowing specialist 'fitters' to be removed from the process of manufacturing a car almost entirely. 'As we cut out useless parts and simplify necessary ones we also cut down the cost of making. This is simple logic, but oddly enough the ordinary process starts with a cheapening of the manufacturing instead of with simplifying the article. The start ought to be with the article.'[12]

Fast-forward to post-war Japan. With capital constrained and demand low, Taiichi Ohno, Toyota's engineer, looked for ways to drive production according to sales, not targets. His team visited the USA to see what they could learn from Ford, only to be appalled at the amount of stock they found sitting idle, the number of faulty cars that had to be repaired before they were dispatched for sale, and uneven work patterns. What impressed them was the supermarket Piggly Wiggly: because goods were only reordered when purchases had been made, there was far less stock sitting unwanted in storage, taking up space and, in some cases, becoming stale and unusable.

The production system that Ohno and his team created turned Toyota into one of the most successful companies in the world and has since become the subject of numerous doctoral theses. Toyota looked at an entire system, broke it down into its constituent parts and then stripped out all forms of waste – which they classified as 'muri' (overburdening the people or the system), 'mura' (unevenness or inconsistency in the process itself) and 'muda' (work that adds no value). To emulate this, you have to measure all aspects of the process – in terms of cost of input and value of output, time taken and so on – so all instances of waste can be identified and their elimination planned. So with a manufacturing process, for example, you start by looking at its design to work out which processes are inefficient (muri). You then study how the process is implemented so that you can make it as smooth as possible and minimise any unwanted variations in volume and quality (mura). Finally, once the process is under way you identify and deal with the work that adds no value (muda). Muda itself can be broken down into seven types, which management students remember as TIM WOOD (transport, inventory, motion, waiting, overproduction, overprocessing, defects). Toyota developed a culture that underpinned this approach. It rested on two themes: continuous improvement – as the process of eliminating waste is never-ending; and respect for people – as sharing problems builds trust and teams in which individuals can learn new skills.

Over the years 'lean' techniques have built on Toyota's experience and learning, as companies have spent millions trying to create more value by cutting out waste. Many companies and organisations have mastered this process – and shown that it is possible to do more for less. Yet the full potential of the lean approach has yet to be realised.

Being lean means going green

One of the best examples of creative lean thinking I've encountered comes from a carpet factory in Shanghai that wanted to install more efficient pumps for its machinery. Rather than tinker with the existing design, its engineer went back to first principles, looking at every element of the system and considering how it could be improved. He examined the pipes the machinery used. Conventional wisdom held that it was best to use thin pipes as these are cheaper to manufacture. The engineer knew, however, that it takes more energy to pump liquid around thin pipes. He then calculated that while fatter pipes might indeed be more expensive to purchase, the fact that they are also more efficient means they can be used in conjunction with smaller (and therefore cheaper) pumps, motors and so on. Overall, therefore, there would actually be a saving if he broke with convention. Next he redesigned the layout, keeping the pipes as straight as possible and placing other elements around them, so that bends – which increase friction and therefore eat up energy – could be kept to a minimum. The result: the horsepower required to operate the new pumps fell by 92 per cent.[13]

In the past, while lean approaches like this one might have made good economic sense, their necessity was not widely recognised. When energy was cheap and plentiful, most businesses did not worry about wasting it – it seemed a marginal cost. Even the oil shock of the 1970s was seen as just that – a one-off shock, not a wake-up call. Similarly, today's supply chains – farms, machines, factories, transport systems, shops – were built on the assumption that natural resources could be used either freely or indefinitely, and that it was cheaper to throw resources away than to use them again.

Now that people are starting to appreciate that these resources are limited, they no longer seem a marginal cost, and they will become increasingly less so in the future. The costs of energy and raw materials are magnified by increasing demand and insecurity of supply. On top of that, people are becoming more aware of the economic and social cost of failing to tackle climate change. The Stern Report on climate change, produced for the British government in 2006, predicted that the overall costs of climate change will be equivalent to losing at least five per cent of global gross domestic product every year.[14]

And this is where lean thinking comes together with the need to 'go green' (be that in the conservation of energy and resources or the reduction of carbon emissions). Lean thinking, which is already built into the best companies' DNA, argues that 'less is more': not less in the sense of limiting consumption, but ensuring that the process of production uses fewer natural resources. A lean approach to manufacturing will cut out waste and inefficiency (saving those scarce natural resources), enabling the process to be redesigned so that it becomes more sustainable, while the products retain their quality and are cheaper to make. A lean approach is rooted in measuring the use (and waste) of resources, and that information – about the amount of carbon that has been emitted during a product's manufacture and distribution, for example – can then help consumers make 'green choices'.

Take concentrated washing detergent, for instance. Traditional washing detergent is bulky and heavy, requires a good deal of packaging and is expensive to transport – all of which eats into the profits of the companies which make and sell it. Concentrated washing detergent, by contrast, is a much more economic prospect, requiring less packaging and therefore costing less to transport – it also allows clothes to be washed at lower temperatures, thereby reducing energy consumption. It has been calculated that if everyone in the world switched to using it, we could reduce CO_2 emissions by over 4 million tonnes, the equivalent of taking one million cars off the road.[15]

This shows the power, economic effectiveness and potential of lean thinking: remove the waste – unnecessary packaging and travel costs – and you save money and cut carbon. Toyota's Ohno knew he needed to get the maximum from the resources he had. In essence, that's the challenge we have on a global scale today. Lean thinking provides us with the route to be green and to consume, and for our economies to grow.

Many would disagree with the premise underlying that statement. They would argue that one answer to the problems we face – the impact of a growing population on our environment, and climate change – is to cut back consumption. They point out that if we continue with the current rate of consumption, our planet will require the natural resources of three planets the same size. They believe we have no choice but to back-pedal: governments should tax more, people should consume less and economies should grow more slowly, if at all. In their eyes, most major corporations – manufacturers, retailers and so on – are the enemy, and are responsible for greedily and inefficiently using up the planet's resources. Even when those companies have sought to claim green credentials they have often been treated with scepticism, their initiatives being dismissed as nothing more than PR-grabbing 'greenwash'. (In fairness, the charge has sometimes been justified.)

This is an understandable view, but in my mind it carries with it an intractable problem of its own: it's difficult to reverse hundreds of years of material progress in the West, and it's very hard indeed to justify denying progress to developing nations. Arguably, an attempt to hold back consumption will hit the poor much harder than the rich.

There is an alternative, and that is for us to learn how to maintain and even increase consumption sustainably. For me, this is the only realistic option, as the irrepressible desire for a better life is part of human nature. History is full of failed attempts to stamp on that wish and give up on our innate craving for personal security, well-being and progress.

Sustainable consumption depends on people accepting and living by the underlying principle of lean thinking: that less is more. This does not mean having to accept 'less' of what they desire, but desiring goods and services that use fewer natural resources. It means making it easier, cheaper and more logical for consumers to go green – to save energy themselves and to buy green goods. And it requires no less than a complete rebuilding of the entire supply chain to make it lean.

So much for the theory. What did this mean for a company such as Tesco in practice? For a start, we had to operate in a lean manner, rooting out wasteful activity that consumed unnecessary resources throughout our operations. The total of all direct emissions from Tesco's UK operations alone adds up to some 2.5 million tonnes of carbon: that compares with around 36 million tonnes emitted by the many businesses which supply Tesco's UK operations. So we set ourselves a challenging target to reduce carbon emissions across our global supply chain by 30 per cent by 2020. Overall, we wanted Tesco to be a zero-carbon business by 2050 – which means that any carbon the business still emits will be matched by extra renewable energy that Tesco generates for others to use. To the cynical, that might sound like a publicity ploy, but it's worth bearing in mind that Tesco's annual gas and electricity bill for the UK alone was £200 million in 2011. The measures we have so far put in place are now reducing the company's global energy bill by £150 million annually.

Various practical steps were – and are still being – taken to bring about greater efficiency. We started to relocate our depots to bring them closer to the stores they service; we looked at the design of our lorries to make them more aerodynamic, thereby saving fuel. Much of our focus, though, was on the stores themselves, which account for around 70 per cent of Tesco's emissions.

Lean thinking started to be applied to store design back in the mid-1990s, and by 2007 we were building new stores that used only half the energy of ones built ten years earlier. But to be zero carbon by 2050 required radical new thinking, not incremental change. We therefore took our whole approach apart and scrutinised our processes closely. In doing so we discovered, to our horror, that only 14 per cent of the average Tesco store was recycled when rebuilding was required. This seemed unjustifiably wasteful. Consequently we introduced a target to reuse everything, setting ourselves the challenge of designing new stores that will be as easy to dismantle and reuse as they are to assemble. (At one store we managed to reuse almost 60 per cent of the materials we shipped out – a big change in well under ten years.) Bearing in mind that, thanks to daily wear and tear, the average Tesco store has no more than a 30-year life, this offers the prospect of huge future savings.

We also wanted to see whether we could achieve our goal of becoming a zero-carbon company immediately, by actually building a zero-carbon store. This was quite a challenge. A modern store has evolved over time and balances carefully all of its many functions. A busy store serves 50,000 customers a week. It may have a turnover of £2 million a week. Something like 200,000 cases of goods containing 40,000 different types of products have to be ordered, delivered, unpacked, displayed and sold. So every store must fulfil the needs of both customers and staff alike.

Thinking 'lean', we looked at an entire store's operations, measuring emissions from all its activities. We were helped by work at our Cheetham Hill store, where we had researched how to save energy and cut carbon.[16] We found that, of the heat used in this store, 37 per cent was lost by ventilation and 8 per cent was lost through the building fabric. As far as electricity was concerned, 23 per cent was used for lighting. Refrigeration was the biggest problem. Refrigerators removed 54 per cent of the store's heat and consumed 37 per cent of its electricity.

We used these insights to design our new zero-carbon store. Out went steel and concrete and in came timber. Out went halogen and fluorescent lights, in came LED lighting technology – a pioneering move for a retailer. In, too, came natural light and natural ventilation – a return to older, more traditional building designs which had to make clever use of nature to light, heat and cool buildings because there was no mechanical alternative. We insulated the store and changed the type of glass to lessen heat gain and loss (which requires artificial heating and cooling). We designed completely new refrigeration systems, using different gases which did less environmental damage, and we put doors on all our fridges.

We also needed a renewable power source big enough to power the store. So we developed a combined heat and power plant. Powered by reusing waste vegetable oil from food manufacturing, the unit produced enough surplus power for nearby housing.

The outcome of all this was the world's first zero-carbon store, opened in 2009 near Cambridge. It operated as we had hoped and met its targets. Just as importantly, customers liked the store, in part because the timber construction created a warmer, more welcoming atmosphere. All the innovations were explained on signage around the store, which reassured customers about its impact on the environment.

Simultaneously, we turned our attention to how lean thinking might cut carbon emissions in the supply chain. To do that, we obviously needed to find out which parts of the production process, and the transport, storage and use of a product, emit the most carbon, and in so doing to measure a product's carbon footprint.

'Footprinting' uses a similar approach to that which Ohno used to look for waste in a production process. Yet this lean approach is harder than it sounds. A T-shirt bought in one country is made from textiles manufactured in another, from cotton grown in a third country. Once home, it will be washed using technology from somewhere else. At each point in the process, carbon is emitted.

Helped by major suppliers, by the time I left Tesco we had calculated the carbon footprints of over 1,100 popular own-brand products – ranging from flowers to fabric conditioners, pasta to nappies and milk to magazines. Measuring carbon output in this way proved an enormous and expensive undertaking, but as we improved and refined the process, the cost dropped from as much as £25,000 per product to as little as £1,000. Our experience underscored the wisdom of Ohno's approach of looking at an entire system in order to eradicate waste.

Some of our discoveries proved to be surprisingly counter-intuitive. For example, Tesco orange juice from concentrate has a lower carbon footprint than non-concentrated juices because less energy is needed to chill and transport concentrated juice. The carbon footprint of Tesco Fresh Sweetened Soya Milk is a third of that of semi-skimmed cows' milk because of the methane produced by cattle. A bunch of red roses from Kenya has a significantly lower carbon footprint than one from Holland: the fuel and electricity used in growing flowers in Holland more than offsets the emissions of air freight from Kenya. The carbon footprint of fresh pasta products is typically 10 to 20 per cent higher than that of dried pasta products because of the need to chill fresh pasta. Cucumbers seasonally produced in Spain without heating have a significantly lower carbon footprint than cucumbers grown here in the UK in heated greenhouses.

All these findings helped us in our quest for a leaner production chain. Such production reflects the principles of 'natural capitalism', an approach advocated by a number of scientists, academics and business people, led by Paul Hawken, Amory B Lovins and L Hunter Lovins. Natural capitalism does not reject the benefits of the market, profits or wealth creation. Instead, it argues that it is in businesses' own interests to broaden the definition of capital to include natural capital simply to minimise waste and boost productivity.

Natural capitalists argue that four principles underpin this approach to the market. First, 'radical resource productivity' – getting as much as possible out of every resource a business uses. Then 'turning waste into value' – any extra resource is recycled, or, if it cannot be recycled, does no harm. Next comes 'the solutions economy', which argues that by wasting less, both producers and customers gain. And finally there is 'reinvestment in nature', so as to make nature more productive, benefiting mankind as a whole.[17]

To these four I would add a fifth: harnessing the power of the consumer – a critical component to sustainable consumption, as I said above. This may seem counter-intuitive: surely consumers are to blame for the problems we face? But if you don't involve them, then you are missing out on the greatest force for change there is.

In the UK, some 60 per cent of carbon emissions are currently controlled or influenced by consumer decisions. Those emissions may be due to how a particular item is used at home – for example, a light bulb or a pair of trousers being washed. They may come as a result of how the product is stored, packaged or transported by a retailer – refrigeration, plastic, air freight. Or they may be in the production process itself – the methane that cows produce, the emissions from a farmer's tractor, the energy needed in a production plant. So when consumers buy green products, that bleep at the checkout sends a signal down the supply chain, telling manufacturers 'Supply more of this product.' The consumer has the power, therefore, to turn the supply chain green.

To unleash that power, you need to get inside the customer's head. Many people grapple with two competing mindsets. In the red corner is the mindset of the modern consumer. A mind that values price and quality but also convenience, mobility and independence. It is the mind of someone who likes buying the latest electrical gadget, who enjoys German beer or Chilean wine, and who enjoys flying overseas on holiday if their budget allows. In the green corner is the mindset of the responsible citizen. A mind that recognises the threat that climate change poses not just to the world but to their children: this is the mind of someone who wants to play a part in protecting the environment and cutting emissions.

These two mindsets are not incompatible. If you listen to what customers say, it's clear what needs to happen if they are to make a green choice. Cut the price of green products, so people on tight budgets can afford them. Next, make green products as easy to use as any other products. Finally, give people information about products that are harmful to them or the environment. If you remove those barriers, the supply chain – and those who provide products and services for it – will become lean to create green products. If you ignore them, you lose the opportunity to transform the world to a lean mindset. Worst of all, if you try to bully consumers into being green, they will see red.

At Tesco we sought to remove the barriers of price, inconvenience and lack of information that deterred customers from buying green products and acting to cut emissions in their own lives. My aim was simple: to make 'going green' something that everyone could do, and would want to do. They would not simply save money, but 'green goods' would be of high quality, convenient to use and fashionable.

We awarded Clubcard points to customers who reused carrier bags. This was a green initiative – but also a lean one: by encouraging recycling and reuse we saved having to buy three billion carrier bags. We also halved the price of energy-efficient light bulbs, and their sales increased sixfold in just three years.

Zero-carbon stores, carbon footprints, green products: these are tangible examples of how lean thinking can help to overcome the challenge of a world that is growing in size, relies on finite resources and is grappling with climate change. Going green should not mean limiting consumption, nor sacrificing high-quality products for expensive, low-quality green ones. By thinking lean, we can go green – and do more, for less. Above all, lean companies are fit companies, ready and able to compete.

9 Compete

Competitors – and the act of competition itself – are great teachers. Don't wait for your competitors to come over the horizon. Seek them out.

Competition benefits the consumer. This is not a sentence you read very often because in many quarters 'competition' has become a dirty word. To me, however, competition is a force for good – not just for companies, but for society, too.

Yes, competition means there are winners and losers and, at times, the result may appear unfair. That, as the cliché goes, is life. Man is not born equal. Attempts to make him so have always ended in misery or, worse, bloodshed. Governments that have ditched the market economy and tried to plan their way to prosperity have usually landed up bankrupting their nations. The late Vaclav Havel, who grew up in the bleak communist years to become the first president of the Czech Republic, came to the same conclusion:

> I have always known that the only economic system that works is a market economy . . . This is the only natural economy, the only kind that makes sense, the only one that leads to prosperity, because it is the only one that reflects the nature of life itself. The essence of life is infinitely and mysteriously multiform, and therefore it cannot be contained or planned for, in its fullness and variability, by any central intelligence.[1]

And yet, despite the lessons of history, many people are suspicious of the market and businesses that operate within it – especially big businesses. 'You take more out of society than you put in' is the criticism often levelled at big businesses. For these critics the pursuit of profit is suspect: the profit earned by one firm, they argue, always comes at a price for someone else in society. Business is, at best, amoral; at worst, immoral. Businesses, the critics say, are selfish in the narrow pursuit of their own interests and have no regard for the interests of others. You have to make a stark choice in life: doing good for others or doing business for yourself.

I believe competition and the market economy benefit mankind. I also accept that many people's faith has been undermined by the reckless acts of some bankers in the early 21st century, whose foolishness and greed did immeasurable damage to the arguments in favour of competition and free markets. The clear failings of financial regulation obviously must be addressed. Just as important, however, is the need to make the case for competition and to explain the benefits that the free market brings.

Since 1950, the world has seen one of the fastest and most sustained periods of economic growth in its history. The basis for that growth has been capitalism, an economic and political system that safeguards private property and permits free trade in competitive markets. It is not a complete free-for-all, but a system in which individuals are free to pursue their own interests while competing within a clear legal framework.

At the heart of this system lies a fundamental belief: trust in people, not in governments. Those people are what the economist Ludwig von Mises called the 'sovereign consumer'. They are the individuals who know what is best for them and their families, and they should be free to make decisions about their lives.

This belief in people, competition and the profit motive broke down the dam of protectionism that was built in the 1930s. As a result, trade flowed more freely, spurring markets to innovate, create and invest. One round of world trade talks – the Uruguay Round – delivered a global tax cut estimated to be worth more than $200 billion a year.[2] Overall, between 1960 and 2003, global per capita GDP more than doubled.[3] The greatest beneficiaries have been those countries that warmly embraced free trade, competition, and the freedoms that underpin a capitalist system. One study found that economies rated 'free' or 'mostly free' enjoyed incomes that are more than double the average levels in all other countries.[4] Meanwhile, the fight against extreme poverty and hunger is progressing, although clearly more needs to be done. According to the World Bank, the number of people living on less than $1.25 a day is projected to be 883 million in 2015, compared with 1.4 billion in 2005 and 1.8 billion in 1990.[5] Competition, free markets, trust in consumers – this has been a winning formula, and has transformed people's daily lives.

Competition is, of course, unsettling. Competitors try to put each other out of business. That's their job. Day in, day out, their chief executives and thousands of their employees are scheming away, trying to outwit you, to win your business away from you and do you down. It is as if you are a politician, but fighting for election every day rather than every few years.

The temptation, therefore, is to shy away from competition. Equally tempting, should you have vanquished your opponent, is to become complacent: as far as you're concerned, you've won, the job is done. Or, engaged in a bitter fight with one competitor, you may neglect to keep an eye open for other rivals quietly creeping up behind you – and, if you do spot them, to say 'Let's not worry about them for now.' All these tendencies are not merely mistakes, but wasted opportunities. Competition should be embraced. Compete, don't retreat.

Years spent in the hurly-burly of retailing made me realise that competitors – and the act of competition itself – are great teachers. I don't like waiting for my competitors to come over the horizon. I prefer to seek them out. Nor am I interested in looking for their faults or spotting their weaknesses – that is not only easy to do, but a sign of complacency. I want to know about them so that I can learn from them. My strongest competitors are the best management consultants there are: I look at their operations, their products or simply visit their website to find out about their thinking, research and planning – for free.

Such investigations can – as I found many times – throw up some awkward truths: a lack of preparedness on my part, ignorance of a new product, the need for investment. But however painful I found it, it was always less painful than the consequences of putting the report away in a drawer to turn yellow while we all kept our fingers crossed that the competition would go away. There is one thing worse than not doing research, and that is doing research and not changing in response to it.

All the preparation, the thinking through different scenarios of what a competitor might do – all this is sadly not enough. The late Sir Michael Quinlan, one of Britain's most influential defence planners during the Cold War, summed up it well:

> A theorem: In matters of military contingency, the expected, precisely because it is expected, is not to be expected. Rationale: What we expect, we plan and provide for; what we plan and provide for, we thereby deter; what we deter does not happen. What does happen is what we did not deter, because we did not plan and provide for it, because we did not expect it.[6]

Apply this to business, and the theorem rings equally true. The more you plan a response to a competitor's move, the less likely it is that the competitor will make that move.

Furthermore, the more you think about competition in the conventional sense, defined by analysts and experts, the less likely you are to spot the hidden competitor. This is the greatest threat of all: the competition you don't know you have. To discover that unknown threat, lurking in the depths of the marketplace, you must think and act like a consumer. Ditch convention, stop thinking in silos and looking at your business from your perspective, and start thinking like a consumer – someone who has a need, wish or demand. And then follow your instinct, be inquisitive, look around you. Intuition and experience, those intangible and unquantifiable human assets, will kick in. Follow the route they take you.

I often found that the unexpected threat did not occur because of another company's actions, but because a new piece of technology came along that created whole new sectors. For example, our non-food, direct to home delivery service – which sold things like washing machines and bikes – was originally aimed at beating Argos, a catalogue-based retailer that sells goods for customers to pick up from a warehouse or delivers them to their home. Eventually, it struck me that this assumption was entirely wrong. Our real competitor, I suddenly realised, was not Argos, but Amazon – which at the time mainly sold books, music and films, but was likely to expand into new lines. If it did that, it would become a far more daunting competitor. We therefore had to confront it. That meant upping our game massively, changing processes, developing entire new categories, online capabilities and logistics.

For retailers, being one step ahead of your competition is critical. Whatever its critics might say, retailing is one of the most brutal industries there is. Retailers parade before an individual consumer, displaying their wares and inviting the consumer to make a choice of whom to visit and perhaps buy from. The power is with the customer. They choose, and their choice passes an immediate and sometimes cruel judgement on each retailer. It is competition in its purest form.

This happens every hour, every day. One moment sales can be going quite well and customers are happy. The next everything has changed: you have failed the customer and they have passed judgement on you by taking their custom elsewhere. This experience hardens retailers: they have to be ever vigilant and fight every day to win over the customer. That fight is intense.

Margins are slim. No retailer can afford to be on the losing side for too long. As a player you feel the pressure when you wake up in the morning. It's a fight for survival.

There are some who argue that such brutal competition – in the UK and around the world – is a bad thing and should be managed and regulated. In supermarkets' struggle to win custom, they are accused of causing many of society's problems. We destroy corner shops. We tear the hearts out of local communities. We concrete over fields and cause millions of people to sit in traffic jams. We squeeze our suppliers and are bad for British farming. We encourage people to eat unhealthily. We are responsible for an epidemic of obesity. And that's just the more polite things people say about us.

Imagine if, back in 1980, the British government had agreed with that and decided to freeze the market as it was. I suspect Sainsbury would be number one, Tesco would be struggling to keep up, and suppliers would have smaller markets to serve. Some might say 'And a good thing too.' Yet consider the impact that freezing competition would have had on consumers.

Back in the early 1980s, supermarkets sold just food, and that food was usually tinned. The supply of fresh fruit and veg was limited. Luxury was a bottle of rather dodgy Riesling. Those days are now history. Competition has turned the luxuries of my youth into affordable items for people on modest incomes, and helped those on low incomes make ends meet. In Britain, food prices declined steadily between 1975 and 2007, falling in real terms by almost a third.[7] Put another way, Tesco saved the typical UK household almost £5,000 on its shopping bills in a decade – ten years in which other household bills rose.

Competition has also led to an explosion of choice. When I joined Tesco in 1979, we sold just one-tenth of the number of products we do today. In the first six years of the 21st century, the largest four UK grocery retailers each introduced, on average, three new products a day. In other words, consumer choice grew on average by a dozen new products a day, every day, for six years.

And it is not just choice of goods that has increased, but choice of stores. In Britain, 95 per cent of people have access to three or more different supermarkets within 15 minutes of where they live. That choice allows customers to shop around more. In a four-week period, customers on average use three different supermarkets. The value of the sales generated by those consumers who switch between supermarkets, and do not stick to shopping at just one, is now worth over £10 billion a year. That £10 billion keeps competition fierce.

Then there are the indirect benefits of competition. Jobs: Tesco created one new job every 20 minutes, every year for ten years. Tax: over one decade, Tesco paid £3.5 billion in tax – enough to pay for 160 new secondary schools in England. And, of course, suppliers. Next time you unload your trolley at a supermarket checkout, think of the number of people who have helped get those items into your hands. Farmers, food processors, brewers, fishermen, small manufacturers, hauliers – the veins of the supply chain spread across regions, countries and continents.

Those, then, are the benefits of competition. But how does it actually play out between competitors in the arena? The toughest competitors I faced at Tesco were the two retail giants: Aldi and Walmart.

Learning from the competition

Aldi and Walmart were – and are – two formidable retailers, against whom we competed in our home market and as we expanded around the world. Although they look quite different from one another and have different ways of doing business, they have one key feature in common. Both are mass-market discount businesses, founded by brilliant entrepreneurs who developed a new, disruptive way of conducting the old business of retailing. I stress the word disruptive: their approach and systems profoundly reshaped their home markets, devastating established firms by keeping costs low.

When you ask someone 'Who are the world's largest retailers?', many people might mention Walmart, but few outside the retail industry would say Aldi. Still privately owned, it conducts its affairs discreetly. Few know that, with revenue of about $60 billion, Aldi is larger than Target, Ahold and Marks and Spencer.

Like Tesco, Aldi began life as a single store – in Aldi's case situated in Essen in Germany and run by a miner's wife. In 1946, her children, Theo and Karl Albrecht, took over the store and gradually grew the business. In 1960, by which time they had 300 stores, they fell out. The row was not about profits, nor strategy, but about whether to sell cigarettes at the checkout (or so the story goes). Rather than one brother walking off in a huff, they did a logical thing: they split the business in two, Aldi Nord and Aldi Sud, each owned by one brother. Since then, while largely keeping the same branding and business model, they have operated in different territories, both businesses enjoying conspicuous success.

Aldi developed the art of the limited-range discount model. Every element of the retail offer is designed to deliver a product of a given quality at the lowest possible price. All retailers try to do this to some extent (except luxury brands, of course) but Aldi have taken the idea to its logical extreme. (Part of the reason for their obsessive focus on low prices may be a memory of the trauma caused by hyperinflation in Germany in the 1920s, and the deprivation and shortages during and after the Second World War.)

This approach has created the purest business model in retailing that I have encountered. There are literally no frills. There are no options. Something is either essential to the model or it is not included. For example, there is not masses of choice of any one product. Nor is there a huge range – traditionally, most Aldi stores have between 1,000 and 1,500 products, compared with up to 40,000 in a typical supermarket. Most of those 1,000 products are brands which Aldi own. Aisles are not decorated, as that costs money: products are left in pallets or boxes, as that saves money.

Aldi's strength lies in the appeal of their mission, the simplicity of the model and the discipline with which it is adhered to. For competitors it is a tough nut to crack – you cannot rely on Aldi to make a mistake. To win you have to come up with something better. So competing against Aldi keeps you honest. You will not be able to command a higher price from a customer, unless you have clearly added something which Aldi has not.

Aldi grew strongly in Germany, gradually spreading their appeal across income groups, and ended up with more than 25 per cent of the market, a remarkable share from a discount store format. Part of the reason for their growth was that other German retailers made a strategic mistake. Instead of reorganising their main formats to compete head-on with Aldi, they viewed Aldi as a niche retailer and developed lookalike small discount chains of stores, entirely separate from their main businesses. This error meant retailers ended up competing on Aldi's terms with a format they did not understand. Before long, Aldi had grown right into their main market, benefiting from economies of scale which other retailers could not match. If Aldi's competitors had innovated they might have played the game on more favourable terms, but they never did.

We first competed against Aldi when they and another limited-range discounter from Germany, Lidl, came to the UK in 1990. They were predicted to take a 25 per cent share of the market as they had in Germany. This would have meant the end for at least one of the major incumbents. At the time, the pundits thought that major incumbent was Tesco.

Aldi did hit us pretty hard when they opened and, with hindsight, this was a blessing. It meant we had no choice but to respond. If the impact had been less, we might have persuaded ourselves to let things carry on as if nothing much had happened – and that, of course, would have played straight into Aldi's hands.

In the recession of the early 1990s, our customers were struggling. They needed to take care of their money – and Aldi was promising 'record low prices'. Thanks to our research (see Chapter 1) we found that customers were thinking 'I like Tesco but I have to shop at Aldi'. We made the right decision. We decided to give customers Aldi prices at Tesco so they wouldn't have to choose but – and here is the crucial point – without losing the extra things we thought we did well. We had to remain Tesco, and not become an 'ersatz Aldi'.

This was no easy task. We developed a special range of products which we called Value Lines. They were no-frills products designed to offer the best possible value. Thanks to our honesty in the labelling, we did not damage customers' perception of our quality or our appeal to, say, Marks and Spencer's customers. Far from hiding the fact that they were designed for people on a budget, we blazoned it on items with bold blue and white packaging. After spending years moving upmarket to emulate Sainsbury and Marks and Spencer, our shareholders thought we had lost our senses when we launched this range. But we had read the market right, learnt from the competition and followed the customer. It was a big success, which wrong-footed Aldi, possibly for the first time.

We then embarked on a long march, slowly driving greater efficiency into every part of our business with new systems and many new management innovations. We wanted to play Aldi at their own game – but do even better. (For example, we copied Aldi's system of using pallets to display goods in store, but made it better by putting wheels on the pallets to help move them around. Simple stuff, but every little helped.) Every penny we saved – and there were lots of them – was ploughed back into the customer offer with better service and better products. For a decade and more, prices went down in real terms year on year. We forced ourselves into a virtuous cycle, lowering prices and increasing volume, which allowed us to lower prices again.

The pressure was intense. Ten years of prices falling in real terms – while wages, energy and the cost of land were rising in real terms – meant that at every budget round people wanted me to ease up so they could get some breathing space. Shareholders asked if we could increase dividends rather than keep cutting prices for customers. I constantly had to remind the business that the only way to keep competitors from squeezing the life out of you is to keep yourself under constant pressure. Thankfully, I was right. We built market share steadily over the period. We also became increasingly profitable, so soon we were able to make long-term investment in our brand to keep it in the best possible shape.

Aldi and Lidl did have some success but it was against weaker, soft discounters. Between 1990 and 2005, the discounter share of the market remained unchanged at around four to five per cent. They were never able to break out into the core of the market as they had done in Germany.

During this time, another front opened up in our fight with

Aldi and Lidl, even more keenly contested and this time abroad. It came about in the wake of the fall of the Berlin Wall in 1989 when we visited the former communist countries of central Europe and realised that these offered potential new markets for us.

I will never forget my first visit to Poland in 1991. If anyone was ever in doubt about the inability of a centrally planned economy to meet the needs of its citizens, a trip to central Europe at that time would serve as a corrective. There were no shops in any modern, British sense. Gdansk, home to the Solidarity movement which eventually helped topple the communist regime, reminded me of shopping in the prefab estate where I grew up during the early 1960s. Yet people were crying out for good shops and something good to buy in them.

Unfortunately we were not the only ones to spot the opportunity. Retailers flooded in from all over Europe. The markets we chose to enter – Poland, the Czech Republic, Slovakia and Hungary – were particularly attractive to French and German retailers. Aldi and Lidl were soon present in some or all of the markets.

There were not too many stores in the early years as each retailer had to start from scratch. But even so there were far too many retailers relative to the size of the countries they were trading in, and profits were therefore correspondingly low. This sparked a desperate war of attrition that took place very much on the discounter's terms: in countries whose populations were on low incomes, all of the competition between retailers focused on price.

Tesco entered these markets with large, one-stop hypermarkets, often in a shopping mall. As a general rule, these are the foundations of a retail network as they give a retailer scale quickly: designed for a one-stop shop by car, they are usually located on the edge of a town. However, in former eastern bloc countries we found that we were being outmanoeuvred by Aldi and Lidl, who were located closer to town centres. We knew from the statistics that many people in Slovakia and Hungary owned cars; what we hadn't appreciated was that few car owners could afford to drive to do a weekly shop. Our response was to develop new smaller formats, essentially compact hypermarkets of 2,000 or 3,000 square metres instead of the large stores of 8,000 or 10,000 square metres. These offered a wide range, combining food and general merchandise, and had the advantage that they could be located much closer to the discounters.

We then introduced not just our Value range (as we had in the UK) but an extra tier of low-priced products built around exclusive brands that we owned. This was a technique which Aldi themselves had pioneered – and we had learnt from them. The competition was relentless.

The German discounters were a little surprised that we paid them so much attention: they had been used to the main players seeing them as a niche and avoiding head-on competition. But we were determined not to make that mistake. Slowly but surely our strategy began to bear fruit and we steadily grew our market share. At first much of our gain did not come at the expense of the discounters, although we slowed them down a lot, but from other competitors (such as other hypermarket chains). We were then helped by consumers gradually becoming more prosperous, which allowed us to appeal to them on more than just price. When we improved our offer, with more upmarket products (including clothing and electrical goods) and better quality fresh food, we really started to put the discounters under pressure. This would not have been possible if we had not first learnt from our competitors how to make our businesses as simple and efficient as possible. Those early days helped us build trust with customers so that when we added more upmarket products at higher prices, customers felt it was a price worth paying for the extra value they received.

After 15 years of hard work and steady progress Tesco is now the market leader in central Europe. It never felt easy. Aldi and Lidl are too formidable as opponents to give you a quiet time. And just as we were winning on that front, an even bigger competitor appeared back in our home market, Walmart.

Walmart is a phenomenon. Founded in 1962 by Sam Walton (a retailing and marketing genius if ever there was one), it grew organically to become the first truly cross-continent retailer within the USA. Walmart started as a seller of general merchandise – clothing and everything for the home except food. Although Walton did not invent the discount general merchandise format in the USA, he certainly perfected it. In the early years he sought out smaller towns to avoid head-on contact with K-mart discount stores (which was a much bigger chain than Walmart at the time). But where K-mart continued to rely on the scale economy of each large branch, Walmart invested in central distribution, central purchasing and logistics. Creating a network over a continent the size of America is a mammoth task. Those who tried invariably failed. So most did not even try – until Walmart.

Walton expanded quickly but methodically out of Walmart's home in the south-east, using a 'hub' (a distribution centre) and 'spoke' (store network) system. Pioneers of logistics and merchandise systems – those things that sound so boring, but are critical to success – Walmart gradually built a system of low operating costs which was superior to their competitors, the largest general merchandisers and supermarkets. And it was not all about systems. Walmart had clear values around which they built a well-motivated, energetic team. Sharp-eyed retailers, with a high morale, they made their stores pulsate with energy.

In 1988 Walmart opened the first supercenter (the American equivalent of a hypermarket), a giant format which sold food as well as general merchandise. By the mid-1990s, there was probably no retailer who felt that they could compete head-on with Walmart. Instead, consultants encouraged retailers to find ways of differentiating themselves from the leviathan to avoid being squashed by it. This strategy played into Walmart's hands, leaving them to be the market leader on 'value'. By the time Walmart entered the UK, they were the world's largest retailer, soon to become the world's largest company, and they were five times the size of Tesco.

Walmart entered the UK by buying Asda for $10 billion. I received the news in the middle of a question-and-answer session in Thailand. It proved a good exercise in how important it is to appear calm while you are thinking 'Oh no, what now?' My initial reaction, I have to confess, was 'I must get out of this meeting and back to the UK.' However, I knew that that would have been a very visible sign of panic. So I forced myself to calm down and completed my schedule. And while I can hardly claim to have felt like Francis Drake completing his game of bowls before taking on the Spanish Armada, that breathing space did allow me to compose myself, get my thoughts straight and put Walmart's move into perspective.

What was the right message to give to the company in the face of this threat? It was clearly serious but I didn't want the business to be consumed by fear. On the other hand I didn't want us to look the other way and pretend Walmart didn't pose a huge threat. They certainly did.

We obviously knew and admired Walmart, but we had never competed against them. We had no idea how much lower their operating costs were compared with our own. Certainly there was a widely held view (which we did not share) that the US industry was much more productive than the UK's and that Walmart would – not to put too fine a point on it – wipe the floor with us.

One thing that definitely worried us was their massive volume of non-food turnover. Tesco's non-food operation was in its infancy and general merchandise lends itself to greater economies of scale than food. We were concerned that Walmart would outgun us on general merchandise, and that they would use the profits to cross-subsidise an attack on our core food business.

We decided nevertheless to remain Tesco – to learn from Walmart but follow the customer. In other words, we decided not to alter our fundamental strategy based around our customers, but respect the competitor and learn all we could from Walmart. And we did. We crawled all over their business. Our most senior team of managers – the people who ran our business each day – visited America, China and wherever Walmart did business to learn as much as we could about them. There was much to admire. Gradually though, our teams gained confidence as reality replaced myth, and we began to see how we could compete. General merchandise was a key to it. We needed to create a competitive global supply chain as quickly as possible.

We didn't sell anything like the volume of general merchandise that Walmart did but we were growing fast. We also knew that we were good at building lean supply chains – after all, we had developed them to deliver fresh food in the UK. We found that we could make up for the higher prices we paid manufacturers (due to our lower volumes) by making supply and distribution more efficient. We quickly increased the size of our stores to offer a full food and non-food range. We introduced new formats, new product ranges, new services and new low prices. We learnt that, although Walmart might place orders with ten Chinese factories to make a household product (like a toaster), we could compete if we simply had a big enough order to fill one factory. The result was a momentum created in our business which was more than enough to withstand the onslaught of Walmart.

Over time, Tesco's productivity compared very well with Walmart's and even exceeded it in food – even though commentators laboured under the impression that Walmart, by being big and American, must have higher productivity. We actually increased our market share, and our profits, more in the five years after Walmart entered the market than before. This struggle strengthened my view that, in the enormous market that is global retailing, there is plenty of room for Walmart, Tesco, Aldi and many more. Walmart drew the best out of us. The battle between them, Tesco and other major retailers has been competition at its best – and the consumer has benefited most of all.

Victory at all costs is no victory

In the thick of the battle, the temptation is to 'win at all costs'. But victory is worthless if in the process you have betrayed what you stand for. The will to win has to be balanced by being true to your values. In all our hard-fought battles, I was crystal clear that we should always act as Tesco. Learning from our competitors should never mean trying to become them, and certainly never putting the interests of winning ahead of the interests of our employees.

Winning brings responsibilities to customers, staff, local communities, suppliers. Strong companies are those which recognise these responsibilities. Tesco's relationship with its customers is based on trust. If we do not act properly towards them and their communities, we will lose that trust. It is as much a commercial imperative as it is a social obligation for us to do the right thing – to treat people how we like to be treated.

For some people, corporate social responsibility is 'compensation' for doing business in the first place. I don't see it like that. Firms are not just passive actors in the market. They do not exist in a moral vacuum. A firm's behaviour reflects the collective beliefs of all who work and invest in it. Such is the scrutiny of business today that more considered judgement and responsible action is expected of a business than of private individuals in their own exercise of moral responsibility.

A good business is most likely to behave in a socially responsible way by innovating, taking risks, competing, investing, hiring, serving and marketing. These everyday activities are the ones which benefit not only the firm and its customer but the wider community.

This explains why the corporate 'mission' of the best companies is seldom only to create profit. Clearly companies know that profit is necessary, but most understand that the pursuit of profit is insufficient to sustain its employees' and investors' morale and motivation over time. Note that I say 'most companies'. All companies' directors will mouth these words, most will mean them, but some will fail to live up to them. Why do some fall short – polluting the environment or making reckless investments? It might be ignorance, poor governance or perverse incentives, but a lot of business behaviour is simply explained by the culture and society it operates in. The moral standards exhibited in business will almost inevitably reflect the moral standards of society at that time. Society gets the kind of business it deserves.

Good companies, however, view the audience they serve as both customer and citizen. They look beyond the immediate demands of the customer and consider how to serve that person as a citizen and a member of a community.

I would obviously like to think that Tesco is one such company. As we grew, so did the importance of our serving the communities in which we operate. It became apparent that this commitment was not some add-on, optional extra, a 'nice to have' that we could issue a report on once a year. It was integral to our business, and had to be reflected in our strategy.

Our Steering Wheel, which we used to manage the business in a balanced way (see Chapter 6) originally had four segments. The fifth, Community, was added to ensure the whole business was doing its bit to serve communities as well as customers. Reflecting our values, our initiatives were shaped by customer feedback and also by our experience in Korea, which I discussed earlier.

The five segments of the Steering Wheel now became:

- what are we doing for the customer?
- how is work being improved?
- what are we doing for our people?
- what financial targets do we have?
- what are we doing for the community?

We then focused our activities on a Community Plan which sets out our strategy and plans in as much detail as our customer plan, and is as professionally managed as every other part of the Steering Wheel. The four areas we chose to focus on at first – local community work, education, diet and health, and climate change – were not randomly chosen initiatives. They addressed the environment that our business operated in and what customers wanted. We recognised that doing our bit in these areas benefitted the long-term viability of Tesco itself.

Race for Life is a particularly good example of the plan in action. We wanted to help people be more active in their lives and to support the founders of Race for Life, Cancer Research UK, in their vital work. Many cancers are affected by people's lifestyles. We have made our products healthier and provided more information on a healthy lifestyle. Helping Cancer Research was a natural extension of this effort.

Cancer Research UK is one of the most admirable organisations with whom I have ever worked. The biggest single independent funder of cancer research in Europe, it puts almost £300 million into cancer research each year,[8] which is a major part of the UK's total cancer research effort. The organisation alone, and in collaboration with others, has made a number of breakthroughs in the effective treatment of cancer. Thanks in large part to them and their fellow research units, the world's fight against cancer is slowly and gradually being won. That success is testament to its management. Cancer Research has organised itself to compare with the very best company in terms of professionalism and strategic focus.

Cancer Research launched Race for Life in 1994 to raise awareness and much-needed funds. The idea is a simple one: a five-kilometre race for women. Some people do race but mainly it is a coming together of women who have been touched in some way by cancer – be it themselves, their family or their friends.

Over the years, Race for Life has grown into a huge national event. Although we have provided money, our biggest contribution has been practical support – publicity, advertising, organisation, recruitment and planning. Like all genuine partnerships, we have both benefited and learnt things from each other. We have both been demanding and got the best out of each other. Many of our customers have participated in the events, and they like the fact Tesco is involved. The same can be said for our employees and suppliers.

But Race for Life – and the Community Plan overall – is really an example of Tesco not simply putting something back into society, but deepening loyalty to its brand. Every successful business will hone its marketing skills on selling products. This activity, though, is not about meeting the usual commercial objectives, which can be quantified by sales or footfall. It is designed to build a stronger, deeper emotional attachment between us, our customers, our employees and communities, which reaps dividends in different ways and at different times.

Some may say this is cynical. I would say it is simply good business, and a clear example of how the free market generates benefits that go well beyond the employees, management and shareholders of companies. Politicians would do well to think of business as part of the solution to life's difficulties rather than part of the problem. Government and business should engage much more closely to find innovative solutions to the challenges we all face. Above all, though, society – like companies themselves, must embrace competition, a force for good that has generated untold benefits for mankind.

The final word belongs to the champion of the free market, Adam Smith. Competition converts 'the private interests of and passions of men' into consequences 'most agreeable to the interests of the whole society'. In a passage that strikes a chord with every shopkeeper, Smith wrote 'It is not from the benevolence of the butcher, the brewer, or the baker that we expect our dinner, but from their regard to their interest. We address ourselves not to their self-love, and never talk to them of our own necessities, but of their advantages.'[9] Competition is a good thing. 'Compete, don't retreat' should be the mantra of every leader. To compete and win, however, every leader needs to understand the importance of trust.

10 Trust

Trust is the bedrock of leadership. When people trust you, they feel that their interests are safe in your hands, and they have confidence in your vision, ability, judgement, drive and determination to see things through.

The final word on my list was going to be leadership. Strong leaders create great companies, win stunning victories and retire showered in glory. You can't have success without good leadership. Field Marshal Montgomery wrote that his entire 'doctrine of command' could be summed up as 'leadership'.

The first taste I had of leadership and real responsibility – when I was asked to be Marketing Director back in 1992 – was unsettling. Ian MacLaurin and David Malpas appeared to be saying they had no idea what the matter was with the business, and they needed my help. Up until that moment I had always had complete faith in Ian and David. They were my mentors. They led me, so I assumed they had all the answers. Suddenly I felt the terrible weight of responsibility, the burden of people looking to me for leadership, for the first time. Like a son realising that his father is looking to him for help, it was a shocking moment.

But what is leadership? Slim argues that leadership is Courage, Will Power, Initiative, Knowledge and Unselfishness. But as I thought about it, I came to the conclusion that there is one quality that leaders need more than any other – and that is trust. Trust is the bedrock of leadership.

Without that trust, people may still obey you but – as the word 'obey' implies – they may act reluctantly, half-heartedly and hesitantly. When people trust you, they feel that their interests are safe in your hands, and they have confidence in your vision, ability, judgement, drive and determination to see things through. That trust rests on a number of the things I have touched upon in earlier chapters: your team's belief in your purpose, your noble objective, their sharing your values, their willingness to act according to set procedures. At that point, you have won their hearts, not just their minds. Montgomery believed that 'it is essential to understand that battles are won primarily in the hearts of men . . . The British soldier responds to leadership in a most remarkable way; and once you have won his heart, he will follow you anywhere.'[1]

There is, though, a missing dimension that many people fail to understand about leaders. Strong leadership does not simply depend on a group of people putting their faith in you. It also depends on you putting your faith in them. You need to trust them to build a store, stack a shelf, buy a company – and I dare say (not that I have done it) capture a trench held by the enemy. When you put your trust in them, their confidence, self-esteem, courage, determination and commitment all grow. When this trust is created, anything becomes possible – but three things in particular begin to happen.

First, a trusted leader is able to take a team further than it would have gone by itself, stretching the ambition, effort and – at times – patience of its members. A leader's courageous goals may at first seem impossible but, because that leader is trusted, the team is willing to try their best to achieve them. Their trust overrides their lack of confidence and judgement of their own capabilities.

Second, people change how they behave. An environment of trust grows – not just between the leader and the team, but within the team itself. Individuals put faith in their colleagues.

Third, and, perhaps most important of all, people become leaders themselves, with the confidence, self-esteem and desire to take responsibility for their actions. That does not mean making everyone equal, tearing up the rule book and allowing anyone to do what they like: as I said earlier, it is critical to give people clear roles and make them accountable for their actions. Within that framework, however, good leaders give their staff the ability to exercise their judgement and to feel as if they are being treated like trusted adults.

This culture is important in any organisation, but the bigger the organisation, the more critical it is. Too many public services have become submerged in bureaucracy and targets. The right targets can certainly focus and motivate a team. However, targets that seek merely to control behaviour, because the management distrusts its team, sap the morale, erode the dignity and undermine the professionalism of those on the front line. Organisations that suffer from this lack of trust find their employees' motivation diminishes and their performance suffers. The result: more missives and diktats, compounding the problem, deepening the mistrust.

Building trust

Did a culture of trust exist at Tesco? Of course I would like to say so, but I am hardly the one to judge. I certainly never had a checklist of the steps I wanted to take in order to build trust in me. But piecing it together today, with the luxury of hindsight, I suppose there are various steps I would recommend leaders take to create trust between them and their teams.

The first is to be yourself, as only by being honest with people all the time will you encourage people to put their faith in you. Leaders are prone to fall into the trap of thinking that ideal management requires a different type of person – a super-executive. They use different words, and sometimes even a different tone of voice. People need to know that their leader is authentic and did not leave their 'real' personality at home. They can spot a mask – and that mask will, in any case, slip at some point: trying to be someone you are not is virtually impossible to do all the time.

You also need to make sure that the whole organisation – not just the senior management team at head office – knows you, and that you are the same person wherever you go and whoever you speak to. You can't have one persona for HQ and another when you're at the coalface. Certainly, I went to great pains to be myself whenever I met our staff in our stores, and in particular at Town Meetings. Opening up to reveal your true self in front of hundreds of strangers, whose trust you are seeking, is an unsettling experience. But if you want their trust, that is the only thing to do.

To win people's trust, some CEOs think it necessary to be seen to be doing a huge amount and to be obviously in charge by making every decision. That can sometimes be counterproductive. It is often better to stay calm – even if that means appearing inactive. By staying calm, managers have time to listen, watch and learn, and see the bigger picture. Hyperactive managers at the centre, who send out commands at the slightest bump in the road or after having their latest 'new idea', are a hindrance not a help in any organisation. Order followed by counter-order creates disorder at the front line of the organisation where the action is.

My trust in the front line was reflected in how we empowered people throughout the organisation. I believe that each individual needs the freedom and power to think for themselves, so that they devise solutions to problems before they become serious and, most important of all, so they gain confidence. Self-confident organisations delegate power and responsibility down to the front line, where value tends to be created. Samuel Smiles identified the need for managers to let go:

> Too much guidance and restraint hinder the formation of habits of self-help. They are like bladders tied under the arms of one who has not taught himself to swim. Want of confidence is perhaps a greater obstacle to improvement than is generally imagined.[2]

We therefore encouraged wide spans of control and responsibility, so that managers were kept busy and did not end up doing the job of the person below them. We kept titles simple so that people did not bother too much about structure and status. Although we had a quarter of a million staff outside the UK, less than one in a thousand were expat managers from Britain, thereby ensuring that decisions were taken by local people who knew the culture and understood the society. People were encouraged to make decisions themselves and take the initiative.

The digital revolution has increased pressure on all leaders to be active, to give their immediate reaction to problems and to meddle. I certainly sent plenty of emails in my time at Tesco, but very few on important subjects. Emails are a wonderful tool for instant communication, but they have their limits: you cannot listen via email, you cannot pick up on someone's feelings and emotions. Nothing beats a face-to-face chat about a tricky issue. Talking to someone is much the best way to maintain trust.

The managers who get drawn into discussions via email on small issues tend to be those who lose sight of the bigger picture. They micromanage, endlessly burying themselves in the details. This is a recipe for disaster. A good manager knows that they need to keep a sense of perspective – and that there are others they can trust to deal with the detail. It is a sign of bad leadership when a manager is dealing with everything and worrying about the tiniest aspects of the organisation. Such behaviour suggests that trust between the leader and the team has broken down, the leader has lost all sense of perspective or – worst of all – control.

That doesn't mean, however, that leaders don't need to know anything about what that detail might entail. If you don't know the detail, then you don't know your business or organisation.

Thanks to spending a lifetime at Tesco, when I walked around a store, I could tell at a glance whether things were working or failing. If you want to see the wood from the trees, it helps knowing the trees in the first place.

A trusted leader therefore knows the detail, is confident to let others manage and does not try to do their job. These leaders watch what is going on, and intervene to help only if things begin to go wrong. Such trust is the bedrock of a successful organisation. Montgomery hits this nail on the head with typical forcefulness – and self-confidence:

> It is absolutely vital that a senior commander should keep himself from becoming immersed in details, and I always did so. I would spend many hours in quiet thought and reflection in thinking out the major problems. In battle a commander has got to think how he will defeat the enemy. If he gets involved in details he cannot do this since he will lose sight of the essentials which really matter; he will then be led off on side issues which will have little influence on the battle and he will fail to be that solid rock on which his staff can lean. Details are their province.[3]

My attempts to be calm meant I would leave people alone to get on with their job – although my door was always open, and I was ready to see anyone at any time. To start with, some people found this approach unsettling: they wanted the reassurance of having their decisions signed off by others. Yet I knew that that sort of culture would not breed leaders or trust. If everyone was forever covering themselves, and seeking approval, I would get exhausted and the company would grow at a glacial pace. Over time, I found people's self-confidence grew as they acknowledged the trust I placed in them.

That did not mean that I was like Admiral Fisher (the commander of the British fleet I mentioned earlier) who allowed people to forge his signature, and had a note in his office which read IF YOU HAVE NOTHING IMPORTANT TO SAY PLEASE GO AWAY AND LET ME GET ON WITH MY WORK. Nor was I quite as sanguine as Montgomery who, fighting in France in 1940, was woken up by a staff officer to be told the Germans had captured the town of Louvain. 'Go away and don't bother me. Tell the brigadier in Louvain to turn them out,' he barked – and then went back to sleep.

A calm environment, and not becoming overwhelmed by the detail, is not always what is required of a leader. Organisations that have lost their way, in which morale is flagging and a sense of purpose is lacking, can respond well to a different kind of dynamic leadership. A notable example is what happened when Winston Churchill became Prime Minister in May 1940.

Britain was facing one of its darkest hours. Nazi Germany had all but conquered France, leaving Britain standing alone in Europe. Churchill's energy, drive and determination were quickly felt across what was an uncertain, wavering government machine as he issued a torrent of messages and minutes, often labelled 'Action This Day'. His Assistant Private Secretary of the time (Sir John – 'Jock' – Colville) recalled:

> Most of the matters were of major importance relating to the battle that was raging or to aircraft production, but he always found time for trivialities too. Could trophies taken in the First World War be reconditioned for use? Could wax be supplied for troops to put in their ears and deaden the noise of warfare? What was to be done with the animals in the Zoo in the event of bombardment?[4]

As Colville noted, while no one complained that Churchill 'neglected the vital for the insignificant', there were 'those who lamented his preoccupation with detail in matters great as well as small'. And yet the impact of Churchill's energy and zeal transformed the machinery of government. According to one member of the Cabinet Secretariat:

> Knowledge of these messages, sometimes peremptory in tone but always pertinent and timely, quickly spread through the administrative cadres of Whitehall. They did much to confirm the feeling that there was now a strong personal control at the centre. This stream of messages, covering so wide a range of subjects, was like the beam of a searchlight ceaselessly swinging round and penetrating into the remote recesses of the administration – so that everyone, however humble his rank or function, felt that one day the beam might rest on him and light up what he was doing. In Whitehall the effect of this influence was immediate and dramatic. The machine responded at once to his leadership. It quickened its pace and improved the tone of administration. A new sense of urgency was created as it came to be realised that a firm hand, guided by a strong will, was on the wheel. Morale was high.[5]

'A firm hand' and 'a strong will' were just what the machine of government – and Britain – needed to restore trust in government. As the Cabinet Secretary noted, this change reflected 'the vigorous sense of purpose which at once made itself felt'. He wrote 'It was as though the machine had overnight acquired one or two new gears, capable of far higher speeds than had ever before been thought possible.'[6]

In certain circumstances – when an organisation is in crisis – this style of leadership is crucial. Most of the time, however, organisations are not facing a fight for survival and therefore this hyperactivity becomes a hindrance. Churchill's peacetime political career was, for example, not as successful as his wartime one. Yet Churchill clearly had one trait which I can fully sympathise with and admire, and without which no leader in any organisation can make a lasting impression: his strength of will.

'It was by his strength of will – it might almost be said that it was by his strength of will alone – that we were carried through the greatest crisis of 1940', wrote one of his closest advisers. When he had a strong view on a policy or action to be taken, he would press his case home. 'Objections were frequent, for he was sometimes wrong and often premature and impatient. Argument was tense and long. But opportunity was always given for full discussion.'[7]

During that discussion, 'he was ready to listen to the arguments on either side. And, even when he had formed his view, he was ready to modify it – usually after a period of reflection which might be protracted – if fresh evidence was brought up or fresh arguments were introduced'.[8] 'I would sooner be right than consistent' was one of Churchill's favourite sayings. As another of his inner circle said:

> In the course of this process it frequently happened that his proposed action was shown to be unsound, or quite impracticable with the resources available – or so seemed to be at first sight. This did not deter him in the least. He drove on regardless, until either he had his way or additional resources had been found from somewhere, or until at length he had to recognise that his proposal was no good, or could be replaced by a better one.[9]

Churchill's drive, his unwillingness to let seemingly impassable obstacles stand in his way, his focus on a supposedly unachievable goal: these traits can madden, exhaust and exasperate those around a leader, but they are critical if a country is to stave off military defeat – or, at another level, if an organisation is to grow and prosper.

I know that I often maddened my colleagues with my obsessive insistence on debating an issue until I felt we had got to the truth. Painful though that process may have been, it was critical if my team was to trust the decisions that followed. I was also stubborn in my insistence that we actually did what we said we would do. If you sign up to values, goals, targets, you have to stay the course. A leader who sets out a strategy and then changes it simply because circumstances become difficult eventually loses the trust of their team. Delivering on your promises is the best way to build trust – be it between a politician and the electorate or between a CEO and their team.

To 'calm' and 'stubborn' I would add 'respectful'. I tried to meet as many of the team as possible, face to face, right around the world. The act of meeting a staff member, though, is not enough. Indeed, for the staff member, the arrival (usually unannounced) of the CEO in their store could be a trifle unnerving. Only by breaking down any sense of suspicion or fear that they might have, and getting them to open up to me about their problems, could I discover how our strategy was playing out on the shop floor. From their perspective, I hope that having a CEO who actually listened, rather than simply talked at them, helped to build their sense of confidence.

Being respectful also means not indulging in juvenile shouting matches and a macho, aggressive attitude. Television reality shows give the impression that a leader needs to abuse, demean and even fire members of their team in public. This behaviour reflects a failure of leadership, and a complete absence of trust. If a mistake is made, a leader should encourage the team to learn from it: humiliation erodes confidence which in turn undermines initiative and innovation. If someone does not agree with a course of action, and refuses to do it, shouting is hardly likely to convince them.

Related to that is something Tesco tried hard to practise: 'to praise more than criticise'. For every ten words of praise someone receives, it is the one word of criticism that will be remembered – and that is especially the case when that criticism comes from the CEO whom the staff rarely see. I was very conscious of this, so I was generally better at 'praising more than criticising' our staff on the shop floor than I was with senior management whom I knew much better.

After that comes 'equality'. I made a conscious point of always trying to treat everyone, at every level of the company, equally. Lobbying people before meetings, having a clique or a personal network is not my style – I am a shy person, which makes me no good at office politics. I have never been much affected by personality, so I never had favourites. I'm also only too aware that having favourites breeds mistrust. When Slim was asked 'Who are your crack divisions?', he would reply 'All my divisions are crack divisions.' Favouring one group above another distorts what a leader hears about an organisation: those in a clique tell the leader what they want to hear, or else they face eviction and life in the cold. Meanwhile, those outside the clique feel – rightly – isolated, unloved, ill-respected, none of which breeds trust.

Finally, you cannot trust someone who does not tell you the truth. The best respect you can show someone is to tell them the truth. Pious and self-righteous though that may sound, I have stuck to that – often to a fault. Whether it was meeting people on the shop floor or discussing an issue at a board meeting, I would say what I thought, unvarnished but I hope politely. Over time, though, as people saw that I did what I said, and that I was straight with them, I'd like to think that my integrity trumped their dislike of what I was saying. People's dislike of you, or of what you are saying, does not matter as much as their not trusting you.

Telling the truth to others is critical. If they find you have led them astray, their trust in you will crumble. Tell them how it is – even if it is bad news – and their confidence in you will grow. Yet the truth that matters the most is being true to yourself. If you know yourself and are aware of your strengths and weaknesses, you make fewer mistakes. You become bolder and more self-assured. Mix that with knowing precisely what you want to achieve, and you soon create a culture of confidence that enables you to ignore the brickbats, carping and criticism that inevitably comes your way.

Respect breeds trust

In the end, however, it is not about the leader and what that person does, but what a leader causes other people to do. A truly successful leader breeds a culture of trust and confidence in the organisation. That is the bedrock of a strong organisation.

Creating that culture of trust depends on giving people what they hope for from a job. At its heart, as I spelt out above, there are four things that most people want – and if you can deliver these, you will win their trust and they will follow you almost anywhere. Those four things are to be treated with respect; to have an interesting job; to have a manager who helps and supports them; and to have the chance to get on and up in their careers.

Some people are better than others at managing people. No organisation should just rely on its employees' natural aptitudes and abilities in management. Constant improvement of management skills and capabilities is imperative. When I became CEO, Tesco was growing fast. I realised that if we were to be sure that our staff had managers who helped them, we needed to do everything possible to equip all our management with the best skills and up-to-date practices. A management consultancy developed a toolkit of bespoke management skills for Tesco's 10,000 managers in our stores, depots and head office. We used this toolkit as the basis for a training programme called Future.

Lasting two years, Future was probably the largest and most intense management training exercise ever undertaken in the UK. A mini-MBA programme, it taught our managers the practical skills they needed to manage people every day – such as how to speak to people, how to chair meetings, how to do analysis quickly and prepare plans, how to implement projects, how to coach staff.

Just one simple technique – managing meetings – was fantastically successful at building trust. We all know how bad a meeting can be. There is no agenda or clear purpose as to why everyone is in the room. The meeting then drifts, usually driven by just one or two people, hopping from point to point and then back again. No one takes notes of what is being agreed – if anything is – and so most people leave the room at best confused, at worst irritated. A manager can hold one or two meetings like this: but if they make a habit of it, they will soon lose their team's trust.

We taught our managers to follow a few simple techniques for the meetings which they would chair. First, to make sure every meeting had a clear subject and purpose. Next, to ask people why they were at the meeting and what they wanted to achieve from it: this immediately engages everyone present, as they can then get something out of the meeting. Everyone at the meeting would be asked to build on what others said, and not to be overly negative or critical. Decisions made and actions to be taken were written up on charts for everyone to see, so people knew who was to do what, by when. At the end of the meeting, everyone would be asked whether the meeting had achieved what they had hoped, and whether they had any remaining concerns – which were then dealt with. Finally, managers were taught to keep meetings short.

The evidence of Future's success is that we managed to change what Tesco did – what we sold and how we operated – incredibly quickly. That success is thanks to the trust we had created between management and our teams. Some very simple practices created thousands of managers with the skills and confidence to provide what everyone hopes for: a boss who helps and supports them.

We devoted as much time and energy to giving people the chance to get on and up in their career – another one of the key components of what people want in their work. Whatever its size, people will trust an organisation that trusts them and gives them every chance to fulfil their hopes and ambitions, whoever they are, whatever their background.

'Everyone is welcome at Tesco' sums up the company's underlying philosophy about how we behaved as an employer. With it, we tried to get across the idea that no matter what your background, age or education, you stood the same chance of doing well – indeed, the same chance of getting right to the top of the business – as anyone else. Our actions matched our words. We encouraged people to get all the training and education they could, to develop and add to their natural talents, as this would help them do better at work and in life. But we also said how you did at Tesco depended on what you did in the business – your attitude, your character, your contribution and your achievements, not simply a qualification. Many businesses, particularly in the professions, have focused on graduate recruitment for their business for so long now that it is virtually a prerequisite for progress. We broke that rule.

Tesco is willing to be different because its history is different, largely thanks to Jack Cohen's immigrant roots. His family came to England in the late 19th century as refugees from pogroms against the Jews in Poland. He started not just at the bottom, but as an outsider. As he progressed, he naturally recruited like-minded people. These tended to be energetic, young people with more wits and common sense than glittering academic prizes, degrees and letters after their name. They all started at the bottom, usually in the stores, and rose through hard work, determination and a resourceful character. We wanted to preserve the meritocratic, classless sense of opportunity that Cohen stamped on the company, but saying that 'anyone can make it to the top' is meaningless unless you provide practical support and incentives to encourage it. So we created this culture in a variety of ways.

In selecting for senior positions we placed a big emphasis on the ability to manage people and lead them. Whenever we considered someone for promotion, one of the first questions we asked was 'Who have you developed?' Word quickly went around that, if you wanted to get up and get on, you needed a record of talent spotting and talent development. Managers were soon on the lookout for new talent in their ranks.

We kept a very simple structure, with just six levels between the jobs most of our people started out in (on the checkout, shelf stacking, warehouse work) and the CEO. Such simplicity makes it easy for people to understand how their careers might progress. They can see the next rung of the ladder they need to climb. Byzantine structures, in which the career progression is opaque, can create a sense that only those 'in the know' get promoted – which in turn breeds mistrust.

To help people progress in their career, we created a system called Options, designed to train people to climb up to the next level of the business. Most training was done on the job, but it was thorough and often involved doing new jobs at the same level to broaden experience. The objective was to ensure a promotion was a success, so a lot of time was spent training a candidate with the right skills. Nor was Options just for those at the bottom of the business. Everyone, senior managers included, can always learn more. So there was an Options programme for every level of management, right to the top. Senior managers became more involved with 'off the job' training, taking executives all over the world over two years with bespoke, tailored courses, some of which were designed by the candidate.

Anyone could apply for Options, and thousands did. At any one time over 6 per cent of the Group workforce – today that is almost 30,000 people – were being prepared for the next level up. And as an engine of social mobility, it purred and hummed. Thousands of people climbed up from the bottom of the business, some right to the top. Mums returning to work as part-time checkout operators became regional directors. Sixteen-year-old trolley collectors ended up years later running our operations in an entire market.

Not everyone wants to get on and up. Some people just want to do a job, but it matters to them that the person who is stacking shelves with them has a chance to succeed. I often witnessed the huge pride a store would express when one of their young starters would return in some senior capacity (though they were still treated by the store staff as if they were 16).

The Tesco workforce still mirrors society, warts and all. For example, it is still easier for a graduate to progress than a 16-year-old joining from school, and for a young man than for a mum returning to work part time. Conscious of this, we have tried hard to give everyone real equality of opportunity. We have created support networks for women and ethnic minorities to help them build confidence, and so we could understand better the barriers to these groups getting on and up in the company.

We learnt that the more you do, and the more time you commit to this, the better the results. You find more role models, more candidates come forward, more people progress.

The success of this approach is borne out by how many women are now managers at Tesco. There was a time, not very long ago, when there were virtually no women store managers, which seems staggering by today's standards. Women are still not the majority, but they are a very fast-growing and significant minority – making up about 40 per cent of management in our stores – and are flooding into the levels above. The success of our values to Tesco's culture has strengthened my view that regulation is not the way to enforce fairness or equity – especially in terms of getting more women on to boards. In Britain, some have suggested that the Government should legislate to force companies to have a quota for the number of women on their boards. This would both undermine the worth of the women and reinforce the prejudice. Instead, companies need to understand why women are not doing better at the moment and change accordingly. Some women lack confidence because they worry about balancing family and work. Others dislike the culture, which can manifest itself in the tiniest of things. When I sit down I talk about football within five minutes – this may well alienate many women. By changing the culture of a company, creating role models and selection panels that are women, a company can begin to change things and generate trust.

As Tesco has moved into new markets around the world, we have found ourselves doing business in societies that are often more stratified than the UK or the USA. The motto 'Everyone is welcome at Tesco' has been even more important in these countries. It is just an expression, a sentence: but backed by deeds, these five words have created a powerful sense of fairness and opportunity which, in its turn, has created a culture of trust.

CONCLUSION

The history of mankind is one of organisation. Nations, companies, city states, churches, charities, armies – people's ability to organise themselves has led to progress and prosperity, as well as war, tyranny and genocide. Organisations have given us wealth and misery, probably in equal measure. I was fortunate to run a large organisation which, even so, is just a tiny dot on history's canvas. Yet the lessons I learnt, which I have tried to summarise in this book, are what I believe any organisation will need to heed in the decades ahead.

A rapidly growing population and the threat of climate change will put even more pressure on scarce natural resources. The digital revolution is empowering people with information and choice, toppling not just companies but governments. The rise of Asia, obvious for so long, is heralding a shift in power from West to East, where an energetic middle class, bursting with aspirations and dreams, is quickly emerging.

Those consumers, like consumers the world over, will need to navigate their way around a global marketplace. To consumers living in a world where they can research what to buy online and then buy in store (or vice versa), spoilt for choice and bombarded by information, the role of brands will become forever more important. Powerful brands will not be those that simply fulfil consumers' material and rational needs – quality, price, convenience and so on. For example, acknowledging that people lead busy lives, in which time is money, will not be enough to win customer loyalty. Brands of any kind will need to form an emotional bond with their consumers, appealing to their hopes, dreams and needs.

To get on and up in life; to give your children a better start than you had; to live in a safe, secure place; to lead a healthy, long life: all of these aspirations are as old as mankind itself – but the demands of the global marketplace, the rising wealth of the middle class and the pressure on space are likely to increase their importance in the future. As the impact of thousands of well-educated graduates in the East becomes felt on the global economy, employers worldwide will increasingly look for the best educated and trained employees. Expect education to become an even more important and prosperous industry than it is now. The emergence of megacities, or certain parts of the world where the population density is likely to soar, will see people put more of a premium on their own security. More people, and more old people, will fuel the already massive health market. State-run health systems are likely to creak or crash, forcing and encouraging citizens to spend more themselves on medicine and care.

Another trend, also not new, deserves a mention: popular protest. The internet has given people more power than ever before to organise, to protest, to revolt. This forces all organisations – be they states or companies – to weigh up even more carefully the consequences of certain courses of action, be it the handling of an environmental disaster, the award of bonuses to executives, whether to build a new airport or how to cut public spending. Get it wrong, and you can quickly find thousands of people online, or on the streets, attacking the brand, boycotting your shops or, worse still, rioting.

The importance of data is another significant factor. In 2010, enterprises globally stored more than seven 'exabytes' of new data on disk drives, while consumers stored more than six 'exabytes' themselves: one 'exabyte' is equivalent to more than 4,000 times the information stored in the US Library of Congress.[1] Data on this scale can be used to improve productivity in a number of ways. Greater transparency increases accountability and choice, allows organisations to monitor and learn from their performance, and enables organisations to tailor their offerings to customers or citizens. In business, as I explained, data gives companies a competitive edge: according to McKinsey, a retailer which makes the most of data on this scale can improve operating margin by more than 60 per cent.[2] Yet this clearly raises big, ethical questions about the rise of an Orwellian 'Big Brother' state: who has access to this data, is it secure, how was it obtained and who owns it?

These changes clearly create new challenges but, as I wrote at the beginning, I am an optimist. Mankind is blessed with a creativity which has overcome such challenges before. The pain of the recent global financial crisis should not hide the fact that the world's economy continues to grow. As Slim put it, 'things are never as bad – or as good – as they are first reported'.[3]

While our past offers some solace, our response to today's challenges will not simply require innovation and fresh thinking. We need to look again at how we organise ourselves – our companies, our services, our cities. More than ever, organisations need people who are not merely motivated to work hard, but have the freedom and encouragement to innovate, to think for themselves and take risks. We need a culture that embraces change, and simple systems that can easily respond to that change. Above all, companies and other organisations that rely on customer or citizen loyalty must not simply have common values, but live by those values. They need to confront the truth head-on, as loyalty and trust cannot be built on the shifting sand of lies and half-truths.

In my view, the strong, successful organisations of the future will be those built on these enduring, simple principles, many of which reflect obvious truths about life – obvious, yet often overlooked or ignored. They will also help people to deal with natural human failings. People are afraid of the truth, of setting courageous goals or of losing in a competition. They get bored by writing down processes, doing simple tasks or focusing on details. Yet all these qualities are essential for success.

I'm also aware that there are broader cultural reasons why key truths get overlooked. Short-termism is one. Leaders – in business, politics, the public sector – have become increasingly focused on the immediate future: the next set of results, the next day's headlines. There is, of course, nothing new in this: the temptation to allow profits to drive decisions has existed in business as long as markets themselves, just as politicians have long been tempted by the lure of immediate popularity to veer away from long-term plans. But what makes the problem particularly acute today is the sheer ease and speed of communication. Social media, and the ability of consumers to communicate with each other directly wherever they live in the world, means that leaders of all organisations feel the need to respond to the slightest criticism and give immediate good news.

Bureaucracy is another reason why these truths have been buried. As I've already said, bureaucracy was created to organise people so that they met specific aims. Bureaucracies have therefore always been an instrument of control. Yet as organisations have grown, so the tentacles of bureaucracy have begun to strangle the initiative, independence and dignity of professionals who work on the front line of these organisations, while simultaneously cutting them off from their leaders. A gulf now exists between managers and managed, which no digital technology can overcome.

Next is lack of conviction – a sense that you must not tell the truth or argue for what you believe is right, for fear of upsetting someone. The case for capitalism is a salutary example. The mistakes and misdemeanours (to put it mildly) of some bankers and investors not only plunged the world into recession, but gave succour to those who believe that free markets, profit and the power of the consumer are intrinsically bad. While the critics of the free market have preached from their pulpits, no one has had the courage to mount a strong or vigorous defence of the benefits of competition, or the simple truths about how companies generate the wealth upon which we all rely.

And that brings me to the most damaging tendency of all: our sleepwalking into the quagmire of moral relativism. An obsession with tolerance, a wish to please everyone, has given leaders the excuse to avoid taking difficult, painful decisions. Without the compass of a clear set of values, too many decisions are taken for the wrong reasons. By wrong, I mean morally wrong. Business, just like politics, does not exist in a moral vacuum. Doing the right thing means not simply obeying the law, but doing the right thing for those who work with you, those whom you serve, and those whose lives you touch. That might mean taking a passing financial hit, or a dive in the opinion polls. If it is right, if the decision is based on truth and – most important of all – if it reflects common, decent values, then the benefits will outlive the pain.

Much of what managers are taught lacks this sense of basic humanity, or a relentless focus on the truth. Numbers, not values, dominate corporate life. 'Do the right thing' has become the industry of corporate social responsibility, full of good intentions, but too often divorced from businesses' way of thinking. Meanwhile, politicians talk of politics being 'the art of the possible'. The very phrase smacks of defeat, of recognising the right course of action but not having the will and determination to see it through.

Truth, loyalty, courage, values, act, balance, simple, lean, compete, trust: these are ten words that reflect my experience of what makes a good organisation. To these, I suppose, some might be tempted to add an eleventh: 'luck'. 'Is he lucky?' Napoleon is supposed to have asked when considering whether to promote an officer. It's certainly the case that you can have a great idea, but be unlucky enough to have it a split second second after someone else. It's also true that you can come up with a great plan, but then be hit by circumstances completely beyond your control – as Tesco discovered in the US when our launch of Fresh and Easy threatened to be blown off course by the financial crisis of 2007. A small mistake may not matter in a lucky environment but be disproportionately punished in an unlucky one.

Luck, then, plays a role in our lives, and most of us will experience it in both its good and bad forms. What matters, however, is not how it operates but how you respond to it. A piece of good luck should generate the courage to make the most of it possible. A piece of bad luck should generate a powerful desire to bounce back from it. Above all, the awareness that things won't always go your way should create the resilience within you to rise to the occasion in tough times.

Certainly, not everything went my way in my years at Tesco. There were the botched marketing campaigns, failure to spot a competitor soon enough, not gripping an IT project – the list, as I said before, is a long one. But we didn't allow the occasional setback or disappointment to drive us off course. The result was that the company which in 1992 was struggling as the third supermarket in the UK, with a turnover of £7 billion, was by 2011 one of the world's largest retailers, with a turnover of £44 billion in the UK. Furthermore, in that time, it had entered 13 new markets, and was number one or two in eight of those.

And that is why 'luck' does not belong in my list. Not because luck doesn't exist, but because it is too arbitrary ever to be considered as part of the tools of management. This is not the case with those ten other words. They reflect my experience of what makes a good organisation, and I believe they have a universal application.

If I had to choose which of the ten words is the most important, I would say it is truth. Getting to the truth about the cause of a problem, and then not hiding it; the truthful answer to the question 'what is the purpose of this organisation?'; being true to oneself and those around you: seeking and speaking the truth is not merely morally right, but is the bedrock of successful management. And often it is those you serve, your customers, who are the source of the truth. Listen and learn from them, heed their advice however difficult it may be, and you stand a greater chance of success. It's that simple.

AFTERWORD

When I first embarked on this book I felt that of the ten key management words I had identified, Truth was perhaps the most important. One year later, and I can't help wondering whether Courage shouldn't be up there as first equal. Let me explain.

As I write this, we're a very long way from achieving global stability. Developed economies are still struggling with the aftershocks of the banking meltdown, five long years after the collapse of Northern Rock in Britain and four years after Lehmans went bust. The faltering recovery has been snuffed out by the huge spike in global oil prices and the Euro crisis. It has been the longest and most severe recession in my lifetime. It has changed how we do business and how millions of people lead their lives. There is no going back to life before the banks went bust and recession struck. Austerity, a difficult decade, a lost decade: call it whatever you like, everyone – companies and governments included – now have to change to meet the challenges.

Tesco is not immune from these challenges and from the need to adapt to meet them. And although it sees change as routine, some of the changes it has made have been painful. Eighteen months after I left, Tesco announced that it was reviewing its Fresh and Easy operation in the US – 'reviewing' being code for pulling out. As I wrote earlier, I take responsibility for Tesco's decision to invest there. I am of course saddened by the fact that our venture has not achieved what we hoped. Had we pulled off our plans, the prize would have been immense. I still believe Fresh and Easy could be successful but understand that, in a difficult climate, my successor has to make difficult choices.

Hindsight being what it is, some now say that our plans were doomed from the start. Well, I prefer perspective to hindsight. Yes, of course we realised that to expand in the US obviously carried a risk – just as any number of other things we did carried a risk. We understood then that success and failure were two sides of the same coin: you cannot have one without the latter. But that risk was one that did not put the entire Tesco operation in peril. Our venture into America was just one part of Tesco's courageous, bold strategy to create a multinational retailer; an on-line retailer; a non-food retailer.

Such courage, and willingness to risk failure, is needed today more than ever. To get out of the slough of economic malaise that is gripping much of the world's economy, we need more people to find the courage to innovate, invest or start a new business. For those who do succeed, and defy the naysayers who see the world as a glass half empty, the rewards are immense.

By way of illustration, some introductions. Meet Patrick Wall, who gave up a well-paid life as a consultant because he wanted to create a virtual supply chain to meet the needs of a booming demand for online shopping. His company, Metapack, is an e-commerce delivery management service bringing online retailers, shippers and customers together through labelling and tracking to improve delivery service and reduce costs. Meet Mike Welch, a former tyre fitter, who thought the old way of ordering and fitting tyres could be dramatically improved by using the internet - the kind of idea you might chat over a beer in the pub. The result: Blackcircles, an online tyre retailer linked to a franchise of independent tyre fitters which reduces the price to consumers by up to forty per cent compared with the traditional market leaders. And, finally, meet Matt Moulding of the Hut Group, who began his career in the cutthroat, competitive market of online entertainment and has flourished as an online retailer. The Hut Group now specialises in selling nutrition, sports supplements, entertainment and fashion clothing to a young, target group.

I've met these people since leaving Tesco. They are typical of many entrepreneurs who, when they enter a room, emit a pulse of energy. Impatient, inquisitive, quirky, they never stop asking 'why can't we do that?' They don't see much difference between work and pleasure because, to them, work is pleasure. They see possibilities in things we regard as ordinary and without potential. They believe they can solve problems the rest of us just accept as 'the way it is'. Above all, they have chosen to take personal risks, to give up their job and their tranquil way of life, to create something new – something many of us are reluctant to do.

Courage is more than just about taking difficult decisions. In its purest form, you need courage to be honest about the challenges and difficulties that you face. And that brings us back to truth. Politicians in many countries have had to summon the courage to look their electorate in the eye and tell them the truly horrendous state of their economy and public finances. Where they have done so, the public has shown a willingness to trust those politicians implement the painful strategies needed to restore stability. Where truth and courage has been lacking, so too has that public trust.

The bleak economic reality means that the public sector will have to do fewer things, and do what remains better with fewer resources. That does not mean our leaders should be frantically doing something in the hope that frenetic activity will yield results. Politicians are there to lead, not manage. They are accountable at elections, yet if they interfere in the administration of services as if they were accountable every day, the results can be counterproductive and chaotic. The Chairman of a plc does not micromanage what happens on the front line, day in, day out: nor should a Minister. Leadership is about remaining focused on big goals, and having the guts to stick to your plans to achieve them, no matter what.

So, yes, unearthing the truth is the foundation of good management. Having the courage to act on the truth, however, turns a manager into a leader. And in challenging times, we need that courage more than ever.

References

Chapter 1: Truth

1 *The Grocers*, Andrew Seth and Geoffrey Randall, Kogan Page (1999), p.24
2 ibid., p.25
3 Jack Cohen quoted in *Counter Revolution: The Tesco Story*, David Powell, Grafton Books (1991), p.119
4 *The Grocers*, Seth and Randall, p.24
5 *The Grocers*, Seth and Randall, pp.25 and 27
6 *The Grocers*, Seth and Randall, p.33
7 *The Guardian*, cited in *The Grocers*, Seth and Randall, p.33
8 *The Grocers*, Seth and Randall, p.35
9 *Sunday Times*, Sri Lanka, 1 April 2001
10 http://www.lga.gov.uk/lga/aio/109536 table 14
11 http://www.slough.gov.uk/documents/room1.pdf
12 http://www.zen99662.zen.co.uk/id/resources/Demographics Summary.pdf
13 http://www.audit-commission.gov.uk/SiteCollectionDocuments/InspectionOutput/InspectionReports/2009/sloughbcaplace-toliveinspection13aug2009REP.pdf
14 *Defeat into Victory*, Field Marshal Viscount Slim, Cassell & Company (1956), Pan Books edition (1999), p.182
15 'An Essential Partnership – The Chemical Industry and Medicine', speech to Division of Medicinal Chemistry, American Chemical Society, 22 April 1935 by George W Merck, quoted in *Built to Last,* James C Collins and Jerry I Porras, Random House (2000), p.48

Chapter 2: Loyalty

1 *The New Rules of Retail*, Robin Lewis and Michael Dart, Palgrave MacMillan (2010), pp.51 and 53
2 http://www.ons.gov.uk/ons/rel/family-demography/families-and-households/2011/stb-families-households.html
3 http://research.stlouisfed.org/publications/review/08/01/DiCecio.pdf
4 http://www.irp.wisc.edu/publications/focus/pdfs/foc201.pdf, p.5
5 *Women and Employment: Changing Lives and New Challenges*, Jacqueline L Scott, p.160
6 http://www.legislation.gov.uk/ukpga/Geo 6/14/28/contents

Chapter 3: Courage

1 *Fisher's Face*, Jan Morris, pp.138–9
2 Quoted in *Built to Last*, James C Collins and Jerry I Porras, Random House (2000), p.98
3 *The Merchant of Prato: Francesco Di Marco Datini: Daily Life in a Medieval Italian City*, Iris Origo, Penguin (1992), p.90
4 Speech at Emory Business School, 1991
5 *The Machine that Changed the World*, James P Womack, Daniel T Jones and Daniel Roos, Simon & Schuster (2007), pp.55–6
6 http://www.pigglywiggly.com/about-us
7 Jack Cohen quoted in *Counter Revolution: The Tesco Story*, David Powell, Grafton Books (1991), p.65
8 ibid., p.79
9 'Closing in 1911–1912', *Daniel H. Burnham, Architect, Planner of Cities*, Vol. 2, Charles Moore, Houghton Mifflin (1921)
10 http://www.mersey-gateway.org/server.php?show=ConNarrative.119&chapterId=804

11 http://www.liverpoolmuseums.org.uk/maritime/exhibitions/magical/quiz/trivia.asp
12 http://www.worldportsource.com/ports/GBR_Port_of_Liverpool_86.php
13 http://www.visionofbritain.org.uk/data_cube_page.jsp?data_theme=T_POP&data_cube=N_TOT_POP&u_id=10105821&c_id=10001043&add=N
14 http://liverpool-consult.limehouse.co.uk/portal/planning/csrpo_consultation/csrpo?pointId=1245921856105
15 http://liverpool-consult.limehouse.co.uk/portal/planning/csrpo_consultation/csrpo?pointId=1245921856105
16 http://www.liverpoolvision.co.uk/
17 http://www.visitbritain.org/insightsandstatistics/inboundvisitorstatistics/regions/towns.aspx
18 Experian, 17 October 2008
19 *Self Help*, Samuel Smiles, Penguin (1986), p.151

Chapter 4: Values

1 *The Political Brain: The Role of Emotion in Deciding the Fate of the Nation*, Drew Westen, Public Affairs (2007), p.15
2 ibid., p.15
3 *Defeat into Victory*, Slim, p.184
4 *Quartered Safe Out Here,* George MacDonald Fraser, HarperCollins (2000), pp.52–3
5 *Defeat into Victory*, Slim, pp.186–7
6 ibid., p.37
7 ibid., p.186
8 *Brand Manners*, Hamish Pringle and William Gordon, John Wiley & Sons Ltd (2001), pp.3 and 36
9 http://www.pwc.com/en_GX/gx/world-2050/pdf/world-in-2050-jan-2011.pdf

10 http://kostat.go.kr/portal/english/news/1/1/index.board?bmode=read &aSeq=245048
11 http://www.lmg.go.kr/2006iaescsi/generalinfo/seoul.asp
12 http://kostat.go.kr/portal/english/news/1/7/index.board?bmode=read&bSeq=&aSeq=252523&pageNo=1&rowNum=10&navCount=10&currPg=&sTarget=title&sTxt=
13 http://www.ft.com/cms/s/0/b5bb3868-3b36-11df-a1e7-00144feabdc0.html#axzz1lAMBH74h
14 *The Guardian*, 5 January 2010 and *Daily Telegraph*, 16 August 2011

Chapter 5: Act

1 *The Machine that Changed the World*, Womack, Jones and Roos, p.239
2 *Sam Walton: Made in America*, Sam Walton with John Huey, Doubleday (1992), pp.78–9
3 *Self Help*, Smiles, p.88
4 *The Loyalty Effect*, Frederick F Reichheld, Harvard Business School Press (paperback edition 2001), p.136
5 *Courage and Other Broadcasts*, Field Marshal Viscount Slim, Cassell & Company (1957), p.28
6 ibid., p.30
7 *Self Help*, Smiles, p.172
8 *The Prince*, Niccolo Machiavelli, translated by George Bull, Penguin Books (1981), pp.96–7
9 http://cep.lse.ac.uk/pubs/download/DP0526.pdf
10 'Webvan's Splashy Stock Debut May Shake Up Staid Grocery Industry', George Anders, *Wall Street Journal*, 8 November 1999
11 'Webvan: Reinventing the Milkman', University of Michigan Business School MBA candidates Denise Banks, Otto Driessen,

Thomas Oh, German Scipioni and Rachel Zimmerman under the supervision of Professor Allan Afuah, McGraw-Hill (2001)

12 http://www.publications.parliament.uk/pa/cm201012/cmselect/cmpubacc/1397/1397.pdf, para 5

13 http://www.publications.parliament.uk/pa/cm201012/cmselect/cmpubacc/1397/1397.pdf, p.3

14 The Failure of the FiReControl Project, National Audit Office, HC 1272 1 July 2011, p.4

15 Roger Hargreaves, National Project Director, FiReControl, Q73, Public Accounts Committee Hearing, 6 July 2011

16 The Public Accounts Committee found: 'The project was flawed from the outset, as the Department for Communities and Local Government (the Department) attempted, without sufficient mandatory powers, to impose a single, national approach on locally accountable Fire and Rescue Services who were reluctant to change the way they operated. Yet rather than engaging with the Services to persuade them of the project's merits, the Department excluded them from decisions about the design of the regional control centres and the proposed IT solution, even though these decisions would leave local services with potential long-term costs and residual liabilities to which they had not agreed.' http://www.publications.parliament.uk/pa/cm201012/cmselect/cmpubacc/1397/1397.pdf, p.3

17 'When you have got 46 different fire services and they have all got very different ways of doing what might well be the same thing, you have to make them all do the same thing in the same way to systematise it, because if you keep saying to them, "You can carry on doing it 46 different ways", you cannot write computer logic, and computers are logical.' Steve McGuirk, Chief Executive, Manchester Fire Service, Board Member, Chief Fire Officers Association, Q 191 http://www.publications.parliament.uk/pa/cm201012/cmselect/cmpubacc/1397/1397.pdf

18 'Governance arrangements in the first five years of the project were complex and ineffective, which led to unclear lines of responsibility and slow decision-making. Additional layers of governance were created in response to emerging issues without clear lines of decision-making, accountability, responsibility, assurance, or internal challenge.' http://www.nao.org.uk/publications/1012/failure_of_firecontrol.aspx, para 9

19 Outline cost 2005: £120m. Full version (1.0) 2007: £340m http://www.nao.org.uk/publications/1012/failure_of_firecontrol.aspx, Figure 3

20 http://www.dailymail.co.uk/news/article-2040259/NHS-IT-project-failure-Labours-12bn-scheme-scrapped.html

21 *Self Help*, Smiles, p.174

Chapter 6: Balance

1 *Defeat into Victory*, Slim, p.413

2 *The Balanced Scorecard*, Robert S Kaplan and David P Norton, Harvard Business Review Press (1996), p.viii

3 ibid, p.viii

4 ibid., p.25

5 ibid., p.10

6 ibid., p.28

7 http://www.nao.org.uk/publications/1012/nhs_ambulance_services.aspx

8 *Defeat into Victory*, Slim, p.294

Chapter 7: Simple

1 *Information Anxiety*, Richard Saul Wurman, Doubleday (1989), p.32

2 http://www.publicfinance.co.uk/news/2010/03/nhs-manager-numbers-increase-by-84-in-a-decade/

3 http://www.nao.org.uk/publications/1012/government_cost_reduction.aspx
4 http://www.bis.gov.uk/policies/growth/growth-review-implementation
5 http://www.taxpayersalliance.com/tolleys.pdf
6 *The Complete Plain Words*, Sir Ernest Gowers, Penguin (1987), pp.2–3
7 *Simplicity,* Edward de Bono, Penguin (1998), p. 61
8 *Self Help*, Smiles, p. 90
9 *My Life and Work*, Henry Ford, BN Publishing (2008), p.50
10 http://www.bloomberg.com/news/2011-01-30/nespresso-will-survive-plethora-of-knock-offs-inventor-says.html
11 http://www.time.com/time/magazine/article/0,9171,2053573,00.html
12 http://www.bloomberg.com/news/2011-01-30/nespresso-will-survive-plethora-of-knock-offs-inventor-says.html

Chapter 8: Lean

1 'Review of Education Capital', Sebastian James, April 2011, para 2.3
2 ibid., paras 2.4 and 2.5
3 ibid., para 2.20
4 ibid., Executive Summary, p.5
5 ibid., Executive Summary, p. 4
6 http://www.communities.gov.uk/news/communities/2009832
7 http://www.communities.gov.uk/communities/troubledfamilies/
8 http://www.communities.gov.uk/news/communities/2009832
9 http://www.communities.gov.uk/news/communities/2009832
10 http://www.communities.gov.uk/news/communities/2009832
11 *My Life and Work*, Ford, p.15

12 ibid., p.15
13 'A road map for natural capitalism', Amory B Lovins, L Hunter Lovins and Paul Hawken, Harvard Business Review, May–June 1999. The company cited is Interface.
14 http://www.hm-treasury.gov.uk/d/CLOSED_SHORT_executive_summary.pdf
15 http://www.unilever.co.za/aboutus/newsandmedia/press release/2011/
16 http://www.sci.manchester.ac.uk/uploads/zestfinalreport.pdf p.117
17 *Natural Capitalism* (Tenth Anniversary Edition), Paul Hawken, Amory B Lovins, L Hunter Lovins, Earthscan (2010), p.1

Chapter 9: Compete

1 *Summer Meditations*, Vaclav Havel, Alfred Knopf (2002), p. 62
2 *Open Markets Matter: The Benefits of Trade and Investment Liberalisation*, OECD (1998)
3 Peter G Peterson Institute for International Economics, cited in 'Free Trade Agreements, Promoting Prosperity in 2008', Daniella Markheim, Heritage Foundation (May 2008)
4 http://www.heritage.org/Index/pdf/Index09_ExecSum.pdf
5 http://web.worldbank.org/WBSITE/EXTERNAL/NEWS/0,,contentMDK:22889943~pagePK:64257043~piPK:437376~theSitePK:4607,00.html
6 'Shaping the Defence Programme, Some Platitudes', Sir Michael Quinlan, quoted in *The Secret State*, Peter Hennessy, Penguin (2003), p.396
7 http://www.defra.gov.uk/statistics/files/defra-stats-foodfarm-food-pocketbook-2011.pdf, p.26
8 http://science.cancerresearchuk.org/prod_consump/groups/

cr_common/@fre/@gen/documents/generalcontent/research-strategy-dnld-version.pdf

9 *An Inquiry into the Nature and Causes of the Wealth of Nations,* Adam Smith, Methuen & Co. Ltd (1904), Book One, Chapter 2

Chapter 10: Trust

1 *The Memoirs of Field Marshal Montgomery*, Field Marshal Viscount Montgomery, Collins (1958), p.89
2 *Self Help,* Smiles, p.199
3 *The Memoirs of Field Marshal Montgomery*, Field Marshal Viscount Montgomery., p.86
4 Sir John Colville in *Action This Day: Working with Churchill*, Sir John Wheeler-Bennett (ed.), Macmillan (1968), p.50
5 Lord Normanbrook in *Action This Day*, Wheeler-Bennett (ed.), p.22
6 Lord Bridges in *Action This Day*, Wheeler-Bennett (ed.), p.220
7 Lord Normanbrook in *Action This Day*, Wheeler-Bennett (ed.), p.27
8 ibid., p.28
9 Sir Ian Jacob in *Action This Day*, Wheeler-Bennett (ed.), p.176

Conclusion

1 'Big data: The next frontier for innovation, competition and productivity', McKinsey Global Institute
2 ibid.
3 *Defeat into Victory*, Slim, p.235

Index